# THE FURNITURE MAKERS

A History of Trade Unionism
in the Furniture Trade
1865 – 1972

## Hew Reid

Deputy Head of the School of Art and Design, Furniture and
Timber, Buckinghamshire College of Higher Education,
High Wycombe

Malthouse Press
Oxford

Malthouse Publishing Ltd.,
19a Paradise Street,
Oxford OX1 1LD, U.K.

First Published 1986

Typeset on a Monotype Lasercomp at Oxford University Computing Service
and printed by The Bath Press, Lower Bristol Road, Bath, BA2 3BL.

Reid, Hew
    The furniture makers: a history of trade
unionism in the furniture trade, 1865–1972.
    1. Trade-unions—Furniture workers—Great Britain—History
I. Title
331.88'1841'00941        HD6668.F9

ISBN 0-948720-06-9
ISBN 0-948720-09-3 Pbk

# CONTENTS

# *Foreword*

by Ben Rubner, General Secretary, Furniture, Timber and Allied
Trades Union.

Hew Reid has the distinction of having written the first history of the
unions involved in the manufacture of furniture in Britain from the early
craft societies to the present day industrial organisation. He brings to life
memories of yesteryear which will evoke in older and newer generations
of those involved in the trade recollections of developments which have
taken place in wages and conditions of employment over the past
century and more.

During that time the changes which have occurred in methods of
production, materials, and particularly in machinery, have been almost
unbelievable. Some day, perhaps, Dr. Reid will turn his talents and
unrivalled knowledge of the trade to writing a further volume showing
just how the unions in the industry, both individually and collectively,
have faced up to new and ever-changing technology which, by the early
nineteen seventies had witnessed such innovations as automatic shaping
machines, wholly revolutionary polishing and finishing methods, new
systems of glueing and drying and more especially of packaging units of
furniture prior to delivery from the factory.

This, Hew's first venture, though it only sketches in the story of such
technological developments as a background to more general historical
events, makes nevertheless a major contribution to the subject which
should benefit all those concerned in the manufacture of furniture,
whether they are students, designers, manufacturers, salesmen or the
shop floor workers who are the backbone of any industry and trade
union. He reminds us, in graphic description, of the sweatshop
conditions which prevailed in some sections of the trade until the second
world war and in some cases even beyond that period. He reminds us of a
persistent and increasing tempo of production which has characterised
the trade, a tempo which would have astonished the early furniture
makers. Has it been mass production, or as one outstanding cabinet
maker who was 70 years old in 1946 once declared to me, mess

production? Certainly political and social pressures have reduced the heaps of wood shavings on the cabinet shop floor and the wood chips behind the machines. But is it the same trade which many of us used to know? A knowledge of change in the industry, of the gains and losses arising from new technologies is well worth while passing on to us, and particularly to the young people who are Hew Reid's daily concern at the Buckinghamshire College. They could not be in better hands.

I have had great pleasure in writing this foreward. It has been a privilege to be associated with Hew Reid in bringing forward a historical study of such important to instruct and to guide those who are present day participants in a great industry and to stir the memories of those who have been involved, often for their whole lifetime, in the affairs of the unions which have brought such benefits upon their members between 1865 and 1972.

'Fairfields',
Roe Green,
Kingsbury.

April 1986

# *Introduction and Acknowledgements*

The art and craft of furniture making is one of the oldest of man's accomplishments and as such finds its memorials in the great museums of the world. For many hundreds of years is was a trade organised for the benefit of the rich and powerful. Early craftsmen are recorded only through their products or their patrons. Changes in the availability of materials prompted new styles and higher levels of production identified with the names of designer-craftsmen, though still for the houses of the affluent and successful. By the beginning of the nineteenth century, however, the situation began to change. The growth of towns, the wider distribution of income, increased supplies of raw materials brought an enormous expansion of the trade and with it a decline in those craftsmen who worked in isolation and a move towards groups of workers producing furniture in major centres of the trade.

Folklore places the furniture maker and the shoemaker in a philosophical and revolutionary position in working class society. This is no myth. It is borne out in the history of their trades. The furniture workers were early in the field of workers' organisations and if their nascent trade unions were no more than transitory this was a reflection of the seasonal and fragmented nature of their calling rather than a lack of organisational zeal. With the coming of the mass market the furniture workers organised around the most skilled areas of the trade, the cabinetmakers and upholsterers and this is where this trade union history begins.

The major concern of the Alliance Cabinet Makers Society formed in 1865 was, for the next 35 years, little more than survival. Every downturn in the economy threatened its very existence. With time and membership stability, political pressures began to be reflected in the work of the union, which could be justifiably proud of its role in the clarification of the laws on picketing as a result of the Jackson and Graham dispute of 1875. It was nevertheless the amalgamation of the Cabinet Makers with

x

the Scottish Society in 1902 and the appointment of Alex Gossip as general secretary which brought a new militancy and placed the furniture trades in the forefront of the battle for the rights of working men.

Though one of the first trade unions to sponsor and support a Member of Parliament, the union became deeply depressed and disappointed with the progress made by parliamentary methods and was forced into the area of extra-parliamentary pressure groups. Not only did it fight aggressively for a living wage and appropriate recognition for its members. It also fought for the cause of national and international socialism with a determination and enthusiasm which earned it a reputation for evangelical zeal in the front ranks of socialist action. In the early years of the century persistent militancy became its watchword at the centre of every significant left wing group and event of the period. The first world war confirmed that position. In the 1920s and 30s furniture trades union representatives were to be found in prominent positions in the Workers'and Soldiers' Soviets, in the 1926 General Strike, in the British Communist Party, in the Hands Off Russia Movement and in the Anti-Imperialist League.

The end of this phase came in 1939 with the intoduction of a Trade Board into the industry. A new attitude could be detected among the employers and a new and more moderate group took control of the union, ushering in a period of mutual co-operation. The value of furniture workers' involvement and assistance came to be recognised in an industry which was passing through a phase of traumatic technical change. A climate of industrial peace made the adoption of new materials and technology practicable. As the market for furniture boomed a sophisticated and far-sighted National Labour Agreement cleared up most of the areas of conflict and misunderstanding between the parties and secured for the workers living standards of which the pioneers of the union could never have dreamed.

The history of the Furniture Union is a story of people, of politics, of pride and prejudices and of commonsense; the story of an industry continuously, and inexorably, in transition. It is a story of men and women with a vision of the future which they pursued against all obstacles. That vision has, at least in part, been achieved and it is to the early pioneers, who set the pace of purpose and action, that those who have followed owe an incalculable debt.

The author wishes to place on record the debt of gratitude which he owes to the many individuals and institutions which have made this work possible. Ben Rubner and the late Jim Kooyman of FTAT made available the union's records and provided unfailing support and encouragement; members of the union, both serving and retired, gave unstintingly of their time and patience in talking through and explaining incidents in the union's past.

My thanks go to Frank Rubner, Dean of Creative Arts at Leeds Polytechnic, for his help with the first Chapter. Also to Professor Royden Harrison, Dr. Tony Mason and Dr. Henry Weisser, without whose continual encouragement, advice and correction this work would never have been completed, and to Arthur Marsh for editing it and preparing it for publication.

This book would never have appeared without the cooperation of Mr.D.J.Everett, my Director, and the staff of the Furniture Technology Department of the Buckinghamshire College of Higher Education who made possible a sabbatical year at the University of Warwick which enabled me to complete a first draft. Th task of transforming my longhand script into a typed and readable state was splendidly undertaken by Mrs Rene Reed.

Finally, to Dorothy, Andrew and Max, who have lived with me and with this work, I gratefully record the debt which I owe for their encouragement, forbearance and continuous support. The attempt to record the achievements of a fiercely independent group of craftsmen over a century of development has been a source of joy and inspiration to me. To them I owe a debt which can never be adequately acknowledged.

H.R.

High Wycombe
23 April 1986

# CHAPTER I

# The Furniture Makers - The First Beginnings

The history of the making of furniture is inevitably tied to the development and decline of the successive civilisations which have punctuated the story of man's emergence into settled societies. In tracing the development of trade unions in the furniture industry it is necessary to provide as a preamble a summary of furniture making through the ages and its development in the United Kingdom. What follows is brief and partial. It is included to set the scene for the emergence of workers' organisations in the middle of the Victorian era.

It is generally accepted that the making and use of furniture is characteristic of an advanced and settled society and that the earliest examples of the furniture maker's craft in the Western World were the products of the civilisations of Ancient Egypt, Mesopotamia, Greece and Rome. The tools and craftsmen to produce these articles had emerged in the transitional Mesolithic (Middle Stone) Age during which a fine range of carpenter's tools, including the adze, gauge and chisel, were developed. That period also added the carpenter's first machine - the bow-drill, in which the drill is rapidly rotated by means of a string wrapped round it, attached at each end to a sort of bow which is moved back and forth.[1]

The Egyptians from early Dynastic times (about 2,700 B.C.) used the bow drill as an integral part of their wood working technique. Judging from the surviving wood work, they used neither nails nor screws, almost everying being fitted together with wooden pins or dowels, a method for which the drilling of an accurate hole was essential. [2]

By this period the craftsmen of Egypt and Mesopotamia were producing a wide variety of articles of high aesthetic and technical quality. They were aided in this task by the skills of the metal workers who were capable of making tools as diverse as axes, adzes, chisels, gauges, drills, knives, saws, clamps and razors. [3] The carpenter of this period was as versatile as he was skilled. His output ranged from boats, chariots and furniture to musical instruments such as harps and lyres. Technical innovation was also taking place. From this time comes the first evidence of the construction of plywoods, a five-ply board of glued wood strips of great strength and stability.

The objects of great beauty found in the tombs of the period demonstrate the degree of refinement which these workers could attain in catering for the luxury - in death as well as in life - which their rulers craved. They also highlight a factor central to the development of the craft of furniture making, namely that for a very considerable period of man's history the commissioning and use of furniture of all but the most primitive and utilitarian kind was restricted to the ruling groups in a society, invariably the most affluent and the most cultured. [4]

The Greeks and Romans added to the range of wood working tools available by developing the rule, the square, and smoothing jack and moulding planes, as well as developing further the sophistication of those tools already available. Indeed it is clear that there has always existed a relationship between tool development and furniture making skills on the one hand and the cultural development and the settled nature of society on the other, which determines the type and kind of work the craftsman is called upon to do.

So highly developed had the trade become that, on the evidence available from archaeological sites, the tool kit of the average Roman joiner in Rome or London was more extensive and specialised than that of his medieval counterpart in a small French or English village 1,000 years later. In such Western European countries the making of furniture of any quality dates only from the Gothic period of architecture, when furnishing to match ecclesiastical and fortified buildings was produced in monasteries. Indeed, one of the oldest known pieces of British furniture is the Coronation Chair made for Edward I (1272 - 1307) by the monk, Walter of Durham, and now in Westminster Abbey. [5]

Furniture making requires a variety of separate skills which at earlier periods emerged as specific trades. The first of these separations or divisions of skills were those of the chairmaker, upholsterer and bedding maker. The date of this separation is not clear; however, by the sixteenth century the work of the carpenter and joiner and that of the furniture maker had become separate and clearly defined. The Norwich Indexes of Freeman list upholsterers and chairmakers from 1640 and chairmenders from 1677. [6] In Bristol the apprentices enrolled in the years 1662 and 1689 include upholsterers, and the first apprentice book of 1540 lists an upholsterer and a bedder. [7] Cabinetmaking as such has a less clearly documented history until the 1600s but this is more clearly understood if the furniture and furnishings of the early Tudor period are examined.

The schedule of the contents of the house of Sir William More of Loseley are available for the year 1556. The most prominent feature of the hall was the large chair of the master of the house, standing upon a dias or raised platform at the top of the room. Before this stood the high table, the 'table dormant' of Chaucer's franklin. To one side of the chair was a second and lesser table for the lady of the house, and guests and family were accommodated at the high table on stools. At the lower end of the hall stood a hutch table, the Armoire, the ancestor of the modern sideboard, acting as a serving table for the household. Near the table stood the cup-board on which the appointments for the high table were kept. Either side of the fireplace were high backed benches, garnished as necessary with blankets and cushions for comfort. [8]

The floor of such a hall was not conducive to the use of good quality furnishings. Erasmus describes it as being laid with white clay and covered in rushes of which the upper layers were renewed with reasonable regularity. The lower layers, however, remained undisturbed, sometimes for as much as twenty years. The private chambers on the ground floor were, however, tiled; those above were boarded. The Parlour, the sitting room of the More family, was sparsely furnished. There was a 'table of Chestnut not a frame joyned to the same'. There was 'one joyned cheyre' and '5 joyned stoles of chestnut' with a supply of 'footstoles', and chests. These chests served as a secure receptacle for valuables as well as clothes and linen:

> In cypress chests my arras counterpoints,
> Costly apparel, tents and canopies,
> Fine linen, Turkey cushions boss'd with pearl,
> Valances of Venice in needle work,
> Pewter and brass, and all things that belong
> to House and Housekeeping.
>
> (*Taming of the Shrew* 1594 - 1600, Act II).[9]

Sparse as the More household was it was relatively well furnished by comparison to the dwellings of the craftsman and the cottager. An inventory of about the same time at a weaver's house at Biddenden in Kent shows the house to have been half workshop, with the looms and tools of the trade occupying a substantial part of the floor area. The domestic furniture was limited to a chair for the master, a stool for his wife, a trestle table with forms for the workmen and apprentices and a bed and two chests in the upper part of the house. A contemporary document records 'Manie farmers thinke his gaines verie small towards the end of his terme, if he have not six or seven years rent lieing by him, beside a fair garnish of pewter on his cupboard, with so much more in odd vessels going about the house, three or foure feather beds, so many coverlids and capets of tapestrie, a silver salve, a bowle for wine, and a dozen spoons to furnish up the sute'. [10]

The furniture of the cottager of the period can only be guessed at since none of it has survived. The painting by Peter Brueghel the Elder of 'Boars carousing in an Inn' and the Tavern Scene from 'Trattato di Arimetica' give a clear impression nevertheless. The furnishings consisted of a box bed for the man and his wife, straw mattresses on the floors for others, some stools and a form, a rough table and a hutch for food and perhaps a chest or two. This visual information is reinforced by the Inquisition records of the town of Montalieu. [11]

The contention that the upholsterer or upholder and bed maker were amongst the earliest recorded trades is supported by both the foregoing inventories and the emphasis given in Warner's *Patient Countess* (1587). The convention which decreed that the master of the house should sit in a cushioned armchair at his board was observed even in the humblest home. The Count lost in a forest is made welcome by a cottager for whom 'browne bread, whey, bacon, curds and milk were set him on the borde'. And for his ease, 'a cushion made of lists, a stoole halfe backed with a hoope were brought him, and he sitteth down beside a coupe'. [12]

The Restoration of 1660 signalled the dawning of the era of the cabinetmaker as we understand the trade description today. As a modern trade it appears to have its origins in Italy and developed strongly in those countries most effected by the Renaissance. The work of Jean Mace of Blois from 1644 to 1672, of Andre Boulle from 1672 to 1732 and of J.H. Reisener c. 1760 under royal patronage is well documented. [13]

In London the evidence for the development of the industry stems from the work of Sir Ambrose Heal. He lists as the earliest business in the trade that of Edward Phillips who had an upholstery shop in Cornhill (1584) and whose example was followed rapidly by others in that area. Royal patronage was as important in London as in Paris and many of the craftsmen in this early period came from the Continent to the Westminster area - Gerriet Jensen of the Pavement, St. Martin's Lane from Holland was the Royal cabinetmaker for Charles II, William and Mary, and Queen Anne. Pauderin of Pall Mall was the French cabinetmaker to Charles II from 1677 to 1685 and in the same period Heal lists Stalker of St. James as a maker of Japanned furniture in 1688 and Spane of St. Giles as a carver in 1682.

The Restoration marked a watershed in cultural and aesthetic matters. 'The long exile of the King and Courtiers', writes Pinto, 'had brought them under diverse foreign influences, principally French and Dutch'. Certainly the swing in fashion and manners from Puritanism with its emphasis on severity of style and minimal decoration to the elaboration in costume and furnishings characteristic of the Restoration period was amplified because workmen were available to meet the demand for elaborate and luxurious furniture. As a result of competition, and in some cases persecution, foreign cabinetmakers, experts in veneering, carvers, guilders, japanners and other specialised craftsmen flocked to England and acted as mentors and examples to a new generation of British craftsmen. [14]

The presence of these foreign craftsmen soon had its effect upon the native tradesmen. 'Joyners, cabinetmakers and the like...from very vulgar and pitiful artists are now come to produce works as curious for the fitting and admirable for their dexterity in contriving, as any we meet with abroad' wrote John Evelyn. 15. Furniture was at this stage in the development of the industry, still a bespoke trade and retailing of the products was unknown. 'The close proximity to the customer was a prime consideration in the selection of workshop sites and choice of urban and metropolitan areas by furniture makers had already become apparent'. [16]

In part, this exclusivity was broken down by a growing market for the product of the furniture makers and this market was both stimulated and, in a sense, standardised by the publication of pattern books. The most famous designers and publicists were Thomas Chippendale and Son who first published the *Gentlemen and Cabinetmakers Directory* in 1754 and who had a workshop in St. Martin's Lane; George Hepplewhite, who died in 1786, and operated from Cripplegate and Thomas Sheraton (1751 - 1806) who had his workshops in Wardour Street and published *The Cabinetmakers and Upholsterers Drawing Book* in 1791 and *The Cabinet Directory* containing an explanation of all the terms in the cabinet, chair and upholstery branches, and a *Display of Useful Articles of Furniture* in 1803.

It is helpful at this point to draw back from the design and product development aspects of furniture and to examine the role of the materials used in the changing nature of the furniture makers trade, since the materials used in the fabrication of furniture influenced the type and nature of the craftsmen employed within it.

Prior to 1660 the timbers used were, in the main, home grown, oak, elm, chestnut and beech being the predominant species. The joiner was the maker of furniture at least as far as the carcase and chair products were concerned and it was as a natural progression from his work on windows, doors and internal panelling that he went on to produce the furniture of the period. Furniture was strong, utilitarian and, as can be seen from the earlier description of houses of the period, intended to be used by many generations and prized rather more for its utility than its aesthetic qualities. Such examples as we can see today in museums and private collections were not without decoration but this was a secondary rather than primary aspect of the articles produced. The construction techniques were those of the joiner and the pegged mortice and tenon ubiquitous. Dovetails ensured that the article would endure despite the limited life of the animal glues used and the damp conditions which it normally had to endure.

As already noted, the return of Charles II from exile on the continent of Europe in 1660 resulted in a complete revision of ideas of that fashion in high society home furnishings. In consequence there quickly developed in London groups of tradesmen who at first copied and then adapted continental influences for a growing home market, and with colonial expansion, for an overseas market also. Walnut and mahogany became the timber with which to construct furniture, and the veneers of these and other more exotic timbers, such as rosewood, tulipwood and ebony, were used to enhance surfaces for decorative effect. Oak and other domestic timbers did not cease to function as furniture timbers, but their use became restricted to articles which were best served by their less decorative, harder wearing qualities. The country house might be furnished in walnut but the chapel had pews of oak.

Methods of construction changed and most markedly because of the use of veneers. Veneers, at that time, and, indeed, until the mid nineteenth century were sawn from a decorative or exotic log, in planks only 1/8th of an inch thick (today they are machine cut at .65 mm.) thus allowing a particularly beautiful log to provide the decoration for many pieces of furniture. A veneer requires a completely flat surface for adhesion, though it can be glued to curves in a single plane and with 'tailoring' made to fit to compound curves. For the purposes of veneering, therefore, the existing joiner's technique of frame and panel construction was unsatisfactory as was the through dovetail technique.

Timber gains or loses moisture across its surface with changing temperature and humidity. Surfaces respectively of radial, tangential or end grain, lose or gain moisture in the ratio of 1 : 2 : 4. It can be seen, therefore, that the end grain of the through dovetail initially absorbs more glue moisture than the surrounding area, making it difficult to achieve a lasting bond with the veneer. Even if such a bond is initially achieved, the loss and absorbtion of moisture of the panel substrate at the dovetails later results in the delamination of the veneer from the panel.

Cabinetmakers, the new breed of craftsmen, developed the lap dovetail and the hidden mitre dovetail, which minimises, and in the case of the hidden mitre, conceals, the end grain to be veneered in any carcase work. The substrate materials used under these exotic timbers were many. Mahogany was employed for the very highest quality work, but softer woods such as cedar, Scots pine, poplar and other relatively absorbant materials were also used. The use of a softer material for the panel was dictated by the need to have it flat and true for veneering and this was more easily accomplished with the hand tools of the period on such timbers, the relative absorbancy of the base also providing a keen bond with its overlay.

Carving has always had a place in furniture decoration from earliest times and this was not diminished with the use of the new materials and development of new fashions. Indeed foreign influences encouraged a new and more dramatic approach to the art. Oak carving had had its roots in ecclesiastical stone carving, but the depth and complexity of the work which can be carried out in oak is limited by the lack of uniformity and texture in the mateiral. Contrary to the views expressed by E.T. Jay it is quite as strong, if not stronger, than any other material used for wood carving. However, its very hardness, lack of uniformity, and above all the relative coarseness of the texture were the features which led to the use of other timbers for the finest carved work. The timbers which came to prominence in the post-1660 period were mahogany, walnut, fruitwoods (e.g. pear and apple), and, above all, lime wood, though oak retained its position as the carving material for ecclesiastical work. [17]

The furniture craftsmen of the eighteenth century were not an easily identifiable group. A cabinetmaker might be a craftsman/shopkeeper, making and selling to a fashionable public, or he might be a shopkeeper who acted as an outlet for a number of craftsmen. He might be a working master who made for such shopkeepers or other cabinetmakers on an 'out of work basis', or he might be a journeyman working for wages in any establishment requiring his skills.

There were, however, by the eighteenth century considerable divisions between the trades in furniture making. A guide for the period states that the cabinetmakers could be making 'beds, chairs, chests, tables and all carcase work'. The work of the upholsterer was as it is today with the addition of providing what would be regarded as soft furnishings in the form of curtain hangings. [18]

The carver was the most skilled of those engaged in furniture making. Campbell writes in 1747 that 'the Cabinet-Maker is much the most curious Workmen in the Wood Way, except the carver'. The carver was always a sub-contractor even when his work was of paramount importance to the finished article as in curved chairs, desks and panelling. 'Tradesmen in this Way are never out of Business'. [19] The other trades discussed in Campbell are those of looking glass frame carver, case maker (for clocks) and japanners. These are described as the 'better trades'. The joiner, turner, chair maker and frame maker have lesser standing.

The best furniture was beautifully made and beautifully finished but even as late as the early 1800's such production was for a limited market and the character which was apparent in the furnishings of the various classes of society in the 1500's was substantially maintained and reinforced. For the rest of the population other than the wealthy, furniture was 'white wooden, wickers and ordinary matted sort, commonly called kitchen chairs'. Indeed, Campbell, dealing with the frame maker, notes that his work 'needs but little ingenuity or neatness as he only joins the deals (soft wood planks) roughly planed' [20].

The hours of working for all workmen were long. By the mid-eighteenth century a twelve to fourteen hour day was a normal with turners working fifteen hours. A six day week was normal, with holidays at Christmas, Whitsun and Easter, and for London workers, eight 'hanging days'. 'It was common for master frame makers, tailors and others who had engaged to complete orders within a given time, to bear in mind to observe to their customers 'that there will be a hanging day and my men will not be at work'. [21]

It is difficult to be specific about wage rates for furnitue workers in the eighteenth century. Seasonal variations apart, much depended on the segment of society for which the work was being done. London rates did not necessarily reflect what was paid in other major towns. However, as some indication the *General Description of All Trades* gives for 1747 the following rates:-

| | |
|---|---|
| Cabinetmaker | 12/- to 15/- per week with up to a guinea a week for the man who knows his business |
| Chairmaker | 12/- per week |
| Frame maker | 10/- to 20/- |
| Turner | 18/- to 20/- |
| Joiner | 15/- |

Campbell suggests that 30/- to 42/- is a possible wage for the most able man on piece work, whilst Collyer gives the rate for 1761 as being similar to those of the *General Description of All Trades,* with the addition of:-

| | |
|---|---|
| Chair carver | 30/- to 40/- on piece work |
| Japanner | 20/- to 30/- |
| Picture Frame Carver | 21/- upwards |

[23]

These wages suggest that the furniture worker of the period was fringing upon the aristocracy of labour. However, this only applied to a small number of highly skilled workers producing for the aristocratic and affluent. As industrialisation widened the market for the number of furniture workers increased and wages were so reduced that it was not until the beginning of the twentieth century that comparable levels of wages were again achieved.

The first evidence of combination in the furniture trades is to be found in the mid-eighteenth century. In 1761 'A number of bills of indictment were preferred against the rebellious journeymen cabinetmakers, who have lately combined together to raise their wages and lessen their hours or working, etc. The combinations amongst journeymen, peruke makers, shoe makers, taylors, cabinetmakers, etc., is a growing evil and wants to be remedied'. Having made its remonstration against the insidious activities of the workers, the *London Chronicle* turned its attack on to the employers and their policy of price fixing and the operation of a cartel. It continued 'but there is a much greater [evil] amonst their masters, who agree together what price they will have for everything they make or sell, and this is universal amongst most tradesmen'. [24]

The unrest of 1761 may have involved the London Cabinet Makers' Society, reputedly founded in the 1750s and the forerunner of other cabinet makers' unions. The *Book of Prices* of this organistion was revised regularly at least until the 1830s.[25] The United Society of Cabinetmakers seems to have existed at much the same time but is obscure in its origin and activities. There is, however, a card in existence issued in 1801 which carries as its main message 'To repair the loss of Tools by Fire, the chief end of our meetings'. This was an undoubted reflection of the times but the objectives of the Society were at least understood by some employers as the following job advertisement shows:-

'Cabinetmakers wanted for constant employ. Enquire at Mr Warffe's No. 168 Ratcliff Highway. None belonging to the Society will be employed'.

The reference to 'constant employ' as an attraction to craftsmen, more important than high wages or short hours, may be an indication that seasonal fluctuation in demand was as severe in those days as it is today. [26] and [27]

It is tempting to see the development of the furniture industry in the 1800's in terms of mass production; in practice it remained a hand based craft industry until the end of the nineteenth century. It is true that rudimentary machinery existed for the working of wood long before that time, but its universal usage was delayed by a number of factors. By nature the trade was diverse and the demand for its products was relatively low. Most makers had little capital. Nor was the pressure for capitalisation great. As a hand based craft industry it had the capability of as much output as was technically required.

Perhaps the most critical bottleneck in furniture manufacture at that time was the production of planks from the round log, the traditional method of conversion being the pit saw, a method used until the earliest years of the twentieth century. An account given by a High Wycombe worker who had been a pit sawyer for twenty years describes the process. 'In the woods a pit was dug, oblong in shape and about six to eight feet deep, roughly lined with planks where the soil was too crumbly to stand on its own. A long log on either side of the pit formed the main bearers, carrying the shorter cross bearers which in turn supported the tree to be sawn. Iron 'dogs' were driven into the tree and bearers to hold everything firm. If really big trees were to be dealt with, a crab winch or rope tackle would be needed to move them into position and to shift them on to bearers when it was necessary to move them in order to avoid cutting through those bearers. Before going on to the pit the trunk had to be trimmed up and this was hard skilled work, in which the operator used a heavy long-handled, wide-bladed axe, known as a siding up axe'. [28]

Once in position on the bearers, the log had to be marked out into planks and this was done by stretching a line from one end of it, rubbing the line with chalk or charcoal black and 'striking a line', that is plucking the line in the centre so that its rebound left a mark, faint enough, but just sufficient to act as a guide to the top sawyer who stood on the trunk itself and steered the saw with the tiller, a cross handle on a two foot extension bolted to the saw blade. Much of the actual work was done by the bottom sawyer, knee deep in sawdust and with more sawdust constantly running down on to him. The lower handle of the saw was simply wedged on to the blade for easy removal when it became necessary to remove the whole blade to allow the tree trunk to be moved over the bearers. The blade of the saw was greased and a wedge was driven into the tail of the cut to ease the work, but it was hard work and slow work capable only of a limited output of planks and for all the skill of the sawyers, it produced a comparatively uneven thickness of plank.

There is some evidence of water powered mechanical sawing in Germany and Sweden in the fourteenth century but this practice was confined to softwoods until the nineteenth century when, first of all, horse power was used and this in its turn superseded when reliable steam power was harnessed to the frame saw and circular saw, for hard wood conversion. The effect of the introduction of a horse-powered and, later, steam-powered sawing was catastrophic to one section of the trade - the sawyers. Mayhew reports, ' The London Sawyers, though not a numerous body, still require full consideration, as belonging to a trade which has been extensively superseded by machinery. [29] At the time of taking the previous census the number of the Metropolitan Sawyers above twenty years of age was 2,180; so that from 1831 to 1841, the London trade had increased by 612. Since then, however, I am informed that the number has declined by nearly one-half. The number of steam saw mills in the metropolis, in 1841, was fifteen; at the present moment they are sixty-eight, including those for cutting veneers as well as timber and deals'. [30] Introduction of machinery was the reason for the fall in numbers employed. The first steam sawmill set up in the neighbourhood of London was established at Battersea, in the year 1806 or 1807 by a Mr. Smart. It was erected principally for the cutting of veneers, and the trade, though aware that it could not fail to take the work from them, found it difficult to believe that it could do so to the extent that it did. 'We knew' says my informant, 'that the mills could cut veneers better and thinner than what we could, and more to an inch, which is a great object of course, in valuable woods, but still we never expected that steam power would be applied to the cutting of timber and deals. Since that time the mills have gone on increasing gradually, year after year, until now there are twenty regularly working between Stangate and London Bridge, and no less than sixty-eight altogether, scattered throughout the metropolis'.

Prior to the introduction of steam-powered sawmills, horse-powered mills were in use. Mayhew reports 'For perhaps twenty years before this period [1806/7] horses had been employed to supersede men's labour. The principle on which these horse mills were constructed was not dissimilar to that now used in the steam sawmills. The horses then did the work of the engine now - working nine saws at once, but with perhaps only half the motive power of steam as regards velocity..Steam sawmills continued to be gradually established throughout the metropolis until they now number sixty-eight - six, at least of the proprietors being also timber merchants. These mills average three 'frames' each, a frame holding nine saws. In case all the means of these mills were called into operation at one time, 1,755 saws would be at work..... A gentleman, himself a conductor of a steam sawmill, took pains, at my request, to calculate the number of sawyers superseded by the application of steam power. These, from the best data, he gives at 750 'pairs' or 1,500 men'. [31]

The process of development of machinery for the wood working trades had been slow and the utilisation of machinery was undoubtedly controlled by the low capitalisation of most furniture makers. The first sawmill in England was erected in 1663 in Hull and was wind-powered. The circular saw was introduced in 1777. James Stangill built a wind-powered sawmill at Limehouse in 1761 for which design he received a premium of £300 from the Royal Society of Arts. This was bitterly opposed by the pit sawyers, who burned it down the same year. [32] [33]

Mayhew reports the sawyers attitudes to machines '....Working men is much disheartened at the increase of machinery, when they're standing at the corner of the streets idle and starving and see carts coming out of the yard filled with planks that they ought to have had. You see, sir, when some are injured by any alteration, they gets compensation; but here is our trade cut up altogether, and what compensation do we get? We are left to starve without the least care. I have paid 1/10d for a quartern loaf before now, and I could get it much easier than I can now. When I get up in the morning, I don't know whether I shall be able to earn 6d. before nightfall. I have been at work ever since I was eight years old, and I'm a pretty good example of what the working man has to look for; and what's the good of it all? Even the machines, some of them, can't hardly raise the price of the coals to get their fire up. When they first set up they had 6d a foot for cutting veneers, and now they have only 1d. Machinery's very powerful, sir, but competition is much stronger'. [34]

The guiding genius of invention for the mechanisation of the wood working industry was General Sir Samuel Bentham who patented a planing machine in 1791, and a rotary planing machine, a moulding machine, a mortising machine, a tenoning machine, a dovetail cutting machine and a veneer cutting machine in 1793. By 1840 Thomas Robinson and Son of Rochdale had produced their first wood working machine, belt driven by steam power. [35]

It would be quite erroneous to suggest that there was intensive mechanisation of the furniture making industry proper by the beginning of the nineteenth century. It was purely at the primary conversion stage of furniture making, i.e. at the conversion of the log to plank form, that mechanisation had any place at this time. While this mechanisation broke the bottleneck imposed by the pit saw, the rest of the industry continued to develop along hand craft lines, albeit with a capability for a very high level of output, for the next hundred years. The resulting contrast between high levels of mechanisation and the persistence of handicraft in the industry is exemplified by the report of the visit of the editor of the 'Journal of the Cabinetmakers' to High Wycombe in 1908. He comments on the factory of R.J. Howland with sixty workmen and a machine shop where 'the machines are separately electrically powered and efficiency is the keynote' and contrasts this with a visit to Henry Goodearl & Sons 'who astonished us with the information that they had no machinery whatever, and here it was that we had the pleasure of seeing some of the methods of fifty years ago still practised and practised successfully even in competition with modern machinery. Here we saw chairmakers wearing what is called a breast bit. On first sight this looks like a narrow wooden life belt across the breast, but on close inspection we saw that in the centre it has a hollow to take the rose of the stock which is one of the most important tools in the kit of a man who makes chairs without machinery'. [36] [37]

'As we pass along we come across a pole lathe, and an adzer hollows a Windsor chair seat held firmly by standing on it. He uses his adze much in the same way that a pick-axe is employed, but to the uninitiated, the gleaming edge after cutting out a long crisp chip at every stroke, came perilously near the foot with which he holds the elm seat'.

Such a factory was, however, even at this time, something of an anachronism and Ebenezer Gomme's new factory, built in the following year, was made by 'sinking a great deal of capital into new machinery to extend the mass production methods from the Windsor and common cane and rush seated work into better class work, and from then on the study of machines and men to increase output per man became the key policies to be pursued by successful enterprises'. [38] The machines were available when the demand for them had truly arrived.

The industry's trade magazine for 1892 carried advertisements for only four distinct and simple machines in the course of the year, - the bandsaw, the double boring machine, the double cut off saw and the shaper and planer. [39] By 1908 it carried advertisements for no fewer than twenty-five different types of machinery. More significantly the machines on offer were of greatly increased complexity, including a 'combined patent spiral cutting, planing and sandpapering machine, a multi-cutter dovetailing machine, and an automatic glue jointer'. [40]

In the hundred year period from 1800 to 1900 the furniture trade, beginning as a luxury, bespoke and commissioned art/fashion form at one extreme and basically utilitarian at the other, developed into a mass production industry. Economic and demographic changes in Great Britain both reflected, and found their reflections in, the furniture industry. As a furniture making centre High Wycombe illustrates this change in a cameo form which was repeated, albeit less dramatically, in other places.

The trade of chairmaker emerged in the 1790's when Samuel Treacher was sworn as a burgess of the town. His description of himself as *Chairmaker* is confirmed by an entry in the *British Directory* for 1784 which records all three Treacher brothers as chairmakers, while a stained glass window in High Wycombe Town Hall records the first chair factory in the town as having been established in 1805 by Samuel Treacher and Thomas Widgington, employing, it is thought, some twenty men. [41] [42]

By 1875 the town directory recorded that there were fifty chair manufacturers in the area, the principal of whom averaged a production of 2,000 chairs a day. There were also fifteen smaller firms with a daily production of 1,500 and twenty still smaller establishments with 1,200 a day, giving a daily ouput in total of 4,700 chairs. The five largest firms of William Birch, Cartwright, Cox, Glenister and Gibbons and Walter Skull each employed over fifty persons in the trade. *Kelly's Directory* for the same year recorded an annual output from the town of one and a half million chairs at an average value of 3/4d each. This output was essentially hand work production since the same directory lists 8 sawmills and 1 boring mill. They were evidently small since the same survey records that there were no more than 3 band sawyers and 6 seat borers at the time. [43]

Oliver's work on the distribution of the furniture industry in the London area replicates over the nineteenth century the High Wycombe situation, showing the number of furniture making establishments as 78 in 1801, rising to 499 in 1846 and 1,304 in 1859. Depression later took its toll, for there was a fall in numbers to 909 in 1871, but by 1911 these had recovered to 1,310, almost identical with the 1859 level. There can be litle doubt that this pattern of growth for the industry was also repeated in the other industrial and commercial centres of the country.

The movement from the countryside and a more traditionally settled way of life, coupled with an overall increase in the population, is demonstrated by the growth of London in this period. In 1801 the Great London Conurbation contained 1,117,000 inhabitants and represented 12.56 per cent of the total population of England and Wales. By 1871 the population had grown to 3,890,000 representing 17.13 per cent of the total population of England and Wales.

'Machinery was overcoming all opposition in the industrial towns' notes Mayes, 'and if it was causing unemployment and want, it was also raising up a new class of wage earners who helped to build and install the machines and kept them running afterwards. These men, earning good wages, were occupying the new and better type of houses which wre being built in long terraces in Northampton, in Leeds, in Birmingham, and wherever the new industries settled, and these were the customers for Wycombe chairs, provided always that those chairs were sound enough to satisfy hard-headed artisans and cheap enough to be within their means'. [44]

This explosion of demand and manufacture during the first sixty years of the nineteenth century was made the more possible because the later years of the Napoleonic wars saw a general erosion of apprenticeship restrictions both in practice and in law, culminating in the repeal of the apprenticeship clauses of the Elizabethan Statute of Artificers in 1814. Artisans, depending on apprenticeships for their situation reacted more or less vigorously to this threat. It was traditional that almost the entire skill or 'mystery' of the trade should be conveyed by precept and example in the workshop by the journeyman to his apprentice. The artisans regarded this 'mystery' as their property and asserted their unquestionable right to 'the quiet and exclusive use and enjoyment of their art and trades'. Repeal was resisted, a nascent trades council being formed in London and 60,000 signatures being collected nationally to a petition to strengthen the apprenticeship laws; the threat also had the effect of strengthening the trade clubs in which craftsmen combined to serve their common interests. Many London artisans emerged from the war period in a comparatively strong position.

For many this apparently strengthened position was an illusion. So far as the woodworking trades were concerned less than one tenth of the trade, or more optimistically one-fifth to one-sixth of the workers, according to Mayhew and Thompson, profited by it, while the woodworking trades began to separate out into 'honourable' and 'dishonourable' branches, a distinction essentially concerned with the high and low quality ends of the market. [45]

The debasement of trades took many forms and was sometimes accomplished only after intense conflict lasting in some cases into the 1830's. When William Lovett, who had been apprenticed as a rope maker in Penzance, came to London in 1821 he could find no employment at his own trade and sought work as a cabinetmaker or carpenter. At that time the distinction between the honourable and dishonourable trades was not so marked. The fact that he had served no apprenticeship weighed heavily against him, but after bad experiences at a dishonourable shop and even worse experiences in attempting to hawk his own products, he finally gained employment at a large cabinet workshop. When it was discovered that he had served no apprenticeship the men 'talked of setting Mother Shorney at me. This is a cant term in the trade, and meant the putting away of your tools, the injuring of your work, and annoying you in such a way as to drive you out of the shop. As soon as I was made acquainted with their feelings, I thought it best to call a shop meeting and lay my case before them'. 'To call a meeting of this description, the first requisite was to send for a quantity of drink (generally a gallon of ale) and then to strike your hammer and hold fast together, which, making a bell-like sound, is a summons calling all in the shop to assemble around your bench'. 'A chairman is then appointed, and you are called upon to state your business'. [46]

Lovett's explanation of his difficult circumstances satisfied the men 'but their demands made upon me for drink by individuals among them, for being shown the manner of doing any particular kind of work together with the fines and shop scores, often amounted to seven or eight shillings a week out of my guinea'. Ten or twenty years later Lovett would not have succeeded in gaining employment in a respectable or society shop. The influential Cabinet Makers Society (of which Lovett himself became president) had consolidated the position of its members in the quality branches of the trade and closed its doors against the mass of unapprenticed or semi-skilled labour clamouring without. At the same time the dishonourable trade had mushroomed, middle men had set up 'slaughter houses' or great furniture warehouses, and poor 'garret masters' in Bethnal Green and Spitalfields employed their own families and 'apprentices' in making chairs and shoddy furniture for sale to the warehouses at knockdown prices. Even less fortunate workers would buy or scrape together wood to make workboxes or card tables which they hawked in the streets or sold to cut rate East End shops [47]

Socially as well as economically the distinction between the 'society' and 'non-society' was most marked. Mayhew records 'The cabinet makers, socially as well as commercially considered, consist, like all other operatives, of two distinct classes; that is to say of 'society' and 'non-society' men, or in the language of political economy, of those whose wages are regulated by custom, and those whose earnings are determined by competition. The former class numbers between six and seven hundred of the trade, and the later between four and five thousand. As a general rule, I may remark, that I find 'society men' of every trade comprise about one-tenth of the whole. Hence it follows that if the non-society men are neither so skilful nor so well conducted as the others, at least they are quite as important a body from the fact that they consitute the main portion of the trade. The transition from the one class to the other is, however, in most cases, of a very disheartening character....society men renting houses of their own - some paying as much as £70 a year, and the non-society men overworked and underpaid, so that a few weeks sickness reduced them to absolute pauperism. Nor, I regret to say, can any other tale be told of the cabinet makers except it be that the competititive men in this trade are in an even worse position than in any other'.

Mayhew gives details of society and non-society organisations in 1850. 'The trade societies in connection with this branch of the art, are those of cabinet, chair and bedstead makers. They are divided into three districts, viz. West End, Middle and East End. The districts contain five societies - one at the West End, another in the centre of the metropolis and the others at the East End. Three of these societies are in connection with the cabinetmaker's trade; the remaining two belonging to the bedstead makers and chair makers. The following table shows the number of men in connection with each society together with the non-society men appertaining to each branch'.

Membership of Societies in the Furniture Trade: 1850

|  | Society Men | Non-Society Men | Total |
|---|---|---|---|
| West End General Cabinetmakers | 300 | 1,400 | 1,700 |
| East End Cabinetmakers | 140 | 1,000 | 1,140 |
| Fancy Cabinetmakers | 47 | 500 | 547 |
| Chair Makers | 130 | 1,428 | 1,558 |
| Bedstead Makers | 25 | 238 | 263 |
|  | 642 | 4,566 | 5,208 |

For the society men of this period, the rewards of exclusivity were considerable, as Mayhew illustrates. 'Those who wish to be impressed with the social advantages of a fairly well paid class of mechanics should attend a meeting of the Woodcarvers' Society. On the first floor of a small private house in Tottenham Street, Tottenham Court Road, is, so to speak, the museum of the working men belonging to this branch of the cabinetmakers. The walls of the backroom are hung round with plaster casts of some of the choicest specimens of the arts, and in the front room the table is strewn with volumes of valuable prints and drawings in connection with the craft. Round this table are ranged the members of the society - some forty or fifty were there on the night of my attendance - discussing the affairs of the trade'.

'The objects of this Society are, in the words to the preface to the printed catalogue, 'To enable woodcarvers to cooperate for the advancement of their art, and by forming a collection of books, prints and drawings, to afford them facilities for self improvement, also by the diffusion of information amongst its members, to assist them in the exercises of their art as well as to enable them to obtain employment; so that both employers and employed may, by becoming members, promote their own and each others interests".

'In the whole course of my investigations I have never experienced more gratification than I did on the evening of both my visits to this society. The members all gave evidence, both in manner and appearance, of the refining character of their craft, and it was a hearty relief from the scenes of squalor, misery, dirt, vice, ignorance and discontent, with which these inquiries too frequently bring one into connexion, to find one's self surrounded with an atmosphere of beauty, refinement, comfort, intelligence and ease'.

'The public, generally, are deplorably misinformed as to the character and purpose of trade societies. The common impression is that they are combinations of working men, instituted and maintained solely with the view of exacting an exorbitant rate of wages from their employers, and that they are necessarily connected with strikes, and the sundry other savage and wily means of attaining this object. It is my duty, however, to make known that the rate of wages which such societies are instituted to uphold has, with but few exceptions, been agreed upon at a conference of both masters amd men, and that in almost every case I find the members as strongly opposed to strikes as a means of upholding them, as to the public theselves'. (This being a reference to the London Chairmakers and Carvers Book of Prices for workmanship as regulated and agreed to by a committee of Master Chair Manufacturers and Journeymen 3rd. ed. 1829).

'The payment of the journeyman cabinet maker is, both by the piece and by the week, 32s. a week, being the minimum allowed by the rules of the Society as the remuneration for a week's labour, or six days of ten hours each. The prices by piece are regulated by a book, which is really a remarkable production. It is a thick quarto volume, containing some 600 pages. Under the respective heads the piece-work price of every article of furniture is specified; and immediately after what is called the 'start' price, or the price for the plain article, follows an elaborate enumeration of extras, according as the article may be ordered to be ornamented in any particular manner. There are also engravings of all the principal articles in the trade, which further facilitate the clear understanding of all the regulations contained in the work. The date of this book of prices is 1811, and the wages of the society men have been unchanged since then. The preparation of this ample and minute statement of prices occupied a committee of masters and of journeymen between two and three years. The committee were paid for their loss of time from the masters' and journeymen's funds respectively; and what with these payments, what with the expense of attending the meetings and consitutions, the making and remaking of models, the cost of printing and engravings, the cabianet-makers book of prices was not compiled, I am assured, at a less cost than from £4,000 to £5,000'. [48]

This picture of organisation, cooperation, and relative affluence was restricted to a small group of craftsmen of the highest skills and the reality of the furniture trade in London and other large centres of population was the emergence of the 'garret-masters'. These were craftsmen who operated on their own or with family labour, with limited capital and produced furniture on a speculative basis. Their output was sold to a new breed of middlemen known as 'slaughterhouse men' who in their turn retailed the articles to the public or to other dealers.

Evidence presented to the 1890 Select Committee of the House of Lords on the Sweating System makes it clear as to how this situation arose. 'The cabinet trade was formerly in the hands of manufacturers employing workmen on their own premises. Within the last twenty years the trade has altered. Some of the large drapery establishments have adopted the system of selling furniture, which they buy from dealers, and do not themselves directly employ workmen. Large (drapery) houses now buy from dealers, who, in turn buy from the small makers. They reside chiefly in Bethnal Green, Curtain Road, and Hoxton.......They work in shops with a few hands, generally several children, including girls, being among them'. [49]

In his evidence to the committee, Mr Parnell, The Secretary of the West End Branch of the Alliance Cabinetmakers Association, explained how the system operated. 'If a firm gets an order to supply furniture to a customer, it gives out to a sub-contractor, who in his turn gives it out to another sub-contractor, who gives it out to a foreman who gives it out as piece work to workmen. This system leads to minute sub-division of labour and renders possible the employment of unskilled and child labour'. Lack of capital also militated against the garret master.

Finished goods had to be sold before more items could be produced, a position of which the slaughterhouse men were well aware. Some placed the garretmaster in the position of having to accept whatever terms he was offered. This situation was in its turn compounded by the seasonaility of and large size of the articles produced. Slack trade forced down prices and the sheer bulk of furniture required that it be moved out of the workshop before anything more could be made.

A garret-master chairmaker described his life to Mayhew thus. 'I work from six every morning to nine at night - some work till ten - I breakfast at eight which stops me for ten minutes. I can breakfast in less time, but it's a rest; my dinner takes me say ten minutes at the outside and my tea eight minutes. All the rest of the time I'm starving at the bench. How many minutes rest is that Sir? Thirty-eight. Well, say three-quarters of an hour, and that allows a few sucks at a pipe when I rest, but I can smoke and work too. I have only one room to work and eat in, or I should lose more time. Altogether I labour fourteen-and-a-quarter hours every day, and I rest on Sundays, at least forty Sundays in the year. One may as well work as sit fretting. But on Sundays I only work till it's dusk, or until five or six in summmer. When it's dusk I take a walk. I'm not well dressed enough for a Sunday walk when it's light, and I can't wear my apron very well on that day to hide patches. But there's eight hours that I reckon I take up every week in dancing about to the slaughterer's. I'm satisfied that I work very nearly one hundred hours a week, the year through, deducting the time taken up by the slaughterer's and buying stuff - say, eight hours a week, it gives more than ninety hours a week for my work and there's hundreds labour as hard as I do just for a crust'.

As evidence of the work done and the under-capitalisation of the garret master, Mayhew reports: 'A general cabinet maker commenced business on 30/-, a part of which he thus expended in the material for a four foot chest of drawers:-

|  | s. | d. |
|---|---|---|
| Three feet six inches of cedar for ends | 4 | 0 |
| Sets of mahogany veneers for three big and two little drawers | 2 | 4 |
| Drawer sweep (deal to veneer the front upon) | 2 | 6 |
| Veneer for top | 1 | 3 |
| Extras (any cheap wood) for the insides of drawers, partitioning etc. | 5 | 0 |
| Five locks | 1 | 8 |
| Eight knobs 1/-, glue, sprigs etc. | 1 | 4 |
| Sets of four turned feet, beech, stained | 1 | 6 |
|  | 19 | 7 |

For the article, when completed, he received 25s. toiling at it for 27 or 28 hours'. [50]

It may be questioned how valid such information is, bearing in mind that it was given to an observer unfamiliar with the skills of the trade. In this instance, however, the object is a standard five drawer chest and on the basis of the materials specification and knowledge of the processes involved of framing up, hand cutting drawer dovetails, hand veneering top and drawers, fitting locks and feet, it would indeed be a skilled craftsman who could produce such a chest to a finished state in the time stated. Furthermore, the earlier reports of a hundred hour week would tie in with this, for only thus could the cabinet maker earn his guinea a week.

The furniture trade had thus become an exploitative sweated trade except where work for the highest quality sales was concerned. The old pattern of making and selling from one establishment had broken down into a new approach of retailing and sub-contracting, all meaningful apprenticeship safeguards had been abandoned outside the 'honourable trade' and the industry was swollen with an influx of the unskilled, of women and of children. Working hours had become intolerably long, Sunday working a norm and conditions quite unfavourable to any form of trade union organisation. The woodworker could obtain his materials cheaply and, with his own tools, become his own sweating master, working himself and his family and perhaps other juveniles for a seven day week, and hawking his products in a competititve situation to a limited number of outlets. A revival of the small factory situation, which in its turn would lend itself to trade unionism, seemed light years away.

In the event the spiral of decline was broken by the need to supply in volume, to a standard pattern, for the new and expanding markets at home and overseas which were then appearing. These allowed for orders to be placed by retailers, by Government, by agents, by military authorities and others, which together with new machinery available to assist hand production forced the development and consolidation of individual garret masters and their workers into a factory situation.

In 1881 B. Cohen and Sons advertised 'A large stock of all styles suitable for home, colonial and foreign markets, with representatives travelling by rail and steamship to all markets'. What these representatives took with them was not the product or the miniature but the catalogue which in its turn established and reinforced standardisation of output. What was happening in the cabinet making side of the industry was equally true of the chairmakers. One High Wycombe manufacturer made 8,000 chairs for the Great Exhibition and transported his production to London, Liverpool, Manchester, Australia, Constantinople and New Zealand. In the mid-1870's Moody and Sankey's evangelistic campaign called for 19,200 chairs, all made in High

Wycombe. [51] [52] [53]

As earlier stated, there is scant evidence of any workers' organisations in the industry prior to 1800. The elaborate Books of Prices of the period and particularly in the Preface and Agreement to the 3rd. ed. there are, however, suggestions of earlier disputes and disagreements resulting in some form of industrial action by one side or the other. 'The Frequent Disputes which have recently occurred in the Metropolis, between various Manufacturers and their Journeymen, in consequence of disagreement of opinion, respecting the value of Workmanship contained in the various articles they severally manufacture are too generally known; and the inconvenience resulting from the want of Rules for decision, have been too severely experienced, to require either particular enumeration of general comment, in justification of the motive that induced the publication of the following pages, which have for their object, the prevention of such disputes in future: as, in many instances, the contentions alluded to have been productive of the most disagreeable and injurious effects to individuals of both parties'. [54]

This exemplary and far-sighted move was reinforced by the setting up of a joint committee of arbitration composed of equal numbers of Manufacturers and Journeymen to resolve disputes 'and that their determination in every such case be considered by each party as final', and by a similarly composed committee to look at and price new models of furniture since they 'have taken into consideration the continual variety which Fancy and Fashion are ever introducing into the various Articles of Manufacture....and from the impossibility of foreseeing the alterations which future fancy may suggest'.

Most of the early records of local workmen's societies in the furniture industry have disappeared. From local newspapers, however, traces can be found of the efforts of the early pioneers of trade unionsim in the industry. High Wycombe has the best documented example. Here the local *Bucks Free Press* recorded in 1854 'A big meeting of chairmakers to consider the conduct of Mr Glenister - a large manufacturer'. The immediate cause of this meeting is not given. However, in December 1855 the chairmakers in the town formed 'The Chairmakers Protection Society' with Robert White as President, William Busby as Vice President and Owen Mead as Secretary. The splendid Certificate of Membership designed by Owen Mead shows two chairmakers with tools of their trade and the Latin motto 'Pro Jure Laboris Certamus', 'We stand for the right to work'. It was, as in London, a society concerned with the mutual improvement of its members. One of its activities was a Mechanics Loan Society from which a member could borrow money to buy tools or any other agreed purchase. [55]

The first years of the society record only meetings and lectures of an 'improving' nature. In February of 1857 however a new situation arose. A manufacturer named Smith 'proposed a reduction in the price of framing odd chairs'. Smith's men objected to the reduction and went on strike. It was at that time, in High Wycombe, as in other towns, custom and practice price for all grades of work, whether formalised in 'the book' as in London or Edinburgh, or not. The Society, now numbering some two hundred members decided to support the seven men on strike against such violation of custom. The necessary 2/4d. per man per day required a levy of 3d. per member. This proved to be far from popular with the membership and the end of this first confrontation was a return to work of the strikers on the basis of a compromise and the gradual disintegration of the Society.

The Society was, however, far from dead. In 1861 it decided to combat the evils of unemployment by providing 'the keen worker with opportunities for taking more shares in an enterprise in which he could be man and master'. A series of meetings resulted in the formation in 1861 of a workman's co-operative, the High Wycombe Chair Manufacturing Co. Ltd. Its capital was £5,000 divided into £1 shares, each share to be paid up by instalments of not less than three pence weekly and 'every shareholder to be a member of the Chairmakers' Protection Society'. Eventually after a series of further meetings the company was formed as 'the Wycombe Co-operative Chair Manufacturing Company'. The aims of the company were stated to be 'the combination of labour and capital, employer and employed, of master and servant, in the recently established Co-operative Societies designed to supersede the system of strikes ruinous alike to both parties, and to elevate the working man to a higher standard and to a more respectable position in society'. The co-operative never became firmly established probably on account of difficulties in raising the capital on the shares. Within two years it had faded from notice and with it the Chairmakers' Protection Society itself. [56]

The chairmakers of High Wycombe remained, however, unhappy with their situation. A few years later they are reported as complaining that their rates of pay were so low that in order to earn a living wage 'we have to start at six in the morning and work till eight at night and cannot get our wage till six of a Saturday evening'. They also protested most bitterly that the 'truck' system was still in operation so that their nominal wages were rarely realised. [57]

In 1872 a new chairmakers' trade union was formed and this proved to be popular both in the town and in the surrounding district. The earliest statement of the union stressed that it was being organised to help the manufacturers as well as the workers by endeavouring to secure uniform rates of pay throughout the trade thus making it impossible for the unscrupulous manufacturer to recruit cheap labour and so undersell those who paid fair rates. It was also its announced intention to take action against truck, and to discourage chairmasters from keeping beer and 'tommy shops'. The first meetings of the union were held jointly with the manufacturers but the latter subsequently refused to consider a new printed list of prices. They (the manufacturers - now 31 in number) had already met privately and now sent the union a letter announcing 'that this meeting respectfully decline the printed list of prices as submitted, but that the question of prices is under consideration by the employers'.

Such an impasse might have remained for some time. However, a local dispute arose in which members of the union were locked out. To this the union replied by removing labour from another factory and the employers then locked out all the union men, putting four hundred chairmakers on the streets. The union was young and impoverished and wished for an early return to work. The deputation it sent to the Manufacturers was most conciliatory. 'It is hereby declared by the Committee of the Chairmakers' Trade Union that they have combined together solely for the purpose of self-defence, and to secure certain prices for their work at the present crisis, and not for the purpose of aggression or with any ulterior object, or to obtain increased prices in the future except under similar exceptional circumstances'.

The dispute lasted from July 1871 until early September of the same year and ended with a gradual drift back to work on a compromise solution. It was too much for the youthful chairmakers' union which, like its predecessors, soon faded away. Trade unionism in the furniture industry in High Wycombe, as in many other centres, was not to become viable until the arrival of the Alliance Cabinetmakers Society with its central organisation and dynamic leadership.

# CHAPTER II

## The Alliance Cabinetmakers' Society
## 1865 - 1901

In the nineteenth century the trade of furniture making made slow progress towards unionisation compared with other industries of a comparable skill in workforce and output. The Amalgamated Society of Engineers formed in 1851 with 5,000 members grew to 54,000 by 1888; the Amalgamated Society of Carpenters and Joiners from 8,000 members in 1850 to 54,000 by the same year and the Friendly Society of Operative Stonemasons which had 5,000 members in 1850 had already had 16,000 members by 1878. [1]

The sectionalised, regionalised nature of the trade, associated with a mobile workforce, low capital investment requirements and highly seasonal demand, all combined to make efforts to build other than local societies seem a near impossible task. Indeed, such were the problems of organisation that despite the development by the end of the century of one of the most vital, politicised and effective trade unions of its time, the majority of workers in the furniture industry were not enrolled into a union until the second world war.

By the mid nineteenth century conditions within the furniture trade in the larger centres of population in the United Kingdom such as Glasgow, Manchester, Belfast and Liverpool mirrored those of London both in products and organisation. This was effectively a three-tier structure. Division 1 consisted of the West End bespoke trade. Small in numbers and highly respected, it had no involvement in any other aspects of the trade. Division 2, comprised the high class, ready made trade. This was essentially a West End grouping around the West End Cabinetmakers' Society which regulated entry and employment within the best shops. Division 3, was composed of the mass of tradesmen, operating individually or in small shops, dependent upon sub-contracting work, but capable of supplying all or any markets. It was against this background that the Alliance Cabinetmakers Society was formed in 1865. [2]

The mid-1860's were years of relative prosperity and good trade for a variety of industries, giving encouragement to workers employed in them to press for increases in wages. 'The upheaving of labour is almost universal throughout the Kingdom. Hardly a trade exists but what is putting up its claim to participate in the large profits now, and for some time past [being made] by the capitalists from the healthy state of trade' reported *The Beehive*.

The furniture workers' organisations in London at this time were the West End Societies of the Cabinetmakers and Carvers who together numbered some 300 members and the East London Cabinetmakers' Society with fewer than 50 members collectively and colloquially known to employers as 'the 40 thieves'. None of these societies responded to the opportunity of the 1860's to promote wage movements either for their own members or for the mass of workers in the capital city. And so, as a London cabinetmaker later recalled, 'The Alliance began with a view to organising the trade in the East End, which had undoubtedly been neglected by the more prosperous body of men in the West End who claimed the exclusive right to work in the West End shops as also did the Manchester Union (Friendly Society of Cabinetmakers) in the best shops in the Provinces'. [4] [5]

This version of the story was not entirely correct. The initial aims of the promoters of the Alliance were not principally to organise the East End but rather to seek a wage increase for the majority of workers who were, of course, concentrated in the Eastern and Northern parts of the city. 'On October 11, 1865, *The Beehive* reported, a meeting was held in the Albion Hall in St. Lukes, Chelsea (just off the Kings Road), to organise a wage movement amongst the city's non-society cabinet-makers. The meeting was crowded to excess with workmen exclusively from the principal shops in the Eastern and Northern districts of the Metropolis. The men decided to seek 'an advance of ten per cent both by day and by piece' [some workers being on fixed day wages whilst others were paid by the piece produced] 'and elected delegates from each shop to direct the movements'.

A movement fund was set up and contributions collected and on October 18th, forty-two shop delegates representing some 600 men met to pay in their collection. It was established that the majority of employers were willing to give the advance, provided that it was adopted by the whole trade. When, therefore, an even larger group of 63 shop representatives met in the following week, they formed themselves into a 'Committee acting on behalf of the Journeymen Cabinetmakers'.

The first task of the committee was to produce and circularise amongst the employers a handbill requesting a meeting to discuss the workers' demands. 'The prosperous state of trade' declared the committee, 'warrants the assumption that the capital of the country can afford to pay a higher price for labour'. [6] On November 4th, 60 employers, including Mr John Maple, met the committee and agreed in principle to a ten per cent wage increase, contingent upon its acceptance by the other employers in the district who were not represented at the meeting, and who numbered some 120.

The tone of the meeting was less negative than this might suggest. An employer conceded that 'when in these districts the cabinetmakers saw the builders, joiners and iron workers, and all other trades have got a considerable advance, they naturally said to themselves - who were they, that they should be excluded from the operation of the seemingly general system, and, therefore, kept in a position which caused them to be looked down upon by those other trades. They considered themselves in every respect equal to them in intelligence and respectability'. Other views were also expressed on the outcome of the concession. 'The higher wages in the East End might encourage cabinetmakers to give up business on their own account and come into a comfortable shop, and thus quit being of use only to upholsterers (that is, having their work covered up!)'.

Though the general tone of the employers' reaction was of acceptance, they were less than happy at the prospect of having to deal in the future with any kind of organisation of workmen and the formal notices of change of rates bore the message, 'The application for an advance was made by the men generally, and not by any society whatever, and the employers do not recognise such societies at all'. This attitude did not deter the men of the trade. A meeting of all journeymen was called for November 22nd 1865, in the Hall of Science on City Road, London. Attended by over 1,000 furniture workers, it resolved by acclamation that 'the only way of obtaining and maintaining the ten per cent advance is by the formation of an association'. The new Society was to be called the Alliance Cabinetmakers' Association 'formed with the avowed purpose to obtain the advance of ten per cent throughout the whole trade' and 'to support those members whose situations might be sacrificed in maintaining the price of work. The allowance to such men to be 15/- per week'. [7]

It was reported that fifty employers had formally agreed the increase but many others were showing a marked reluctance to meet the demand. The chairman (unnamed) stated that 'every measure should first be tried before extreme steps are taken, but if necessary, we must not flinch from taking these steps'. The meeting ended with over 800 furniture workers agreeing to join the new Association.

The new Alliance met formally for the first time on November 29th 1865. This was only two days before a deadline that had been set for the payment of the wage advance and so a small committee was set up, empowered to withdraw as many men as was necessary from the shops that refused. In the event such drastic action was not called for by such a young and inexperienced union, and by the end of December the increase had been won for all the members.

Membership of the Alliance cost 3d. per week in these early formative years, and for the first two years of its existence was a 'dispute pay only' society, since it was reported 'they have confined themselves for the present, to the purpose of creating a fund for the protection of trade' and 'the committee are very anxious that the whole of the non-society men in the trade should join, in order to enhance the wages and social position of their class'. [8]

There is no mention of qualification for entry. By taking this position the new society was showing that it was neither in conflict with, nor aping, the exclusive attitude and ideals of the older more conservative societies such as the West End Cabinetmakers or the Friendly Society of Cabinetmakers. This evangelical approach was mirrored in its resolve not to hold its meetings in public houses, as was the common practice of the times, but rather in the Alliance Hall in Old Street Road, East London. The buoyancy and optimism of the new society was swiftly deflated, with the return of a trade depression in 1866. This threw into relief the inherent weakness of the organisation. Unlike the West End societies, its members were unable to exert enough pressure to force an overall acceptance of an agreed price for a specific type or piece of work within their sector of the trade. The only course of action open to them was to imitate the approach used by the East London Society, the '40 thieves'.

This system worked on the basis of each individual shop drawing up its own price list and attempting to enforce these prices as standard within that shop. The system could be very effective but it had the inherent weakness that it depended upon the condition of trade which was in its turn dependent upon the general level of prosperity in the country, and in the final analysis upon the reasonableness of rapacity of the employer.

This shop bargaining approach of the East End '40 thieves' was graphically described in the *Cabinetmaker*. 'Provided a new hand does not underwork another by occupying a job at a lower price than that already paid in the shop to others, even if that price be a bad one, he does not infringe upon the society rules. But of what practical utility is such a system? It does not even keep up the prices to a fixed standard in more than one factory: for supposing that one employer gives twenty shillings a foot for a sideboard of a certain pattern, another may, if he thinks proper, fix his price at 18/- per foot for the labour upon the same description of article, and yet the Society has not got a positive right of interference'. [9] These problems of organisation and enforcement were effectively beyond the capacity of a broad general society in a period of depression and within two years of its formation the Alliance had adopted a more craft society profile, more capable of sustaining a membership in period of recession as well as prosperity.

By 1868 the Alliance had 159 members organised into two branches, No.1 Central London, meeting in Finsbury, and No.2 West End, meeting in Fitzroy Square. The Society now charged a joining fee of 4/- and contributions of 71/2d. per week but it offered to its membership a comprehensive range of benefits:-

| | |
|---|---|
| Strike Pay | 18/- per week |
| Unemployment Pay | 12/- per week |
| Sick Pay | 10/- per week (for an extra contribution of 3d. per week) |
| Emigration Gift | 30/- |
| Tool Insurance | £7 |
| Death Benefit | £3 widow; £2 widower |

In terms of benefits and contributions the Alliance was now much more in line with the exclusive craft societies of the trade but whereas they, the craft societies, adopted rigid qualifications for entry, the Alliance did not require any evidence of apprenticeship as a prerequisite of membership. Members were simply required to be employed in the trade, and not to employ boys other than their own sons. This inclusive rather than exclusive approach was the undoubted reason for the Association's growth over the years to come. Coupled with careful husbanding management it ensured that from a faltering beginning the Alliance would grow from strength to strength.

The evangelical aspect of unionism was not forgotten however. In 1872, within the new organisation of the union, it began to form libraries of books in each of its branches. By the following year these amounted to over 500 volumes of a suitably improving nature, obtained by purchase and by gift. The General Secretary of the Alliance, J.R. Smith, reported, 'Your committee believes that the more the members are educated the more they will see the advantages and benefits of this Association'. The books could be borrowed free for a period up to 4 weeks and 'members are particularly requested to keep the books as clean as possible'.

Although a very small group of craftsmen, the Alliance also took the major step forward in 1872 which was to put the society at the very centre of furniture trade unionism. It amalgamated with the East London Cabinetmakers Society (the 'forty thieves'). General Secretary Smith reported, 'this is the most successful step that has ever been taken by the members, not only to benefit our own individual interests but also to promote the prosperity of the whole Cabinet Trade'. [10]

This new found strength and an improvement in trade prompted the Alliance to promote a general trade movement in the London area in the same year for higher wages. Circulars were distributed in every furniture making establishment in London and a meeting of over 2,000 cabinetmakers declared its determination 'To rescue the Trade from its present degraded condition', [11] by a demand for a reduction in working hours as well as an increase in pay. To these ends a delegate committee of Alliance and non-society men was formed 'to direct the movement for a ten per cent increase in wages', the question of hours being left for each shop to pursue separately. A levy on each workman of 2d. per week was authorised, monies to be held apart from normal Alliance funds and the committee was empowered to withdraw workmen from the shops as necessary to secure the increase. [12]

The movement was most successful and by August 24th some 91 employers had complied with the men's demand, though there were others who remained unmoved. One employer told the committee that he intended 'to remove to the West End and pay West End prices' whilst another, a parquet floor manufacturer, refused to accept the increase, telling the committee that he could hire boys to do the work. [13] By November 1872, however, almost all the Alliance members had won their ten per cent increase and their delegates on the wage movement committee declared an intention to end the 2d. per week levy and to bring the movement to a close. The non-society men on the committee bitterly opposed this, but as the Alliance men claimed, 'As by the united efforts of Society and non-society men the ten per cent cause has been almost entirely won, there is no longer any need for the continuance of the existing mixed delegate system, and those who are outside and wish to continue to have protection, have nothing to do but to come into the Society'. [14] The non-society delegates responded that the Society would not take them in since the 300 men involved 'had an apprentice or two'. This was indeed true since an Alliance rule provided that 'under no circumstances will the rules of this Association permit a member to employ a lad or have anyone working for him (unless he be his own son), as by employing a lad, he becomes as employer, and a sub-contractor, and is no longer a Journeyman receiving wages for his own personal labour'. [15] Though the non-society men pressed for a continuation of the wages movement, it was wound up on November 30th. High-handed the action of the Alliance executive may have been, it was no more than realistic in so young a society. [16]

The Alliance Association had set itself a series of objectives which it had effectively attained. It had organised a mass wage movement which was overwhelmingly successful; it had sustained this effort over a period of seven months without the movement disintegrating; it had recruited a substantial number of new members, and shown itself to the furniture industry as a coherent and virile organisation. So positive an identity paid dividends almost immediately. The Fancy Cabinetmakers of London, up to this time no more than a loose amalgam of men in this sector of the trade, dropped an earlier intention to form its own association and decided instead 'that the interests of all the decorative furniture trades are identical' and formed Branch No.3 of the Alliance with 91 members. [17]

This decision was of particular significance, not only in terms of an increase in the numerical strength of the society, but also because these highly skilled craftsmen had chosen to join the generalist Alliance rather than the more conservative West London Society. J.R. Smith, recognising the significance of this move, noted that 'there is every prospect of it (the Fancy Cabinetmakers Branch) becoming a large and powerful branch, which we trust will do a large amount of good in that branch of the trade, and at the same time form a strong support to the Association'. [18] His hopes were soon realised. Within weeks the London Society of Continental Cabinetmakers with some 80 members had joined the Alliance to form Branch No.4 and with the founding of Branches in Hastings, Reading and Bath, the Alliance moved from its position as a London based society to become a more nationally representative organisation.

The trade conditions in the early 1870's continued to be prosperous. Taking advantage of this, branches were formed all over the country in the next few years at an almost bewildering speed. Eight branches were added in 1873, twenty in 1874, twenty-eight in 1875 and forty in 1876. With this growth of membership amongst hitherto unorganised workers, the Alliance was also able to attract into the fold a number of old local societies. The Manchester Amalgamated Society of Cabinet and Chairmakers was followed by the East London United Society of Chairmakers and Carvers, the Cutlery Cabinetmakers Society of Sheffield, the Manchester and District United Cabinet and Chairmakers Society and the Nottingham Local Cabinet and Chairmakers Society. Within a few short years the London based Alliance had grown from two hundred members to almost 2,000 and had become both a national union and the largest single union representing workers in the furniture trade. [19]

The Alliance was not only expansionist in outlook but also saw itself as a part of the trade union movement as a whole. As early as 1867 it had joined the International Working Men's Association, and as its finances improved began to make donations to other groups of workers in the throes of the struggle for recognition. J.R. Smith reported 'The Association has voted the following sums to other societies - £35 to the Agricultural Labourers, which with voluntary subscriptions of £33.13s.1d. makes a total of £68.13s.1d. (and never did a cause demand our sympathy more), £20 to the Elastic Web Weavers Association, Leicester, and £10 to the Gold Beaters Society'. The executive of the union may have been more enthusiastic than the membership since there is no record of the latter voting on these sums of money. Nevertheless a large sum was raised by the membership for the Agricultural Labourers which suggests that the executive's wider view of the working class struggle was well accepted by the rank and file as a whole, and in 1874, the Alliance and five of its members found theselves at the very centre of the struggle of the trade union movement to maintain its legal rights. [20] [21]

The action centred over the right to picket. This had been in jeopardy since 1867 as a result of the case of *Regina v. Druitt* which outlawed any picketing 'calculated to have a deterring effect on the minds of ordinary persons by exposing them to having their motions watched, and to encounter blacklooks'. The Gladstone Criminal Law Amendment Act four years later had enshrined this principle in the law of the land and the Alliance, in common with other trade unions, had been active in agitating for its repeal, participating in numerous demonstrations and sending regular deputations to lobby Members of Parliament. [22] [23]

The incident that proved to be the turning point in the 'right to picket' campaign arose in 1874 at the firm of Jackson and Graham in Oxford Street, London. At this furniture making company the men 'had waited on the firm in reference to some more definite understanding about the payment for overtime. They had also complained to the firm that they were compelled to lose much time waiting for the machinery in a machine assisted hand production situation. If the machinists had not got the next work 'roughed out' or 'converted' the men had to wait until they had done so, but without receiving any payment for this waiting time'. As pieceworkers they were losing a great deal of money, a situation which the firm could only alleviate by employing more machines and machinists, or by producing work for stock. [24]

On Friday 13th November 1874, as the Alliance Journal reports, 'the men met with the foreman, expecting an answer to the overtime question, but were told that they were all discharged at one o'clock on the following day, but would be re-employed on the following Monday under a new system of 'lumpwork'', i.e. a piecework system with no provision for waiting time or for overtime. The men informed the Executive Committee of the Alliance which sent a deputation to the management of Jackson & Graham on the Monday morning, but failed to persuade the firm to change its policy. The union then withdrew the men from the premises and they remained out on strike until February of the next year.

A series of letters was exchanged between the Alliance and the firm which culminated in the following threatening response from Jackson & Graham on the 10th February, 1875:-

'....on consideration I think it would be a waste of time for me to confer with a deputation from your Society. We have resolved to put an end to that system of organised idleness (I should be justified in using a much stronger term) which has, I believe, been instigated and supported by your Society, ever since we opened our manufacturing in Ogle Street. We have never sought to reduce wages, but on the contrary, have always been amongst the first to advance them, and I think your Society will have reason to regret the hostile course it has adopted and continues to pursue towards our firm'. [25]

The threat was made good when some few days later, five members of the Alliance were arrested on the charge that they 'did conspire to molest or obstruct the prosecutors, by watching or besetting their place of business and that they did this in order to coerce them to alter their mode of carrying on their business'. *The Times* reported the case. 'At the Old Court of the Central Criminal Court on 5th May 1875, before the judge, Baron Cleasby (who normally sat in the Court of Exchequer), Messrs. Ham, Hibbert, Mathews, Read and Weiler, were charged with conspiring together to molest workmen in the employment of William Edgar Graham and others, with attempting to coerce the employers to cease to employ their workmen and to molest workmen with a view to induce them to leave their employment. The prosecution opened the trial by explaining that Jackson and Graham were a firm of cabinetmakers and upholsterers of Oxford Street, London, employing some 100 hands. Until November 1874 they had paid their workmen by the day but after 13th November they had introduced piece work. This method of payment gave great offence to the association (the Alliance) of which all the defendants were members and Messrs. Ham and Read were on the executive committee. This decision resulted in a withdrawal of labour by the Alliance and a deputation called upon Mr. Jackson on the 16th November asking whether the prices paid might be arrived at by a shop committee. This Mr. Jackson refused and the Committee of the Alliance wrote to Jacksons to say they could not consent to their members working under such terms. Mr Jackson went on to report that for the next 3 months the five defendants were observed walking up and down outside the factory between the hours of 9 a.m. and 5 p.m. and particularly during the dinner period'.

The trial continued on the following day and the prosecution brought forward a number of witnesses, all of whom were men working for Jackson and Graham under the piecework system. They all confirmed Mr Jackson's contention that picketing was taking place and that the defendants had tried to explain to them the reason for the dispute, and to persuade them to leave the firm. All referred to the picketing as a 'nuisance' but all agreed that the picketing was peaceful and that there had been no physical interferance with any workman. [27] The prosecution summed up their case as follows: 'A workman is undoubtedly free to make terms with his master and the employer is equally free'. It went on to suggest to the jury that the question was whether the 'pernicious and abominable system of picketing was to be permitted, with all the vexation and annoyance which was implied in such a system. This picketing was coercion of the vilest form, a quite sinister mode of tracking the artisan, which made him a marked man for life. There could be no question that the men charged had been guilty of molesting the defendant by watching and besetting'.

When the defence opened its case the jury was reminded that the medical and legal professions were both trade unions with written and unwritten rules which included debarring any member from practising for the rest of his life if he was found guilty of breaking the rules of the profession. Mr Wright, Q.C. defending Harry Ham touched the kernel of the matter. 'Watching and besetting could not surely be regarded as a crime. No picketing could be criminal within the meaning of the Act (i.e. Criminal Law Amendment Act 1871), unless it was accompanied with or used in such a way as to actually amount to personal and physical molestation'.

Baron Cleasby summed up the evidence by stating 'This Act has made it an offence to molest or obstruct any person with a view to coerce him to quit any employment he was engaged in. The Act laid down quite clearly that such molestation includes following a man about from place to place, and includes the watching or besetting of the workman's home or a master's business'. The five defendants were found guilty. In sentencing them Baron Cleasby declared 'I don't know what would become of society if any number of persons could be allowed to watch and beset the premises of people in business....certainly nothing could be more injurous to a man's business than to have day by day, morning and night, his premises watched, and persons going there and going away, accosted and addressed.....and to some extent threats held out'. The defendants were sentenced to 30 days in prison. One of the defendants, as he was being removed 'declared in a loud voice and excited manner that they were morally right though legally wrong'.

The subsequent release of the five Alliance members from the Cold Baths Field Prison was 'the occasion of a remarkable demonstration of working class outrage' at the 'class made laws'. The prison authorities released the men several hours earlier than they announced 'in order to avoid boisterous crowds of working people' but despite this tactic over 400 trade union delegates met the men at the prison gates and escorted them to a celebration breakfast in their honour, sponsored by the Alliance. Later in the day Professor E.S. Beesley presided over a dinner to honour the released men in the Co-operative Hall. This was attended by 'a large crowd including H. Crompton, F. Harrison, A. MacDonald, J. Chamberlain and G. Howell' and the five members were presented with a 'handsome purse of money of nearly £140'. The celebrations culminated in an open air meeting that night in Hyde Park 'in which over 100,000 working people, including many representatives from Alliance branches in the provinces, demanded that in future legislation should place the workman and the employer in equality before the law'. [28] [29]

The case of the five cabinetmakers and the public sympathy engendered by their trial and commital was vey largely responsible for the changes which subsequently took place to modify the Criminal Law Amendment Act, but the young Alliance society was faced with a heavy bill for the defence and support of its members and their families. The final sum amounted to nearly £800. Happily very many individuals and trade societies contributed to a Defence Fund of some £550 and so enabled the Alliance to remain solvent and active as a trade union.

Activity was at the centre of the union's growth. In a particularly modern and progressive step it produced a publicity brochure which was distributed throughout the trade, encouraging non-society men to join. Describing it, the Monthly Report noted, 'Your committee are of the opinion that if the advantages and benefits to be derived by joining the Association were better known and understood, that there are many towns that would join our Association, and hope that the members will circulate the prospectus showing the benefits and progress of the Association as much as possiible and trust the whole of the members will co-operate with your EC in prompting and extending the principles and interests of the Association'. [30]

The Alliance was a centralist society in that the union dues were collected locally from members, payments on a prescribed scale then being paid by the branch and the surplus, after the payment of branch expenses, passed on to headquarters. In branches where subscriptions did not cover the benefits paid, the balance was sent out from headquarters and in this way strict and stringent financial contrtol was exercised from the earliest and most vulnerable years of the Society. Central control became even tighter in 1876 when, as the economy turned down the Alliance became involved in strikes in Bolton, Oldham and Torquay in defence of wage rates which the employers wished to reduce. These actions cost £1,064 in strike pay and reduced the net worth of the society by nearly half within a year. As a result of this financial setback the Alliance adopted a policy of centralised sanction for action to improve wages or conditions. Branches might vote for a wage claim but the Society would only sanction such action if in the opinion of the executive committee it was economically viable.

Whilst the first ten years of the Alliance was a period of good trade and general prosperity, this was followed by a long and painful decade of economic depression. The value of a strong central control became evident during the latter period. 'Several Branches have been desirous of asking their employers for an advance of wages, but in most cases your EC have recommended them to postpone their movements until trade improves'. [31] Yet in the midst of its problems the Alliance was prepared to help other societies in greater difficulties than itself. 'Several other Trade Societies have been in difficulties, and have appealed to us for assistance, whilst many for the want of better organisation, have completely disappeared. Although trade has been so bad with us, we are pleased to state that we have been able to assist the following societies - French Polishers, Nut and Bolt Makers, Razor Scale Pressers, Silk Throwsters, Miners and Stone Masons....to the amount of £83.17s.1d.'

Under the general secretaryship of J.R. Smith the union was disinclined to adopt political attitudes and the depression years were noteworthy for their lack of political message to the membership. 'There can be no doubt that the cause of the great depression of trade in this and other countries at the present time, is owing to the unsettled state of affairs in the East of Europe, but it is not our place in this respect to give an opinion in reference to political matters, although our members have to bear the burden of the same'; and again 'the great depression in our trade in this and other countries....is chiefly owing to the very unsettled state of affairs in the East, but it is not our place to give any expression on political matters'. [32] For the Alliance under Smith political activity in the seventies and eighties was a closed book and the political outlook of the Trades Union Congress of this period finds no echo in the records of this particular furniture workers' society. The explanation for such neutrality, or indeed refusal, to consider political matters, stems from the defensive position that the furniture workers had to adopt during the period. From 1877 to 1887 the membership of the union fell by one-half to 1,101 members only, a down turn not experienced by other parts of the trade union movement. The Carpenters and Joiners grew from 10,000 to 18,000 between 1870 and 1880, and the Amalgamated Association of Operative Cotton Spinners from 11,000 in 1870 to 17,000 in 1888 to name but two societies which expanded during the period.

Such growth was not, however, general among amalgamated societies. While affiliated membership of the Trades Union Congress was just short of one million in 1874, it had fallen to 379,000 in 1884 and rose only to 568,000 in 1888. 'Much of the explanation lies in the trade cycle, since unions tend to flourish in prosperity and wither in depression' note Clegg, Fox and Thompson, and this was certainly true of the young Alliance Society. Indeed, so severe were conditions at the depth of the depression for the furniture trade in 1886 that the society had to borrow £400 from Birbeck Bank to meet its liabilities, despite the fact that members were paying double contributions. Fortunately such was the volatility of the furniture industry in those hand production times that this debt was paid off within six months and by 1890 the union had well over 4,000 members and was worth nearly £2000. [33]

The early leader of the Alliance, J.R. Smith, retired in 1886 and was replaced unopposed by Harry Ham as general secretary. At the same time the post was made a full-time appointment with a salary of £117 per annum; thus replacing the situation in which the whole of the organisation had been run on a voluntary basis, the EC and the General Secretary receiving expenses and loss of earnings only. The union had adopted from the start a three-year term of office for all officials, and elections on a national rather than a regional basis. EC meetings were held on Saturdays and Sundays to enable members to get to London but economic and social necessity tended to result in the society's officers being London or Home Counties members rather than more widely representative of the membership.

While this generated a strong local autonomy within a centralist structure which was democratically acceptable, it left the question of recruitment in the hands of the local branch, which was not always in a position to expose local members to the possible consequential victimisation as a result of their activities. To overcome this particular problem part-time trade organisers were drafted into various areas from outside during the late 1880's and the names of Parnell, Walker, Adams and Robson are shown in the account under the heading of 'Trade Organising Wages and Expenses'.

The position of 'trade organiser' was regularised in 1891 and Tom Walker, a London cabinetmaker, was appointed as the first organiser of the union at the salary of £117 per annum. His role was to aid recruitment and this appointment strengthened the society substantially. The amalgamations of a number of local societies followed in its wake. The Photographic Cabinetmakers, the Newcastle Polishers Local Society and the Hebrew Cabinetmakers Society joined the Alliance in 1893 bringing in 423 additional members. As the records show this latter society did, however, result in the union incurring some extra expense. The translation of Alliance rules into Hebrew cost £5.5s.0d. and the printing of 1,000 copies of the rules in Hebrew a further £7.10s.0d.

The existence of a trade organiser within the union could not, however, change the transient nature of much union membership within the furniture trade. Harry Ham wrote in 1888: 'The Cabinet trade is not one of the great staple trades of the country. Therefore, except in the large towns, our numbers must be comparatively small, but our average benefits will be found to be equal, if not in advance, of those of any other Society'. The Alliance had introduced a new graduated scale of contribututions and benefits in 1880 as follows: [34]

'Entrance fee 4/- : one shilling when proposed, one shilling on election and remaining 2/- within six months'.

| Standard Wages of the Town | Contribution | Out of Work Support | Dispute Support |
|---|---|---|---|
| A. 35/- and over | 7d. | 14/- | 21/- |
| B. 30/- and under 35/- | 6d. | 12/- | 18/- |
| C. 25/- and under 30/- | 5d. | 10/- | 15/- |
| D. Under 25/- | 4d. | 8/- | 12/- |

'Emigration £1.10s.0d. Tool Insurance £7 for an extra 1/- per £1 per annum. Death Benefit £5 to widow, £2 to widower. Six month membership before coming into benefit'.

Despite this delay before benefits became operable, and the existence of an entrance fee, a pattern of drifting in and out of membership became established within the trade that was to continue until the 1940's. In the 1890's this phenomenon of turnover was at its worst relative to overall membership. In 1893 the Alliance, with 4,800 members, gained 2,303 'new' members but lost 2,390 who were struck off from membership for being in arrears of dues. Such shifting sands of membership were, however, stabilized by a solid core of members who prided themselves on 'never being in arrears'; a fact which was always mentioned in any notice of retirement and must be seen in the context of the crude industrial relations climate within which the industy operated. An indication of the difficulties which this latter produced was seen in a dispute between members of the Alliance who were wood turners in London and their employers. The Alliance took the employers to court for deducting 4/- per week from the wages of the workers for the use of steam power (to drive the lathe) and won the case. In consequence of this decision, some of the employers sought to reduce wages by 4/- per week whilst others locked out their men for refusing voluntarily to return up to 4/- per week wages already earned.

Despite these backwoods conditions, a new recognition and respect for the joint interests of unions and employers in the industry was beginning to emerge. Until the mid-1890's all agreements had been of a loosely regional but effectively factory-based nature. In each town it was recognised that wages, as provided for in the contributions and benefits section of the Alliance rules, provided a local yardstick. This was, however, no more than a conventional arrangement. It had little effective force against the laws of supply and demand.

In 1896, as a result of 'the most prosperous period known to any of our members', the Alliance was able to secure a London agreement with the re-formed London Cabinetmakers Federation. This agreement established day rates for cabinetmakers and shop fitters, a fifty two and a half hour week at a minimum rate of ninepence halfpenny per hour and fixed rates for overtime. The agreement was accepted without dispute in the majority of the London factories but the 'Hebrew shops' required a four week withdrawal of labour before the agreed conditions were applied. By fighting this battle under the leadership of Tom Walker, the Alliance noted, 'our Hebrew members have been rescued from the grip of the sweater and placed under the same conditions enjoyed by their fellow members of British and other nationalities'.

The concept of a Federation of employers was new to the Alliance in the 1890's. At first it seemed benign and useful enough. A darker side of the development of employers' organisations was brought home to the furniture workers by the grreat engineering strike of 1897-98. Its Annual Report records: 'This year will always be memorable in the annals of Labour in consequence of the great struggle which took place in the Engineering trades between organised capitalism on the one side and organised labour on the other, wherein the Federated Employers, backed by the wealth accumulated as a result of the past labour of the workers, and aided by traitors to the cause of Labour, were able to inflict a severe defeat on the organised workers in those trades, backed only by the funds they had been able to accumulate by years of self-denial from their barely subsistence wages, and the aid of others of their own class in the same position'. Of the £116,000 subscribed by British and overseas unions in support of the Engineers, the Alliance raised nearly £500. The Employers' Federation whilst ostensibly rejecting a claim for an eight hour day, declared the union, was 'determined to obtain the freedom for employers to manage their own affairs which has proved so beneficial to the American manufacturer'. It was an attack on the unions' rights to collective bargaining which was to find an echo in the assault upon the furniture workers in Scotland in the following year. The challenge presented, this new employer militancy was quickly identified by the furniture workers. Harry Ham ended his report for the year by calling for a fighting fund for organised labour to resist the threat of organised capitalism. This call found its answer in 1899 with te establishment of the National Federation of Trades Unions (subsequently referred to as the General Federation of Trades Unions or GFTU). The Alliance was one of the first societies to join the Federation. The entry fee was £16.18s.8d. £400 was paid in the first year and the union came into benefit after twelve months' membership enabling it to claim support in the event of an official strike at the rate of 5/- per member per week. [36] [37] [38]

The engineering lock-out also had the effect of jolting the leaders of the furniture workers from their non-politcal stance. 'There is another lesson which the workers should learn from the action of the Government during this struggle, and that is not to let their organisation and combination end with Trade Unionism alone, but to use it effectively at all elections for Governing bodies, both local and Imperial, so that they shall as a body, have a powerful voice in directing the future relationships between Capital and Labour, and obtaining for every citizen in the country the right to labour so that they may live as human beings'. The immediate task, however, was to come to terms with the new employers' federations themselves, and in this the Alliance was particularly effective.

As a result of trade movements regional agreements were signed with the Federation in other centres outside London. The West of England, Nottingham, Liverpool and the North Eastern employers all made such agreements. The Manchester Furniture Makers Federated Association did not, refusing to recognise the union. The Alliance then withdrew its members from the affected factories. The dispute lasted for six months and cost £3,700 in strike pay before a settlement was reached. Though expensive, the prosperity of the times allowed 'members in dispute to work in other towns and thus not be a drain on funds'. As a result working hours were reduced to 53, day rates agreed for cabinetmakers, chairmakers and carvers, overtime rates, travelling allowances, and lodging allowances established, whilst for their part Alliance members agreed 'not to work at night for another employer after leaving their ordinary employment, nor to make any job at home'. [39] [40]

Conditions of employment were now well established in England. The same could not be said of Scotland. The main furniture union north of the Border was the United Operative Cabinet and Chairmakers Society of Scotland, a generalist society with similar aims to those of the Alliance, with which it had signed a working agreement on transferability in 1875. This co-operation extended to a mutual action in Glasgow and on the Clyde in 1893 in defence of wage rates as a result of which talks were held on a proposal for amalgamation. The membership appeared to be in general agreement with such a merger and in 1897 a formal vote was taken. Though the active voting figure cannot be found in the records, these evidently lacked the numbers of members to satisfy the legal requirements for amalgamation. Whilst arrangements were being made for another Scottish vote to be taken an unexpected legal difficulty presented itself, it was discovered that it was unlawful for a non-registered trade union, i.e. the Scottish Society, and a registered society, the Alliance, to amalgamate. The Scottish Society was compelled to go through the procedure of changing its rule book. in order to allow it to become registered and follow this by a vote of the membership in favour of amalgamation.

The pursuit of this lengthy procedure was overtaken by events in the

Spring of the following year. The employers had now formed a National Federation of Furniture Makers of Scotland and on 30th March, 1898, notices were posted in all workshops stating 'all men starting work the next day must comply with the following conditions'. These were twelve in all and which can be summarised as follows:- An abandonment of any restraint or restriction on production especially the 'shop limit' used by employees to regulate earnings and protect older workers; acceptance of the right of the employer to adopt piecework or timework as he wished; the raising of the union's limit on overtime from seven hours to ten hours per week; the abandonment of the closed shop where this was operated by union members; and finally, the acceptance by workers of deductions from wages for any spoilage of work or breakage of glass. [41]

The ACMA Annual Report noted that 'the men were required to start straight away next morning under these conditions....but with keen Scottish foresight, be it ever said to their credit, they seemed to intuitively grasp the full meaning and import of the Employers demands, and there and then resolved to resist them with the strength borne of the knowledge that to be forced to accept such conditions would be to absolutely destroy all the work that our Association had been doing for years, in increasing wages, lessening hours, and improving conditions of employment, as well as the fact that the proposals, apart from the slavery to which it would reduce the men, was a subtle and insidious attack having for its object the destruction of Trade Unionism, by the substituting of Individual in place of Collective Bargaining'. [42] 'The struggle lasted ten months, and proved to the hilt the existence of a spirit of solidarity which the employers never anticipated. Had they done so it is highly probable that the lock-out would never have been entered into, as it ruined some of them, and much exclusive English trade was lost to the manufacturers and has never been regained'. [43]

The catalyst for this dispute was a wage claim presented by the General Secretary of the Scottish Society, Alex Gossip, to the employers in the town of Beith. Aged 36, Gossip was a militant Socialist, founder member of the Independant Labour Party, friend and close associate of Keir Hardie, Tom Mann and Ben Tillett. He was also a founder of the Socialist Sunday School Movement and a formidable and spell-binding orator. Of the dispute he recalled later that, 'very few of our people blacklegged and this was the more remarkable, as after the first few weeks no member knew how much, if any, dispute support would be forthcoming from week to week'. [44] The dispute quickly exhausted the Scottish Association's dispute fund and it was forced to borrow £1,610, but the main burden of expense fell upon the Alliance which spent £5,097 in dispute support, lost £1,820 in income from its locked-out members and paid out another £500 in expenses associated with the dispute, which the Scottish society was unable to meet.

The Alliance levied its membership at 3d. per member per week throughout the dispute. The Scottish society went even further. 'Members who secured jobs in the shipyards or across the Border were levied at 2/6d. per week in addition to their ordinary contributions'. There was meeting after meeting to resolve the dispute, but the deadlock continued until January 1899. The means by which the strike was ended remains a matter of some controversy. Clegg, Fox and Thompson quote Norman Robertson, who states that a three day conference 'produced a compromise on piecework and overtime but the societies were compelled to give way on non-unionists and the limitation of output. At a time of prosperity this was a noticeable setback'. [45]

Alex Gossip writing some years later presents the events in a totally different light. He, (Gossip) issued a challenge to the employers' leader, Mr John Reid, to a public debate on the questions in dispute. 'I spoke to such effect, that all the obnoxious points were swept away'. Even if Robertson's account is correct, the employers seem to have won a Pyrrhic victory. 'Shop limits' [46] are easily reimposed by a determined workforce and non-cooperation with men who refuse to join the union is almost imposible to prevent in the day-to-day manufacturing situation. The strike did not represent a defeat for the joint unions. They still retained collective bargaining; they still existed as a strong organisation, and they had obtained a working agreeement with the employers. [47]

Nevertheless the cost of the conflict was heavy on workers as well as employers. Harry Ham recorded that 'the suffering endured by the men and their families, the worry and anxiety of the union officials, the bad feeling engendered betwen employer and workman, the loss of trade by the employers that possibly will never be regained, all these costs can never be accurately gauged, and should make sensible reasonable men pause before ever lightly entering on such a struggle again. Indeed nothing would justify such unles some vital principle was at stake, and because in this case it was so, the Scottish lock-out was faced and fought out to the bitter end'. [48]

The Alliance was less than happy at the level of antagonism engendered between employer and employed by this, the first truly major confrontation with organised employers. Harry Ham and Jim O'Grady, the Trade Organiser appointed on the death of Tom Walker in 1898, were at pains to avoid a reccurence, as the Annual Report makes clear. 'During the past twelve months, many advantages have been gained for our members. This fortunately has been accomplished at litle cost, mainly through the businesslike way in which our Branches, assisted by the advice of your EC and General Officials, have conducted their movements'. [49]

'In London', the Report went on, 'we have been successful in obtaining a code of working rules that will bear comparison with any town or trade in the Kingdom. Whilst retaining all the advantages won in 1896 (a minimum rate of ninepence halfpenny per hour and fifty-two and half hour week) we have been able to increase the minimum wage by halfpence a hour and had the hours reduced by two and a half per week; but the most valuable part of the working rules in our opinion is the elaborate machinery that provides against stoppages of work either by lock-out or by dispute, until the matter is first submitted for consideration to a Board of Conciliation and Arbitration'.

The national trend towards federation amongst employers had resulted, with the notable exception of Scotaland, in an immense strengthening of the position of the Alliance. Once adversaries, now, for the time being at least, union and employer were co-partners within the industry. The strength of the mutual understanding behind this new role is revealed in the same Annual Report for 1899. 'The Alliance has set up similar codes of working rules (to those in London) in Manchester, Newcastle, Nottingham, Bury, and in Gloucester and achieved a 48 hour wek in Manchester. We (the EC and General officials) are of the opinion that the acceptance by the employers of a code of working rules is of far more importance than an increase of wages. We commend this policy to our Branches, as we are sure, speaking in the light of experience, that such a course would not only be of advantage to the members concerned, but result in an enormous saving of funds now paid away in dispute support'.

This 'financial accounting' approach to trade union organisation remained during this period unchallenged by the membership. Yet it presented an image far removed from the crusading spirit which is popularly supposed to have prevailed at that time. The reality was that local societies coming into the Alliance were rich in numbers but poor in assets. The amalgamation of 1893, for example, brought 462 new members but only £125 in assets. The lesson of financial prudence was rubbed in to the membership by an unsanctioned dispute in Leeds in 1898. The gain of an additional halfpence per hour for 58 members was won at the cost to the Alliance of more than £1,500 in dispute support. 'It is becoming more clearly evident than ever', noted the Annual Report clearly but ungrammatically, 'that such disputes once begun, the result, so far as the men winning, is extremely doubtful'.

The messge of the times for the membership of the Alliance was that of consolidation. Theories relating growth of membership to militancy were hardly applicable to the furniture trade and no political and economic philosophy for the rank and file had yet been developed. The period was for the union a kind of interregnum which ended with amalgamation with the Scottish society and the panoramic vision of Alex Gossip. The foundation for change was, however, being laid by the Taff Vale judgment which burst upon the trade union scene in 1901 and opened up a prospect in which, as Harry Ham explained to his members, 'Any branch or general official acting within the scope of his authority, can involve their union in an action in law with the certainty, in the present state of the law, of a verdict for damages and costs being given against us'. [50]

The Alliance had from a very early period required EC sanction for any trade moveement, local or national. By the turn of the century enforcement of the rule had been made easier by a kind of lethargy at branch level. Indeed such inactivity over improvements in local conditions was unacceptable and unofficial actions without EC sanction resulted. These were roundly and publicly castigated by Harry Ham as hopeless failures. 'The movements at Hadley and Dublin ended in a fiasco not least because they were mismanaged'. 'Hopeless struggles' were made worse by 'local misunderstandings' and by failure to work out 'clear lines of action to be followed in the event of a refusal by the employers to concede the men's demand'. [51]

The reason for a policy of EC control lay, not only in finance and the dangers of local branch ineptitude; it also related to the changing nature of the furniture trade. 'During the past years', wrote Harry Ham, 'the employers' organisations (local federations) have been quietly forming themselves into line, so that disputes in future will be on a more extended scale. Side by side with this we see the gradual absorption of the small by the large employer.....the whole trend is towards the elimination of small undertakings. The unit of capital is thrust out of production unless it will federate with other units.....the cash nexus becomes the only relationship between employers and employed.....most of their (the large companies') energies are applied to the commercial aspect of the question; when this is nearly completed they will undoubtedly turn their ambitions to the big corporation of the men in the unions'. The clash of the Titans was yet to come.

The final event of this period was the amalgamation of the Alliance with the Scottish Society. After the abortive vote of 1897 the Scots had changed their rules, registered as a trade union and voted for amalgation with the necessary two-thirds majority. The Alliance had hoped that it might be able to pursuade other furniture societies to join this new national group but with no success. 'The fact is, however, that some of the Unions in our trade do not, as yet, see the necessity of amalgamtion', but, 'two of the National Unions have become one, and give eminent promise of effecting greater things for its members than if they were still separate'. Harry Ham could hardly have envisaged the impact that the National Amalgamated Furnishing Trades Association was to have as a furniture trades union, as an influence on trade union organisation and politics, and upon the national political stage. A new dynamic society had been born which was to have an influence and a role far in excess of its size and nominal power.

# CHAPTER III

## NAFTA 1902 - 1913:
## A Gathering of Strengths

At the end of the nineteenth century the furniture workers union was essentially a craft society primarily concerned to maintain the interests of its members. Its involvement in the political movements of the period was small. The formation of the National Amalgamated Furnishing Trades Association and subsequent amalgamations brought together within one society a group of dynamic, effective and advanced socialist officials who, with the backing of their members, created an organised body of furniture workers with an influence far beyond its numerical strength. In the decade 1902-1913 NAFTA found a voice, a militancy and an identity which was recognised at national and international level as that of a union of dedicated, determined and politicised socialist workers which has remained with the union to this day.

Initially these were the years of the Taff Vale judgment, described by Harry Ham as a period 'in which the legal profession backed up by the employing interests represented in Press and Parliament, did their level best not only to intimidate the unions by attacking their funds, but also, to so weave the meshes of law around our organisation as to make it impossible to move without fear of running foul of legal decisions'. [1] NAFTA, in common with other unions, decided that the only way to change the law was to 'pay for direct representation in Parliament'. The pages of the monthly reports for 1902 carried the debate amongst the membership, with lucid, lengthy and reasoned arguments in favour of the proposal, of which the following are a sample:-

'It has always seemed to me to be one of the strongest anomalies that the workers should be of the political opinion that the best people to make laws for their welfare are of the class whose interests are diametrically opposed to their own, and that they should believe it possible that those who live on the profits made out of the labour of the workers would ever be likely to formulate and carry out reforms which would be of real service to the workers themselves'.

'None of us would dream of sending our employers to represent us at our Trade Congresses or conferences to formulate plans for our future guidance and welfare, yet the majority of our class seem to consider they are the proper persons to make the infinitely more important law of the land, which should have the same object in view. The idea that they ever will do so of their own free will is utterly fallacious'. [2]

'The old cry of 'no politics' in Trade Unionism was proper enough when the introduction of politics meant the division of unionism into more Liberal and Conservative camps, but the old order changeth, giving place to new, and the cry of 'no politics' must be relegated to the things of the past. Political action is now consciously and continuously used by the capitalist class in defence of their own selfish interests; why, therefore, should the workers be afraid of defending their own interests in the same manner'. [3]

Many contributors to the debate referred to Taff Vale, and all drew the same conclusions that reform of this judgement lay through parliamentary representation because 'in trade disputes, now we have not got an individual employer to meet, but in most cases a combination of employers. The great lesson to be derived from this is the absolute necessity for direct labour representation. The old struggles have been for political emancipation. The coming struggle will be for political emancipation. We are slow to recognise the immense power we possess in the franchise'. [4]

In the rolling tones of the evangelical preacher one member wrote 'Thanks to the economic evolution, we are now on the edge of a precipice and have to choose between an ignoble death and a straight fight, a fight in which there can be few casualties on our side if we march solidly, for we shall be as an avalanche; once set rolling we are bound to gather strength and power as we go along, and the Labour Representative Committee is the via media by which the practical and the ideal may meet on neutral ground and forget the calumnies they have heaped on each others heads and the epithets that have often taken place of argument. Let us try it as an experiment, believing with Carlyle that the good will alone live'. [5]

'I am pleased to see we are awakening from our torper, and commencing to recognise the necessity for the workers of having capable men of their own class to represent them in Parliament. Never was a time more propitious than the present to put this grand scheme into practice'. [6]

A vote was taken in September 1902, and by 3,155 votes to 467 of a total membership of 6,200 it was agreed that a fund be set up, 'the Labour Representation Fund' levied at the rate of 3d. per member per quarter, with effect from the first quarter of 1903.

In May 1904 J. Ramsay Macdonald in his capacity as Secretary of the Labour Representation Committee wrote to the union asking it to nominate a candidate to be placed in a constituency 'most likely to yield good results'. This period was but the dawn of the young Labour Party and a nomination was no sinecure, nor was it a guarantee of success, as the letter made clear. 'The success of the movement to which we are all pleded mainly depends how far we can consolidate the rank and file. As you know, we have met with a considerable amount of success in inducing trade unionist, who used to be divided between the Liberal and Conservative parties, to find a common meeting ground upon our Labour platform'. [7]

This appeal was followed by a further letter in which Macdonald asked the Executive to commend to the members the Labour Maintenance Fund. This fund built up from contributions of 1d. per member per year was made available to pay a salary of £200 per annum to MPs and contribute to the election expenses of the Labour candidates. Members of Parliament were paid no salary until 1911. NAFTA membership in July 1904 voted on the proposals of the EC that a candidate be selected and that the Labour Representation Committee Maintenance Scheme be adopted. It passed both items on a vote of only 17 per cent of the members. (Maintenance Scheme 1,054 for and 47 against, Parliamentary Candidate 1,052 for and 54 against).

An overwhelming mandate had been received for the Labour representation fund but on a minority vote and this remained one of the characteristics of the union over the years. A highly politicised and active minority made the running for a total membership which acquiesced and accepted without challenge the lead of the activists.

The first six months of this political levy brought in only £77.3s.2d., just under half of what ought to have been collected, despite the fact that the rule provided that non-payment would render a member liable to be placed out of benefit. Such an extraordinary sanction was alien to the spirit of the general application of the rules on union welfare payment, and there is no evidence that it was every applied; indeed to have done so would at one time or another have placed 75 per cent or more of the membership out of benefit!

Initially the list of nominated Parliamentary Candidates comprised nine members including Harry Ham and Alex Gossip, but the final vote was taken by the membership on only three, the remainder declining to go forward to selection. These were A. Eades, Birmingham, F. Fountain, Leeds, and J. O'Grady, East London. Eades obtained 59 votes, Fountain 149, O'Grady 1,232.

The Alliance had often held votes of the membership but with the coming of NAFTA the determination to refer all issues to the full membership became a democratic passion. Until the outbreak of the second world war hardly a month passed without the members being required to vote 'en masse' on at least one proposition from the Executive.

Jim O'Grady, having been elected as the NAFTA candidate, was selected by the Labour Representation Committee to fight Leeds East at the next parliamentary election. The cost of the election was estimated as some £650, of which the Association offered £250 if the election was in 1904 and more if it was held at a later date. The National LRC would pay £30 towards the Returning Officer's fee and the rest would be raised locally within the constituency. The Executive had high hopes of this candidature 'The Member holding the seat, which is a purely industrial centre, is a Conservative, and is bitterly opposed to trade unionism. He is also strongly in favour of the introduction of Chinese slavery into South Africa, so the chances of our candidate are fairly good'. [8]

The election took place in 1906. There were 51 Labour candidates, of whom 15 received no support from the LRC, mainly miners' candidates who were not happy with the LRC itself. It was fought on tariff protection, Home Rule for Ireland and a Trade Disputes Bill to reverse the Taff Vale decision. The result was a Liberal-Labour Alliance majority in the House of Commons of 271. 29 LRC candidates were elected and 25 candidates on the Lib-Lab ticket. This excellent and, in some ways, astonishing result was produced mainly because of a secret agreement betwen Ramsay Macdonald and Herbert Gladstone which permitted LRC candidates to stand in a number of seats without Liberal opposition. One of the beneficiaries of this arrangement was Jim O'Grady in Leeds East.

The union journal complained that the local press gave his candidacy little coverage. It was left to the local Labour Party to produce newsheets which encouraged the voters to come and hear 'The wild revolutionary expounding the newer political gospel'. In fact, this allegation was the only mention of O'Grady in the *Yorkshire Post* while *The Leeds and Yorkshire Mercury* made no comment upon his campaign at all beyond a list noting the places, dates and times of his meetings, a service which it rendered to all the candidates in the campaign. [9]

The Conservative candidate and sitting member, Henry Struther Cantley did not, it seems, inspire confidence even in the Conservative *Mercury*. 'The dreary Mr. Cantley meeting last night was a little more long suffering than usual' and, 'The progress of Mr Cantley's campaign had made the result a foregone conclusion.....Mr. O'Grady will top the poll'. The Liberal *Yorkshire Evening Post* was most enthusiastic in its reportage of O'Grady's candidacy. 'All thro' the campaign Mr James O'Grady, the labour candidate, has had most enthusiastic meetings and even when he has been addressing the electors in parts of the constituency which in later years have been noted for their very conservative element, the result has been the same, there being a unanimous vote on practically every occasion' (the practice of the time was to take a vote on the speaker's candidacy at each meeting). On polling day it reported: 'The prospects of Mr. J. O'Grady, the Labour candidate, are extremely rosy.....Mr. O'Grady's workers, of both sexes, to the number of more than 200, were early astir' Announcing the result it reported 'Enthusiastic scenes at the Committee room of Mr. O'Grady. He arrived after the announcement of the result to a great storm of cheers and his wife then led a torch light procession round the division'. 10 11 12.

The *Post* had branded him as a revolutionary. It was hardly revolution which Jim O'Grady espoused, but rather the ILP socialism of his colleague Alex Gossip. His was the socialism of the heart and of the emotions, evolved in the language of the King James's Bible. He wrote to the membership, 'I came out of the stress and heat of that glorious fight, purified in spirit and mind. I had felt the pulsing of the great soul of Humanity; I had heard the cries of the vast toiling millions, of which East Leeds is a microcosm, struggling towards the light. It was the dumb become articulate. I saw the great giant Labour, straining to burst the social and economic bonds that have held him slave so long. I discerned, actually, the sun of emancipation creeping slowly above the social horizon, and I dreamed of a near future full of the possibilities of joy and contentment for the common people'. Jim O'Grady received 4,299 votes, Cantley 2,208, a majority of 2,091. So popular was the rhetoric of the new Member of Parliament that 4,000 copies of his election address were printed and sold to members at 1d. each, the proceeds being devoted to the Tom Walker's Children's Fund. 13

With the election of Jim O'Grady to Parliament there remained the question of whether he could carry out his work for the union as well as that of an M.P. The Executive Committee considered this question and decided that for the time being it was possible to combine both jobs. It noted with complete seriousness, 'the House (of Commons) does not meet till late in the day, closing early on two nights, and not sitting at all on Saturdays. This will permit of at least 36 hours per week being devoted to his work. Of course, members well know that the Parliamentary Session only lasts six months in a year, therefore the T.O. can and will put in his full-time during the other six months in carrying out the usual duties of his office'. 14 'The undoubted gain to the Association will be readily appreciated by our members, and its effect will not be lost on the employers as a body'. 15

Alex Gossip in his monthly report noted the emergence of the 'Labour Party - with the right man in the right place at its head (Kier Hardie). Already they have made themselves felt, though the capitalist newspapers do not give them much of a show and prefer to report dreary inanities by men like Asquith & Co.' Despite this lack of sympathy with the Liberal Party, it did as a Government pass most of the legislation which had been canvassed by the TUC as a programme of progress for the working man.

The Trade Disputes Act passed in 1906 reversed the Taff Vale judgement giving protection to unions in trade disputes and re-establishing the position of peaceful picketing. Also a much enlarged Workmen's Compensation Act brought into scope many more industries and workers than the 1897 Chamberlain Bill. A Pension Bill was introduced in 1908 and enacted in January 1st, 1909, and the same year the Government also passed the Trade Boards Act which enabled such boards to be established for the so-called 'sweated industries'. These boards had the power to establish minimum levels of pay that were legally binding upon the employers whose industries fell within the scope of the Act. Surprisingly this latter piece of legislation was not very enthusiastically received by the trade union movement. It received no comment from NAFTA. The major reason for this antipathy was the fear that the minimum wages would become maximum wages. Originally the Trade Boards mainly covered the work of women who did not feature predominantly among trade unionists at this time. Perhaps there was a feeling that legislation of this kind might make trade unions redundant among the lower paid, though it was always possible to argue that it was designed to encourage trade unionism. [16] So far as NAFTA was concerned, the new boards did not cover the furniture trade.

The Standard of Living 1890 - 1914

'Real' wage index 1890 = 100

| Year | Building Workers | Engineering Workers |
|---|---|---|
| 1900 | 101 | 100 |
| 1901 | 102 | 101 |
| 1902 | 102 | 101 |
| 1903 | 101 | 100 |
| 1904 | 100 | 99 |
| 1905 | 100 | 99 |
| 1906 | 99 | 99 |
| 1907 | 96 | 97 |
| 1908 | 99 | 100 |
| 1909 | 98 | 99 |
| 1910 | 96 | 97 |
| 1911 | 95 | 97 |
| 1912 | 93 | 96 |
| 1913 | 93 | 93 |

Sources:— A.L. Bowley, *Wages and Income in the U.K. since 1860*, Cambridge University Press 1937, p.30; *Annual Abstract of Labour Statistics*.

The government of the day was nevertheless one of the most sympathetic to the working classes that there had ever been. Ironically the industrial strife which accompanied the end of its term of office was 'the start of one of the greatest outbreaks of industrial unrest ever known in Britain'. [17] Prices of commodities had been rising since 1896 and with a stagnation in wages through the period up to 1910, particularly in the high unemployment years of 1907/8/9, real wages and living standards had fallen. With an improving trade situation after 1910 the working classes used the opportunity to win back the losses in living standards that they had suffered.

Correspondence in the union's *Monthly Reports* show that NAFTA members were clear in their understanding of the problem facing them. Alex Gossip had the measure of the situation. On the problems of unemployment he wrote, 'The capitalist does not enter into business from any feeling of sentiment, and the hungry may die of starvation or the naked and homeless of cold and disease for all he cares if no profit is going to accrue to himself by his granting permission to the worker to use his tools and and raw materials. The ability to produce, which our acquired power over the forces of nature has given us, is such that in a very short time abundance of everything is forthcoming, but as the propertyless worker has not sufficient remuneration for his past labour to enable him to buy back the things he has produced or the equivalent, he must remain idle until over-production has been consumed, mainly by those who had little, if any hand in its production'. The solution as he saw it was to put 'the Means of Production and Distribution in the hands of the people as a whole, and to carry on production for use instead of profit'.

Such concern for the underdogs of society was not exclusive to the political left or to the Liberals. Even the Saturday Review commented that 'no system can be more demoralising than the present, when the poor man, self-respecting and loafer alike, knows that, whatever his efforts to save, it is a hundred to one he will end up in the workhouse' [19]. The unemployed were more sinned against than sinning.

Alex Gossip also drew the attention of his members to an article in *The Engineer*, a paper which was looked upon as the organ of employers generally. Referring to unemployment the journal stated 'It is, as every works manager knows, a very bad state of affairs when there are no spare hands in his district; there are no reserves to call out, and there is the constant danger that his men may be tempted away from him by some other employer who is also short handed. Dearth of labour must be regarded as a worse evil than a fair excess of it. It will be accepted that a certain minimum of unemployed is essential to the welfare of the country. That minimum we have put at 2 per cent of the workes engaged in any trade ....of willing workers two to two and a half per cent must always be idle'. With such philosophies publicly articulated, it was the task of the trade union officers to point the way forward and when there was an opportunity to improve conditions, to lead the fight for their acceptance.

The death of Sir Blundell Maple, head of Maple & Co., and the news that he had left a fortune of £2,153,292.19s.2d., was yet another opportunity for Alex Gossip to point out to the membership the iniquity of the system under which they laboured. [20] At a time when 11 per cent of the membership was out of work his point was easily taken, though not everyone - as Gossip pointed out with some scorn - was sympathetic. 'And yet the finger of scorn is oft times pointed at those who feel their whole souls in revolt against this miserable soul-destroying system. Oh the pity of it! Oh the shame of it! In the view of the continued bad trade all over the country, the action of the government in refusing to support the Right to Work Bill of the Labour Party becomes all the more reprehensible'. [21]

The trade union leaders of the day eschewed oratory which was mainly revolutionary. They concentrated on the immediate problem of the need and the right to work, 'our one common need, the need of living and being happy'. Alex Gossip still saw these aims as achievable through the parliamentary process. When, therefore, a general election was held in January, 1910, the membership was exhorted to 'strive with might and main to return only those who understand the cause of poverty, and are prepared to apply the remedy. Nature is prodigal with her gifts and we only require free access to the raw materials and means of production to banish for ever the accursed thing known as poverty'. [22]

Believing as they did that in an ideal society remedies were possible, the reality of the present bore hard on union leaders such as Gossip. Nearly 14 per cent of NAFTA membership was out of work; half of them had run out of benefit with the consequent misery and hardship which all too clearly followed in its train. Yet resolution of this continually recurrent nightmare for the working man, seemed beyond human control. O'Grady, in his 1910 election address noted that the road to socialism was the way forward for the people 'After an experience of four years in the House of Commons, I am more than ever convinced that there is no real remedy for unemployment while a system of production and distribution of commodities for purposes of individual profit exists, and not until the public conscience is awakened to the brutality and immorality of the wild scramble to be rich, with all the socially evil consequences that have followed in its train can a system of national ownership and control of land and capital be substituted, and unemployment banished from our midst'. Was this mere rhetoric? To many it seemed that it was no more than a poor substitute for well thought out programmes of legislation and action which might have had some chance of success in alleviating the suffering which existed here and now.

O'Grady was returned with an increased majority of 3,065 votes in a straight fight with the Conservative candidate. In the *Monthly Reports* he was at pains to point out his independence of the Liberal Party. 'I want to state that the (Labour) Party did not have any negotiations, actual or otherwise, with the Liberal Party to avoid three cornered fights. In East Leeds, no approach was made to the Liberals to withdraw their candidate (which they did).....although it is a fact that Liberal and Tory workmen did vote for the Labour candidate'.

The country went back to the polls in a General Election less than a year later and Jim O'Grady, with the financial support of NAFTA, again retained the seat, albeit with a majority reduced to 925 in yet another straight fight with a Conservative candidate. With 42 Members of Parliament in the House of Commons the Parliamentary Labour Party of 1911 was now a voice to be listened to and a voting body to be considered where legislation was concerned. This was less a tribute to its numerical strength than to the fact that with the Irish Nationalists it held the balance of power which kept the depleted Liberal government in office. In fact the Labour Party members returned at the December 1910 election, collected only 323,000 votes and were still without a clear platform on the solution of these problems of unemployment. So much is clear from the Conference on the Abolition of Destitution and Unemployment held in London on 7th and 8th October of that year.

The conference was arranged by the ILP and attended by 250 delegates from trade unions, trades councils, constituency labour parties and co-operative societies. Under the chairmanship of Macdonald, Barnes and Hobson the conference spent most if its time listening to papers on the problem by George Lansbury, Miss MacArthur and Sidney Webb. It was to the paper of Sidney Webb on unemployment that Gossip and Bramley (the NAFTA delegates) most strongly objected. Their socialist view contrasts strongly with the bland Fabian view put forward by Sidney Webb. The Webb resolution stated, 'This Conference declares that unemployment is a chronic disease of society and that the Government should take steps, as far as practicable, to prevent this grave social disease.....etc.'. The Gossip/Bramley amendment read: 'This Conference declares that unemployment is a chronic disease of the present system of society; that the Government should at once take steps to prevent this grave social disease by introducing measures which must not be merely palliative, but which must contain the germs of the orgasnisation of a Socialist Commonwealth, and be the beginning of the permanent organisation of National resources, and production, industrial and agricultural, on a co-operative basis'. Five minutes remained at the end of the conference in which to move this amendment. It is scarcely surprising that it was lost and the Webb resolution was accepted. The amendment does, however, mark the emergence of NAFTA as one of the most militantly socialist trade unions of the period. [23] 'True and unashamed Socialism was the only salvation for the working classes', was the message to the union's members. A recognition that the blandishments of the Liberals and Tories were no more than a sop to the working classes was, year by year thereafter, urged upon the rank and file.

On the industrial front the period was marked by poor trade and substantial sums were paid out in out-of-work support, reaching a peak in 1908. Industrial action was only undertaken during those years defensively in support of the maintenance of wages and hours and conditions of work. After 1908 trade gradually improved, and there was general reduction in unemployment. With returning prosperity workers of all trades took the opportunity to reverse the fall in real wages that had occurred from 1896.

Disputes require funding, as the executive of the union was very well aware. NAFTA paid out of work support and dispute pay, from the same general fund. A substantial reduction in the out of work support was therfore required before the union could undertake any action that would result in a heavy expenditure in dispute pay. The actual disputes and their outcomes have been charted for the period 1909 - 1913 and it can be seen that for the first two years the results achieved were mixed. Nevertheless by 1911, a general trade movement was under way and the results achieved were, indeed, impressive. The costs, however, were high. While 1911 saw an expenditure of £4000 in dispute pay, 1912 required £16,697 and 1913 £17,248.

The major disputes concerned were in Nottingham, Manchester and Liverpool and were fought against Federated employers who adopted a common platform of union breaking. In each area an application to the Federation for an increase in wage rates was met with a lock-out and the requirement of any who returned to work to abandon unionism and collective bargaining in favour of individual bargaining. The disputes over money therefore became a fight over union recognition. In none of the three areas was any attempt made to bring in blackleg labour; instead 'they are going to play the waiting game, they are trying a new way, namely that of exhausting us by a long dispute and a return under the most hateful conditions they can impose'.

NAFTA won these battles and improved the hours and wages of its members. Perhaps more important, it was able to demonstrate that it had the funds, the organisation and the membership to fight long battles without being broken. This point was not lost on the employers and though in the future there were to be some smaller disputes of a purely workshop nature , major disputes found the union opposed by Employers' Federations which were increasingly effective.

# CHAPTER IV

## *Lock Out at High Wycombe 1913 - 1914*

By 1913 High Wycombe had overtaken London to become, in terms of output, the major furniture making centre of the United Kingdom. Conditions of work and remuneration had, however, lagged behind those of the capital city and elsewhere. Hours were long, twelve to fourteen hours per day were common. Turners worked anything up to a fifteen hour day. Rates of pay were poor and had not improved with the times even though the quality of work and levels of production had changed out of all recognition from the early days of furniture making in the town.

In High Wycombe in 1913 the trade of furniture making was at a crossroads. The 'bodgers', the makers of windsor chairs and chair parts, were still operating their lonely independent trades in the woods surrounding the town. Some factories were little better than shelters under which the trades practiced in the open air by the bodgers had been moved under cover. Others operated extensive and punitive outworker systems with caning, rushing, carving and sewing all being 'sent out'. Some companies managed their workshops in the most autocratic manner whilst other owners saw their role as paternalistic and benevolent. The complete absence of machinery in some factories contrasted with others equipped with the modern machinery which dominated and subordinated workers to its demands. Factory units were small and specialised, few employing more than 150 workers and most under 100. Originally based on chairmaking, the trade had by the earliest years of the twentieth century extended into cabinetmaking and upholstery. Ship furnishing was becoming increasingly important and the area had gained a high reputation for the quality and quantity of its production.

An indication of wages and conditions in the area is given by the survey carried out in 1909 by a Social Services Committee reporting on rates of pay and working hours in the Borough of High Wycombe which reported as follows:

Wage Rates for 2,645 men plus estimated figures of Turners
and 2nd grade Framers: some 3,000 men in all

| | | | |
|---|---|---|---|
| Chairmakers | 1st grade | 150 men | 30/- to 32/- per week |
| | 2nd grade | 350 men | 25/- per week |
| | 3rd grade | 150 men | 16/- per week |
| Framers | 1st grade | 600 men | 25/- to 30/- per week |
| | 2nd grade | (not known) | 8/- per week |
| Upholsterers | 350 men | - some earning 32/- | - average 24/- |
| Polishers | 500 men | - some earning 28/- | - average 22/- |
| Carvers | 1st grade | 35 men | 38/- per week |
| | 2nd grade | 50 men | 20/- to 25/- per week |
| Turners | 3 grades (numbers unknown) from 15/- to 32/- per week after deductions where the turner pays for the power used for his machine! | | |
| Cabinetmakers | | 60 men | 31/- to 32/- per week |
| Benchmen & Packers | | 200 men averaging 18/- per week | |
| General Machinists | 200 men | (largely unskilled) | 18/- to 20/- per week |

The Report found the average wage in High Wycombe for furniture workers to be 21/- to 25/- per week of 54 to 60 hours. Rates in other towns were much higher. The average wage in Birmingham was 36/- and in London 43/- for a fixed week of 52 hours. (NAFTA estimate 1913) [1] As the NAFTA trade organiser, Fred Bramley, stated at the time; 'It is the close proximity of Wycombe to London, with the cheapest labour, long hours and bad conditions which has inspired our activity in this district. We are determined to organise and by organising improve the conditions of the men employed in the most important furniture producing centre in the country and the desire to protect the interests of our members in all parts'. [2]

Conditions were, indeed, primitive. The factories had windows 'glazed at the expense of the workers', the employer supplying only oiled calico. Lighting was by oil lamps fuelled by the workers. When gas came into general use each worker paid 6 pence per week from his wage for the privilege of its use for illumination. The grindstone was available to all at a deduction of 1 penny per man per week and boy labour in the workshop was paid for by the work groups rather than the employers. Bench space was paid for at 2 shillings per week, and electrical power when this became available was also paid for by the worker.

This inequitable state of affairs was accepted, particularly by the older workers, as part of the custom and practice of the trade. An old chair framer is quoted in the local paper as saying, 'I couldn't make chairs without I had a roof over my head, so it was only fair that I should pay for my bench room; likewise if I wanted to frame on after dark I needed light to do it by, and it seems to be only reasonable that a master would jib at paying you for chairs that you had made by the light he had paid for'. [3]

A major area of discontent was loading and unloading. Piece work was the most common method of payment. Yet the workers were expected to load and unload raw materials and finished goods without payment. The same framer confessed with resignation, 'as to unloading, well, you wanted to work indoors and that chair stuff wouldn't get up and walk in to you, and when the chairs were made, they were precious little use to the master or to you till they were up on the van and away'. It was such apathy as this which had in the past resulted in the failure of the local societies in High Wycombe and the difficulties which continued to beset the small union Branch (No.72) in the town. The largest manufacturing centre in the country was not only setting a bad example; it was placing in jeopardy the advances in pay and conditions which had been achieved elsewhere.

In 1913 the furniture industry was going through a busy period. As the Organisers' Report in the June NAFTA journal noted, 'the bulk of employers are afraid of any long struggle.....never before in the history of the furnishing trade has there been such a tremendous demand for furniture products'. A decision was therefore made in early 1913 to attempt to 'improve High Wycombe'.

In common with NAFTA practice a piecemeal, one-target-at-a-time approach was used. In this approach an objective was decided upon - an improvement in the hourly rate or a reduction in hours - and with this target in mind the trade organiser would visit a few firms. If the visit was successful all well and good; if not, a meeting outside the factory gates, a lightning strike and normally capitulation. In such a way an unorganised town could be tackled quickly, inexpensively and effectively. When a good majority of the firms had been won over sets of working rules for the area could be established as guidelines for the future. Such an approach was not only economical. With limited finance it was an economic necessity. But it could only be attempted when trade was buoyant and any disruption of production resulted in a loss of orders and sales to another company. [4], [5]

The need to improve wages and conditions in High Wycombe was made the more necessary by agreements reached in Bristol, Birmingham and London in 1912. These were substantially in advance of those in existence in High Wycombe, and so in January 1913 NAFTA and the Joinery Trades Organiser took on Wainwrights of Wooburn Green, a firm some three miles from the centre of High Wycombe. After a short, sharp struggle, the firm conceded a reduction in hours from fifty-six and a half to fifty hours per week and a wages increase from eight pence and eight and a half pence to nine and a half pence per hour with a further increase to ten pence per hour in May 1913. Overtime rates were to be paid at time and a half for the first two hours and double time thereafter, a substantial improvement which undoubedly did not go unnoticed by the High Wycombe & District Furniture Manufacturers Society which had recently been reconstituted.

The union at this stage had neither the local strength nor the solidarity that was necessary for any prolonged struggle and the incidents which followed at Wainwrights were without doubt noted by the Manufacturers Society as well as the union. In the Trade Organiser's words, 'I have to report the most dirty action on the part of the non-union workers I have ever heard of or ever thought was possible'. [6] The advance in wages had scarcely been paid and the reduction in hours applied when a deputation of cabinetmakers, joiners and polishers went to the Managing Director to protest at the reduction in hours. The whole episode was extraordinary in that the rates had moved from 37s.8d. for fifty-six and a half hours to 41s.8d. for fifty hours, plus payment for overtime which had never existed before. The astonishment of the union organisers was matched by that of the Managing Director of Wainwrights who admitted; 'I could not help being surprised that men should oppose and attempt to defeat the men who were fighting their battles'. In the end goodwill and good sense prevailed on both sides and the agreement was formally signed, but the incident was a clear indication of the lack of trade union identity which was prevalent in this rural area of Buckinghamshire at the time.

In January 1913 union strength in High Wycombe was no more than 121 members. A massive recruiting campaign was therefore mounted and by June of 1913 that year the unions had 2,321 fully paid up members in the town. The Manufacturing Society's minutes no longer exist but we know that they also were recruiting members; and by the time the dispute broke out they had 31 members out of a town total of over 80 manufacturers. It evidently assumed that any dispute would be a short one on the assumption that the anti-union group at Wainwrights would be paralleled by similar groups elsewhere.

Battle had been joined in High Wycombe but in keeping with NAFTA traditions it was low key and localised. The first firm to be tackled was Parkers. The issue at stake was the extensive use of low paid outworkers and the low rates of pay of carvers. The dispute was successfully resolved with an increase in pay and increases of the factory personnel and the abandonment of outworking. One point of interest in this particular action was that Parkers, in an attempt to break the dispute, sent an agent to France to recruit carvers in the Paris area. He duly hired ten and proceeded to England with them. At the station in Paris the Paris Wood Carvers' Association representative appeared to tell the men of the true reason for their recruitment. The men attacked Parker's agent who, poor man, ended up in a Parisian jail for causing a breach of the peace.

A matter of some importance, however, was the editorial article of the *Furniture Record* for 10th October which spoke out most strongly against the guerilla war approach of the trade unions and of the need for the National Association of Furniture Manufacturers to fight this threat. The union had recognised that the hour was right but the employers had organised quickly. The October 17th issue of the *Furniture Record* carried a letter from Thomas Restall, Secretary of the Birmingham Employers' Federation in reply to the 'guerilla war' article. 'You are mistaken', he wrote, 'when you say that we in Birmingham are acting independently of the National Association - on the contrary, the National Association are rendering us both financial and other assistance. The Employers of the town recognise that we are fighting not only for our own city but for the trade in the country and that they are doing their share in helping us'. The Birmingham dispute was, in fact, settled with useful gains by the furniture workers, but as the *Birmingham Furnishing Employers Journal* commented 'the lessons of the conflict are being studied by both parties to the dispute'. [7]

Although the actual decision to fight for better conditions and wages in High Wycombe was tactically considered and agreed earlier in 1913 a formal ballot was held within the newly strengthened branch in the town. The choice was simple: in favour or not of a 'trade movement'?. The result was astonishing; 2,331 for and 0 against. A new will to fight and win in the light of the poor wages and conditions existing in High Wycombe had evidently appeared.

The trade movement decision was taken in May, yet even by November the industrial relations situation was being described by the local *South Bucks Herald* as 'quiet'. The NAFTA organiser, Fred Bramley, explained in the Journal - 'We have selected the lower rated (work)shops one by one, and dealt with them, in all cases with such conspicuous success as to fill the others with alarm!'[8] In November however, this softly, softly approach was countered by the Employers' Associaiton in an instruction 'to pay no further increases in wages without the consent of all members and to refer all Union officials to the Association'. Battle was finally joined when it was decided to withdraw labour from the firms of Stratfords and C. Smiths - 'two shops which refused to consider improving conditions'.

Union funds were limited for such a fight. The permission to withdraw labour was given by the EC with the rider that 'All possible means to avoid dispute however, to be first taken'. The need for caution was self evident, in June the funds of NAFTA stood at £1,134 on current account and £10,595 on deposit. It was agreed that a general levy of all members should be made of 3/6d. payable at 6 pence per week. This was, however, the third general levy of the year and the financial position worsened as the year progressed. By December the union had little more than £5000 in funds and expenditure was £2,500 in excess of income. In six months of disputes the assets of the union had dropped by one half. [9]

By mid-November 400 men were out in High Wycombe and at a meeting on the 21st the unions presented to the Federation a schedule of wages and conditions desired as a pre-condition for a return to work. It was not an extravagant claim - indeed no figure was included which was not at the time being paid somewhere in the town. This schedule was received by the Federation which countered with its own schedule. Though discussion took place deadlock ensued and each side retired to consider the other's proposals.

At this point the employers moved to the offensive. One cancelled the morning break of fifteen minutes (in a five hour morning shift) unless the men worked this time as an unpaid extra at the end of the day. Another ordered his men to parade in front of him and publicly to tear up their union cards or be discharged. In both cases the provocation resulted in the workers walking out and picketing the factory.

The Federation and the unions held various meetings over the next few days. All were inconclusive. They terminated when a Federation notice was posted in the works of all 31 of its member firms. The essence of the notice was, 'The Federation will no longer continue to negotiate and will terminate the engagement of all members of the union in this company. In accordance with the above resolution, all Union men employed in this firm are hereby given one hour's notice to terminate their respective agreements'. 2,000 men and 300 women workers were immediately affected. Over 3,000 members of the various furniture unions were locked out of work.

The workers were not despondent. Public meetings were held and many thousands attended. Picketing was an occasion for singing and the playing of the workers' brass band. At the High Wycombe 'Electroscope' Zola's *Germinal* played to packed houses every night of the week. The band went on to tour London and South Wales to raise funds for the strikers and exhibition games were played at Loakes Park, High Wycombe, by the Wycombe Wanderers football team in aid of the strike fund. 'Cycle parties went long distances to make collections at factory gates in towns where considerable support was forthcoming'. Homes of blacklegs were visited in an attempt to persuade the few who remained in work to come out in support. This sometimes caused intense excitement, especially since the womenfolk were as bitter as the men! [10]

# HIGH WYCOMBE FURNISHING TRADES' LOCK-OUT BAND.

*Arrival in London January 12th, 1914.*

# HIGH WYCOMBE & DISTRICT
# FURNITURE MANUFACTURERS' FEDERATION.

The under-named members of the above Federation in General Meeting held the 28th day of November, 1913, unanimously resolved that in face of the facts

(1) That the Union men rejected the Employers' proposal that with a view of assisting an amicable settlement the men on strike should return to work last Tuesday ;

(2) That the strikes continue ;

(3) That the Union men rejected the Employers' principle of grading which through their delegates they were informed was a vital principle with the Employers ;

(4) That the Union men have rejected the Employers' offer of a Standard Wage as per Schedule sent them ;

(5) That the alternative proposals of the Union are impossible for acceptance by the Employers,

negotiations by the Employers be no longer continued, but that the Members terminate at once the engagement of all Members of the Union in their employ.

| | |
|---|---|
| Messrs. W. Birch, Ltd. | Messrs. R. J. Howland and Co., Ltd. |
| „ Wm. Bartlett and Son | „ Joynson and Co. |
| „ Birch and Cox | „ Joynson, Holland and Co. |
| „ Caffal and Keen | Mr. W. Keen |
| „ J. Cox and Son, Ltd. | Messrs. G. H. and S. Keen |
| „ Castle Bros. | „ V. M. Millbourne and Son |
| Mr. Walter E. Ellis | „ Nicholls and Janes |
| Messrs. James Elliott and Sons | „ B. North and Sons |
| „ Thomas Glenister, Ltd. | „ F. Parker and Sons, Ltd. |
| „ H. Goodearl and Sons | „ Randall Bros. and Co., Ltd. |
| „ Goodearl Bros., Ltd. | „ W. Skull and Son, Ltd. |
| Mr. John Gomm | „ Stratford and Brion |
| „ C Gibbons | Mr. Cecil Smith |
| „ William James Goodchild | „ R Tyzack |
| Messrs. R. Howland and Sons, Ltd. | „ C. P. Vine |
| „ Hill and Butler | |

## In accordance with the above resolution ALL UNION MEN employed upon this Firm are hereby given ONE HOUR'S NOTICE to terminate their respective engagements

DATED this 29th day of November, 1913.

(Signed)

*W Skull Son Ltd*

The police issued notices on the legal penalties for obstruction and intimidation and in an atmosphere of rising social tension various attempts at conciliation were made, ministers of religion and shop-keepers and trades people presenting petitions to both sides. The Federation Chairman, C.E. Skull, rejected these stating that the Federation terms for further negotiations were acceptance of its schedule of wages. But not all manufacturers shared this negative stance as evidenced by the actions of the Mayor of High Wycombe, John Gomm. Though a furniture manufacturer and member of the Federation he resigned from that body, settled with the unions on their terms and opened his factory on the following day, hiring extra workers in the process. A strong element of self-interest may have been involved which he rationalised by declaring that in the event of a protracted dispute his membership of the Federation must of necessity prejudice his position as Mayor.

Association meetings and picketing remained so far peaceful and relatively good humoured. The Chief Constable anticipated that this would not remain so, informing the Watch Committee on 1st December of the possibility of disturbances arising in consequence of the strike and receiving authorisation, after consultation with the Mayor, to obtain the assistance of 50 Metropolitan Police. His prediction proved correct. On 16th. December, after two and a half weeks on strike, the mood changed. Some 1,200 workers assembled at the West End Street factory of Goodearl Brothers where the workers were still working at the old rates, and when 'lights out' came at 7 o'clock and the men left the factory there was what the correspondent describes as a 'hostile rush'. Some injuries were sustained, windows were broken and the police, when called, cleared the street with repeated baton charges. *The Herald* reporter noted that 'Amongst the crowd were a considerable number of women caners and upholsteresses and they encouraged the demonstrators with their approving cries!' [11], [12]

The local Chief Constable, alarmed by this development called for his reinforcements. Ten mounted and fifteen foot officers arrived from London and were quickly in action at a public meeting the following night. After the meeting the police ordered the crowd to disperse. When they failed to do so to their satisfaction the mounted officers rode at the crowd to break it up. The Mayor appealed for calm, but to no avail. A very serious situation was saved by the intervention of Fred Bramley, the Trade Organiser, who persuaded the workers to disperse. The *Times* reported the incident; 'Last night after a meeting of the men had been held, the police were subjected to hostile demonstrations. Further disorders are feared'. [13]

The unions, recognising the gravity of the situation, now formed an anti-violence brigade to provide 'a physical force for the workers'. Whilst Alex Gossip likened the police action to that of the Czarist police of Russia, it was accepted that the anti-violence brigade was intended as marshals and that it was in everyone's interests to avoid confrontation as far as possible. Yet with only a proportion of the workforce, albeit a large one, on strike, tempers began to rise. A striker was reported in the *Daily Herald* as stating; 'We have reached the limit of our patience. If all the non-union men were out, the trouble would be over in a week. If they won't come out quietly, they must come out by force. We're fighting, not only for ourselves, but for the women and the kids'. [14]

Christmas in High Wycombe that year was a bleak and joyless time. The effects of the strike were hitting the workers and their families very hard. Never well paid, they had few reserves to fall back on and strike pay was sufficient only to keep families from starvation. The Strike Committee opened a soup kitchen in the yard of the Swan Hotel and appealed to local allotment holders to donate what they could spare to feed the children of the strikers. Before the end of the strike several soup kitchens were operating in the town and 1,500 children were being fed in this way. Some kitchens were in schools; others, like the Swan kitchen, in local pubs, and some were run by the Salvation Army. Unfortunately, because of the loss of the Poor Law records, the full extent of the poverty resulting from the dispute will for ever remain a matter of hearsay. However, the children were not forgotten at Christmas. Toys were collected nationally and on Boxing Day the unions, the Workers Educational Association and the Sunday schools of the area fed 1,000 children in the Town Hall and presented each with a toy.

The lock-out continued into the New Year with no signs of weakening or lack of resolve on either side. However, on 7th January 1914 the Employers' Federation met and announced that an offer had been received from Lord Rothschild, the Lord Lieutenant for Buckinghamshire, who had also sent £100 to the Childrens' Feeding Fund, to convene a conference under his chairmanship. A decision on this was deferred as Sir George Askwith had, in his capacity as mediator and representative of the Board of Trade, already asked to meet the parties in the dispute.

The Metropolitan Police contingent had left High Wycombe before Christmas but renewed agitation on 6th January resulted in its recall. Tempers ran high and there were repeated clashes between police and workers. Injuries were sustained on both sides and crowds were dispersed by charges of mounted police. In a town of chairmakers in which the traditional weapon of the working man was a beech chair leg the clashes must indeed have been fearsome. When arrested it appeared that the workers could expect scant justice since, as Mr Bramley pointed out, the law officers could be expected to be hostile. 'The prosecuting solicitor is a Mr A.J. Clarke who is doing his duty as a professional man; but the bench is composed of five Magistrates. One is Mr Clarke's father, another his father-in-law, a third a personal friend of Mr Clarke's and a fourth man is quite prejudiced against Trades Union Principles - What can we expect from such a bench?'. In fact sentences were light and arrests few. *The Times* reported the assault of a Police Inspector. 'The Inspector said he was called to the recreational ground where there was a disorder. The accused, Enos George Pusey, chairmaker, threw something which struck him on the cheek with some force. He rode forward and carried him out of the recreational ground'. After conflicting evidence, the Bench dismissed the case. Two others arrested on the same night for window breaking during the disturbance were bound over to keep the peace. Sir George Askwith makes only a passing mention of this dispute in his memoirs. Both parties to the dispute met on 9th. January. The meeting came to no conclusion and the lock-out continued. [15]

Support for the Wycombe workers was widespread. At a meeting in the Town Hall 2,000 people were addressed by Fred Bramley, Trade Organiser of NAFTA, Louis Leckie, General Secretary of the Amalgamated Union of Upholsterers, Mr Fear of the London Defence Committee and Mrs Lewis of the Women's Federation. Their most heartening news was a grant of £1000 to the Strike Committee from the AUU and £2000 from the Amalgamated Society of Engineers. To ensure that all workers were still in good heart and to demonstrate solidarity to the employers the strike committee held a ballot on the following questions: 1. Are you in favour of accepting the employers terms? 2. Are you in favour of accepting the committee's proposals? Forty-two votes were cast for the first proposition, one thousand five hundred and ninety one for the second. This result was sent to the Employers' Federation which was in turn equally uncompromising. 'Inasmuch as the so-called ballot taken by the men on Saturday evening last shows such disinclination on the part of the men to return to work, this Federation unanimously resolves to adjourn until the Standard Schedule of Rates of Wages is accepted by the men'.

The deadlock was in practice less complete than it appeared. Sir George Askwith was due to visit the town in a few days. On the streets the confrontations had diminished to the point at which the Metropolitan Police reinforcements again left the town. Hopes for peace were quickly shattered for at the beginning of February violence returned. On Monday 2nd February the town was again reported in the press to be 'in a state of uproar, with the police quite unable to cope with the situation'. The reasons for the violence and destruction which followed were unexplained. We can only suppose that with the return of a period of very cold weather the patience and tolerance of the workers finally broke. Be that as it may the troubles started at midday with the assault on a blacklegging employee of Edgerley's of Frogmoor. The men then proceeded on to Randall Brothers factory in Victoria Street, broke all the windows and smashed chairs found in the factory. The crowd, now large, headed by Councillor Forward, the Workers Bank and the Anti-Violence Brigade, marched through the Western Ward of the town. The windows of William Bartlett's factory were smashed, followed by those of John Williams' factory and those of the factory of Castle Brothers. The crowd successfully dealt with the factory windows of Joynson & Holland, Ebenezer Gomme, Stratford & Brion, James Cox & Son, Worley Brothers and, finally, Thomas Glenister, all factories with blacklegging workers.

In Frogmoor the crowd, estimated at 2,000, was confronted by the Metropolitan mounted police with truncheons drawn. Two charges were made and calm was finally restored by the Lord Mayor after fighting had gone on from seven in the evening till eleven. During the very troubled week that followed the crowd, despite the appeals of the union officials remained quite out of control. The obdurate attitude of the Federation, the absence of any prospect of settlement and the hardships arising from a hard winter, had left the workers bitter and violent.

The disturbances were thus reported in *The Times*; 'A crowd of about 3,000 proceeded to the residence of Alderman Birch, the head of the leading chair factory in the town, and chairman of the Employers' Federation and broke a number of panes of glass in the house. Later, a number of youths made a hostile demonstration outside Messrs. Glenister's factory'. [16] And again on the following day: 'There has been renewed violence here today by strikers in the chairmaking industry. A van load of chairs was captured by a party of rioters this morning and some of the contents thrown in the river. Later a wagon load of material for chairmaking coming from the country was attacked. At an open air meeting of the unemployed held shortly before midday the leaders advised the men to 'go for a nice walk and not throw stones'. After the meeting a procession marched through the town to Desborough Street. Two non-unionists leaving work for their dinner were met by the procession and were 'booed and hooted'. When they were actually threatened with violence, the police intervened. Stones and bottles were thrown by the crowd at the police who had been augmented by officers of the Metropolitan force, and several constables were hit. Some of the strikers were armed with parts of chairs, and as the situation threatened to become increasingly serious, a baton charge was made. Some among the crowd were injured, one man being badly cut on the head and rendered unconscious. Mounted police were called to clear the main streets of the town'. [17]

A lighter side of these incidents sometimes revealed itself in the Magistrates' Court to which a number of workers were duly summoned. A Mrs Annie MacPortland was alleged to have broken windows in Joynson & Hollands factory. In her own defence she claimed, with some indignation, that *she* could not be guilty of such an act - *she* 'was no militant suffragetist'. Mrs. MacPortland was set free. Not all the defendants were so fortunate. Ten workers were found guilty of a breach of the peace and fined £5 or £10. Their fines were paid by the union and Fred Bramley was reported as saying; 'After Saturday's burlesque of justice the unions have decided not to recognise the local court as a court of justice at all. The Masters have domination over the bench and control the decisions irrespective of the evidence. In future the union will not employ solicitors to defend their men: the principles of justice are no use before Wycombe magistrates and the men would be advised not to plead, but to inform the bench that they had no confidence in or respect for a tribunal incapable of impartial adminstration of the law'. [18]

Sir George Askwith came to High Wycombe on 17th February and spent the day in separate meetings with the two sides to the dispute. On the following day he visited various factories 'to ascertain the character and quality of the work being done' and on the 19th informal proceedings were resumed and a draft agreement submitted to both sides. This was formally ratified on Monday, 23rd and the factories re-opened and work recommenced in the town on Tuesday, 24th February.

After 91 days in mid-winter, there ended the most bitter lock-out to be recorded in the history of the furniture trades. The union and the furniture workers had won a great victory. When the dispute began Wycombe was a town of low pay without formalised pay or conditions of work. With the settlement came improved rates and a schedule of working rules setting out not only hours and conditions but also giving the area a dispute procedure whereby 'in the event of any differences arising.....the matter will be dealt with by the Employer and Employees in the shops and if still unsettled and prior to the National officials of the men being called in, shall be referred to the Employers Federation and the men's Local officials'. The rates of pay and conditioons were to apply 'to all employees in the district within a radius of ten miles of Wycombe Guildhall', thus ensuring that the small workshops in the outlying villages around the town did not become village sweatshops, and, indeed, ensuring that no undercutting of the principal employers of the town could take place by local village entrepreneurs.

Hours of work were set at 54 hours per week - higher than in London but better than ever before. After 54 hours, overtime was to be paid. Apprentices and learners and improvers were to be limited to one for every three journeymen, thus putting paid to the tradition in busy times of setting on as many young men and women as necessary and sacking them when trade was slack.    The agreement ended with the clause: 'Should any difference arise.....no cessation of work shall take place before the matter has been dealt with by the representatives of the Union, and failing agreement submitted to the Chief Industrial Commissioner'. This clause predates the later National Labour agreement *status quo* clause which with its various provisions proved to be so helpful in containing local disputes before they became major confrontation.

The union was willing to end in the dispute because it had exhausted its funds but gained its main objectives. It is less easy to say precisely why the employers settled since their records no longer exist. Locally it was suggested that manufacturers in other furniture making centres were happily taking over the trade of the Federation and, in a period of good trading conditions, were gaining customers who would normally have their furniture needs supplied by High Wycombe.

Rates of pay were not dramatically increased as a result of the dispute. Overall, however, they were an improvement on the original offer from the Federation - which had itself been a dramatic improvement on the original situation in the town. Fred Bramley reported to the Victory Meeting in the Town Hall. 'Prior to the 29th November we had working in High Wycombe 328 machinists at seven pence per hour or less, 200 of them working below sixpence halfpenny per hour. The rate is now eightpence per hour. We had 282 polishers at seven pence or less, nearly 200 of them at sixpence halfpenny and several at fivepence halfpenny per hour. Their rate is now eightpence halfpenny per hour. We had 187 upholsterers working for eightpence halfpenny per hour or less and they will now receive ninepence per hour'.

In resolving the dispute NAFTA spent £3,032 and was overdrawn on the National Strike Fund of the GFTU by over £500. High Wycombe represented a major victory in the fight against regional pockets of low pay and conditions for furniture workers and the union now turned its attention to the West Country where cabinetmakers paid 3/- per week for bench space, polishers 1/- a pint for ordinary polish, 1/3d. a pint for red polish and wood machinists working bandsaws, fret cutters, panel planers, and dovetailers earned 14/- per week of 55 hours. The solidarity of the workers in the High Wycombe dispute had been remarkable. Such resolve was not necessarily permanent. John Collings, who, as a chairback maker, had worked in the trade for 46 years, made very clear in a letter to the press during the lock-out how important it would be to maintain the union's strength. 'It is most essential that every member shall keep up his membership. Should it become defunct, the experience of the strike of 1872 will follow. In 1872 we were receiving 8/- per dozen for regular backs; we struck for 9/- which we obtained after several weeks. This increase gave me an average increase of 3/6d. per week. That price I received for 9 years. After the local union became defunt (i.e. the Wycombe Chairmakers Union) about this time a great depression in the trade came in the latter part of the Tory government (1891). The employers took advantage of the situation and took off the extra scales and the men had no alternative to help themselves *(sic)*. About ten years ago another depression in the trade occurred and several firms took the opportunity to make substantial reductions in prices. In the firm in

which I worked they reduced the rates by another twelve and a half per
cent. I think these facts should bring home to those in the trade that if the
workers do not stand united against such oppression, they will be
crushed'. [19], [20]

The news of the dispute settlement was received in High Wycombe in
the afternoon with unbounded gratification. There was singing and
dancing in the streets. The Lock-Out Band and the NAFTA choir were
on the steps of the Guildhall and gave a concert of popular melodies, and
there was some wonderful community singing. When the union
delegates returned to High Wycombe station, they were met by a
cheering crowd of several thousands and a monster procession was
formed, led by the Anti-Violence Brigade and the Lock-Out Band.
Wherever it went in the town there was the same signs of rejoicing, wives,
mothers and children sharing in the happy demonstration. [21]

This was Fred Bramley's dispute. Just as the union response to the
Scottish lock-out was mastermineded by Alex Gossip, so in High
Wycombe the main burden of organisation rested on the shoulders of
Fred Bramley, Trade Organiser and ex-General Secretary of the
Polishers. The Anti-Violence Brigade, the marshals, the peace keeping
force, but above all the band of fit, strong and committed young
furniture workers who were recruited and organised by Fred Bramley in
High Wycombe, and the only known instance of the formation of a
workers brigade in any dispute in this area was his creation. [22]

The actions of the local and Metropolitan police in this dispute are
well recorded in the union journal and the local press. Their dispersal
tactics of mounted men with riot sticks riding at a crowd would
undoubtedly have led to many more injuries or to much more severe
intimidation had there been no band of furniture workers surrounding
the crowds ready, willing and able to fight back and protect the ordinary
men and women gathered together to protest their right to organise.
Reinforcement of the local police from the Metropolitan area was, at
various stages in the struggle, reduced at the urging of the High
Wycombe Furnishing Trades Joint Committee of unions against the
opposite urgings of the Furniture Manufacturers' Federation. Damage
to property was much less significant than local and national press
reports indicated and claims under the Riot Damage Act from some 20
firms amounted only to £45. The cost, however, of the attendance of the
Metropolitan Police in the Borough was a staggering £1,600.14s.11d.
though it was passed and paid by the Watch Committee without
comment. [23]

The events which occurred in High Wycombe in 1913 can be seen as
the telescoping of whole epochs of industrial organisation. As a result of
one extraordinary event there appeared a core of sophisticated and
organised workmen in the town furniture industry in the form of
NAFTA Branch 72, at the head of a mass body of newly organised

workers with limited industrial experience. In the fight for recognition extremes of behaviour became the norm, frustration expressed itself in violent forms and scenes. It was thus that a coherent industrial force emerged from the primitive and repressive workshop structure traditional in the furniture manufacturing trade.

# CHAPTER V

# *NAFTA: 1914 – 1918*

The years of the first world war were a watershed for NAFTA. Some sixty per cent of all the firms in the industry were involved in war production of some kind and experienced changes in product, method and technology. New glues, improved plywoods and framed construction changed the philosophy of the firms using them and also affected firms still involved in furniture making. In common with other trade unions the Association found itself involved with government and legislation to an extent previously unimaginable; the net result was to limit its scope as a workers' organisation in some directions, whilst extending it in others.

The first action of the trade union movement of the country on the declaration of war was taken on August 24th 1914 by the Parliamentary Committee of the TUC acting together with the Labour Party through the Joint Board which declared an industrial truce. The official leadership refused to take advantage of the fact that labour now had the whip hand in the war situation. Labour supported Britain's involvement in the war, and took the decision not to exploit its improved bargaining position through industrial action that would disrupt production and impair the war effort. NAFTA in common with a number of other unions obeyed this call, and closed down all disputes then current at Wrexham, Manchester and Warrington.

The support given to the war effort by NAFTA at this time contrasts strongly with its anti-war stance in the latter years of the conflict. There is no clear explanation for the union's initial stance in the union records, but certain inferences can be drawn from the statistical returns. By 1914 the funds of the union were heavily depleted by industrial action. It was prudent and opportune to call a halt at this stage to all disputes in order to retrieve the financial situation and, by removing the need for supplementary levies on the membership, to rebuild the numbers paying into funds. The most compelling reason, however, for this initial support for the war was the numbers of furniture workers who enlisted in the armed forces. In 1914, 1,519 members were in khaki. By 1915 this had grown to 2,086 and by 1916 to 4,282. This represented an extraordinary 33 per cent of total NAFTA membership. No other trade union had so high a percentage of volunteers for the war, a good deal higher than for the population as a whole. [1]

Population and Recruitment for the Army 1914 - 1918

|  | Numbers | % of males between 18 and 50 |
|---|---|---|
| England | 4,006,158 | 24.02 |
| Wales | 272,924 | 21.52 |
| Scotland | 557,618 | 23.71 |
| Ireland | 134,202 | 6.14 |

[2]

Against such a background of patriotism, no matter how misplaced the leadership may have considered it to be, the Executive may have felt that there could be no other stance than acquiescence in supporting the war effort. The number of disputes for the remainder of 1914 and into 1915 was kept to a low level, though there were some minor disputes during the early part of 1915 in Barnstaple, Halifax, Leeds and London.

In March, 1915 the industrial truce was reinforced by the signing of the so-called Treasury Agreement by the leadership of the trade union movement. This Agreement, which formally relinquished the right to strike for the duration of the war, was effectively ignored by NAFTA, but the Munitions of War Act brought in by the Government in July, 1915 could not so easily be disregarded. It required all disputes in firms engaged in the production of munitions of war (and for the furniture industry this, in effect, meant anything produced under government contract ) to be settled by arbitration. A graphical presentation of dispute pay per member indicates very clearly the effect that this Agreement and subsequent legislation had in reducing the freedom of action of NAFTA to pursue wage movements throughout the war years other than by arbitration. Nevertheless, with the rapid increase in food prices as the war continued, industrial unrest and tension grew apace and by 1916 NAFTA was taking action in the uncontrolled sector to improve wages by negotiation or confrontation as well as by arbitration in the contract work area. By 1917 the government was forced to raise wages over a wide area of the economy because of steeply rising prices. The furniture workers benefited from this change so that by the end of the war wage levels in the industry were generally some 80 per cent higher than they had been in 1914, though in real terms workers were little better off.

Trade union membership grew during the war period from 4,145,000 to 6,533,000. NAFTA participated in this trend with 13,796 members in 1914 and 22,442 members in 1918, approximately 25 per cent of all workers in the trade.

Military conscription was brought in by the government in early 1916. NAFTA membership in the armed forces was 1,591 in 1914, 2,086 in 1915, 4,287 in 1916, 4,572 in 1917 and 4,693 in 1918. By the end of the war the upper limit for conscription stood at 50 years of age, yet few furniture workers were affected by it after 1916. This was due to the vast amount of government contract work and the development of the aircraft industry. Warplanes, in these early years constructed of wood, were complex and highly labour intensive in their construction and attracted and recruited the younger craftsmen of the industry from all branches of the trade. The wood machinists, cabinetmakers and chairmakers had the obvious tasks of fabrication and construction, but the upholsterer was employed in the covering of the plane wings and body in doped linen and the carver in propeller laminating and shaping. Workers in the industry may be forgiven for thinking that work in an aircraft factory or on government contract was preferable to the trenches of France. Massive recruiting by the aircraft industry from within the membership coupled with the lower rate of entry to the armed forces after 1916 (only 400 members between 1916 and 1918 despite the raised upper age limit of 50 years of age) make it quite clear that those liable for conscription moved to reserved occupations in the new industry in large numbers and that non-government contract furniture making became the province of the older tradesmen.

The leadership of NAFTA, as represented by its officials and Executive Committee, was uncompromisingly pacifist throughout the war. In November 1914 Alex Gossip wrote that 'It is only the profiteers, landowners and capitalists who will benefit from this war. We have no quarrel with our fellows elsewhere. We give the right hand of friendship and comradeship to the comrades in Austria, Serbia, Germany, France, Russia and all other counties who see that the war is not determined in the interests of the workers.....the landowners and capitalists are the real and only enemy'. [3] Furniture trades officials of different unions did not necessarily see eye to eye on the matter. Walter Wentworth, General Secretary of the Woodcutting Machinists in one of the few wartime policy statements still extant expressed a more pragmatic view; 'The country is at present involved in the European war which will have serious effects upon employment of our members. This war brought the trade union world in to an unfortunate position - as provision was never made in our Rules for a war of this description'.

It must, however, have taken some observers by surprise in this early period of the war when jingoistic attitudes had been whipped to unprecedented heights by the popular press, that a union leader such as Alex Gossip could be so outspoken in his contradiction of popular opinion. In November he wrote to the membership: 'One would think that everyone was fighting for freedom, but it is exceedingly difficult to see how the poverty stricken and oppressed classes can gain their freedom by fighting for their own oppressors and against the down-trodden and exploited classes of other countries'. This view was respected by the membership. No record exists of any criticism of his sentiments despite the 1,500 members who had enlisted by December 1914. Nor should it be thought that correspondence stating a contrary view to that of Gossip was suppressed. The union journal openly and regularly printed dissenting opinions though these rarely involved major issues of this nature. The Executive viewpoint was seen as honestly held, if not universally accepted.

The officials made no secret of their anti-war sentiments. At the Food and Coal Supply Conference on 13th February, 1915 it was reported that 'Mr Alex Gossip - in the course of his speech used the words, 'Some of us who are opposed to this war'. He was stopped for fully a minute by the wild and enthusiastic applause which broke out from every part of the Conference'. Backed by such support Alex Gossip and Fred Bramley on behalf of the Executive Committee prepared a *Manifesto on Peace* which can be summarised as follows:

1.  There should be no new racial hatreds or sores created as result of the war. To prevent this no province shall by military conquest be transferred from one country to another without the consent of the population of such a province;
2.  No treaty, arrangements or undertakings shall be entered into in the name of Great Britain without the consent of Parliament and the people. Democratic control of foreign policy is essential;
3.  Any alliance of Britain with other countries shall be made with the object of peaceful relations with all and hostility to none. It should presage the setting up of an International Council whose deliber-ations and discussions shall be made public and which shall include machinery for securing international agreement as a guarantee of abiding peace;
4.  Any peace settlement should embody a plan of armament reduction and an attempt should be made to secure the general nationalisation of armament manufacture, and the control of the export of armaments from one country to another. Trade unionists had no quarrel nor any conflicting interests with the workers of any country, which would justify the reckless slaughter presently taking place as a means of settling a dispute they had not created, which concerned issues they did not understand, and which affected interests which

were not theirs. Humanity should, in future, be protected against such crimes and calamities. If organised labour will not work with the object in view, who will? The EC desired in the name of the membership to declare war on the causes and consequences of war. [4]

The *Manifesto* was endorsed by the EC, sent out to the Branches and accepted and endorsed by the membership with a majority vote of two to one, though on a vote of 10 per cent of membership only. It corresponded to the majority view in the ILP (of which Alex Gossip was a prominent member), yet NAFTA seems to have been the only organised group of industrial workers in Britain to adopt such a position at so early a stage in the hostilities.

Not all of the membership was totally convinced of this point of view and a strong protest was expressed to the EC of NAFTA by No.2 Branch (London West End - 400 members) over a pamphlet *Class Cohesion versus Spurious Patriotism* issued by Fred Bramley. However, the EC took the view that in publishing it he had acted in his individual capacity rather than that of the union, and took no action on the protest.

By 1915 the war had come closer to home. The *Monthly Record* of NAFTA No.87 Branch (Walthamstow) and No.135 Branch (East Dulwich) had been informed that the Tool Insurance Premium covers the case of possible damage by Zeppelin raids. Though the 1915 Trades Union Congress held in Bristol in September endorsed overwhelmingly the policy of support for the war effort, the votes of NAFTA and its delegate Fred Bramley were cast in opposition. This opposition appeared in a more concrete form in the Executive's moves against conscription. Alex Gossip put forward the view that conscription represented the ultimate enslavement of the working people as pawns of the 'Capitalist Classes'. He quoted from the *Daily Telegraph*; 'When the armies pile their arms and the navies resume the peace routine, the old competition of the factory, the mart, and the counting house will be resumed with an intensity unknown before. In such a contest there can be no armistices, no surrenders with all the honours and no peace treaties; the industrial war must continue to an end without respite and without mercy'. [5]

Such, argued Gossip, was the reality of life. The war was real and the conflict in Europe and elsewhere no more than 'a temporary halt in the continuing battle. The protagonists of the working people have not forgotten this, neither should the workers of all lands'. In order to establish the feelings of the membership on the question of conscription, a poll was held at the instigation of the EC on the question 'Are you in favour of conscription?'. This resulted in one of the lowest polls recorded (7 per cent of the membership) with 784 against and 303 for conscription. Low as the poll was, the EC view was formally endorsed and the union, in common with a number of other societies, put forward a resolution to the Trades Union Congress which was accepted and became official Congress policy; namely that 'We affirm all our previous opposition to conscription in any shape or form, and resolve to do everything in our power to defeat all attempts to enforce compulsory military and industrial service, and recommend the Labour Party to prevent, if possible, the passing of the Government Bill'. [6]

Alex Gossip, recognising that the time for exhortation was over and that practical measures were now required, counselled members to push hard to become members of their local committees on conscription and on war pensions so that justice might be done. He deplored 'The mute aspect of Trade Unionists on these committees when faced with problems which warrant a Socialist and an Internationalist viewpoint'. It was not good enough that those coming before the committees should be 'bullied and insulted by the Chairman and other members of the Tribunal, with the so-called Labour representatives sitting dumb'.

Conscription was seen clearly by the Executive as an anti-working class weapon. 'It will be used as elsewhere to break the strength of organised labour, so let us be warned in time. Never let us forget that these folk hate us and fear us, when they do not despise us'. And conscription was the area over which the union and its Member of Parliament first publicly and acrimoniously disagreed. Initially Jim O'Grady's attitude was in line with that of the EC, especially as the 1915 Trades Union Congress at Bristol had rejected conscription 'by acclamation'. O'Grady was no pacifist. Initially he saw the war as being one for volunteers and the reduction of voluntary recruitment as a deliberate act of the War Cabinet which had deliberately closed down the work of recruiting committees when it had resolved upon conscription. Nevertheless, when the Military Service Bill was set before Parliament he voted for it at each of its various stages. In his defence he wrote: 'I felt that the opposition to the Bill from the working classes of the country came over the possibility that it would be used not only for Military Conscription but also for industrial conscription'. He went on, 'I, along with a number of other Labour members, agreed to vote for the Bill based upon the written assurances given by the Prime Minister that the Bill was never intended to allow an employer to exercise coercion over the free action of his workmen'. [7]

O'Grady knew very well that his support for the Bill would alienate him from the officials, from the Executive and, indeed, from many of the members of the union. 'For myself, I have to say, my vote for the Bill was only given after much thought and deliberate consideration of the national and wider issues involved. I gave that vote at the risk of breaking personal friendships that are very dear to me. There are other risks as well; but these are always with the men who have an opinion of their own, and ought always to be taken, unless the man be craven'. He was caught in the familiar parliamentary dilemma of a sponsored M.P.

Should he reflect the views of his constituents, his sponsors or of his conscience? The relationship of the union with James O'Grady was never again as cordial or intimate as it had once been.[8]

The opening shots in NAFTA'S new relationship with its MP were fired by the EC 'The EC is very concerned over the position taken by its Parliamentary Secretary James O'Grady on the vote in the House of Commons on Conscription; this being necessary in view of the number of branches who had written us on this matter'. It was decided that the Standing Order of 1st February, 1912, would decide future action. 'It must be definitely understood that delegates to Congress etc., must act in accordance with any mandate which may be given by the Association'. James O'Grady had, of course, cast his votes for the Bill before the final results of the conscription poll of the union's members were known, though he had been aware which way the vote was likely to go, and he could hardly have claimed to be ignorant of the attitude of the EC or the officials of the union on the matter. His mention of the 'risk of breaking personal friendships' suggested as much. Nevertheless, by pointing out that at the time of the vote in the House there was no union mandate, the quarrel was patched up and James O'Grady remained as Parliamentary Secretary. It is worth conjecturing whether, if James O'Grady had been instructed to vote against the Military Service Bill by NAFTA, this would have been referred to the Parliamentary Committee on Privilege. Such pressure as the union could bring to bear upon him was as nothing compared to that of the various pro-war groups within Parliament and the press. [9]

Glasgow was the biggest single centre of opposition to the war in mainland Britain. It is, therefore, not surprising that Branch No.23 (Glasgow) was not satisfied by James O'Grady's explanation of his voting behaviour on the Conscription Bill. The EC recorded its resolution and published it in full for the membership, to the discomfiture of O'Grady himself. 'Whereas organised labour in this country had with no uncertain voice, declared its intense opposition to the Munitions Act, and through its conferences, declared its intentions to actively oppose both military and industrial compulsion, and whereas Mr James O'Grady, MP, Parliamentary Secretary of the NAFTA has, in supporting those acts, acted against the best interests of those who made it possible for him to enter Parliament, be it resolved that this Branch No.23 urge upon our EC the advisability of asking for the resignation of Mr J. O'Grady, MP from the position of Parliamentary Secretary of the NAFTA'. To which O'Grady replied: 'I consider the censure expressed is harsh and unjustified.....I have only supported a Military Service Bill which is a measure of compulsion. Conscription and compulsion are not the same thing'. (Though the world was never informed as to where this distinction lay). 'At least that is my view. I would point out to this Branch that I am not in Parliament solely as a representative of our association but of a constituency, and together with my colleagues of the Labour movement generally'. He went on: 'The constituency and the general Labour movement allow me to have an opinion of my own and to use my judgement. I have insisted upon that liberty on all questions not vitally detrimental to organised labour and shall continue to do so'. O'Grady then went on to point out that Branch No.23 had paid political levies in 1913 of 2/9d.; 1914 of 16/4d. and in 1915 of £2.15s.3d. 'So some 53 paid the levy, but 184 members who presumably assisted in carrying the resolution want both to call the tune, and refuse to pay'. [10] The effect of transferring a workers' representative from the union headquarters to the 'best club in Britain' was, his opponents claimed, plain for all to see.

The Executive Committee of NAFTA was so disturbed by the situation that a special meeting was called in June to discuss the problem. Protests over the stand of James O'Grady on conscription had been received from a number of branches and an attempt was made to discuss the question. However, 'it was agreed in view of all the circumstances and differences of opinion, that the next business be proceeded with'. By this device, an insoluble problem was disposed of without a vote which would possibly have been close and certainly devisive. As a result Messrs. A. Barker and C.F. Hawkins, both anti-O'Grady men, resigned from the EC and for the time being the matter remained closed. [11]

In its stand against conscription NAFTA endorsed the role of Alex Gossip and Fred Bramley in the National Committee of the *No Conscription Fellowship* and agreed to vote on a proposal that it should affiliate to the Fellowship for a fee of £3 per annum. [12] The President of the NCF at this time was R. Smillie of the Miners' Federation. Alex Gossip was a member of its EC and Fred Bramley of its General Council. 742 votes were cast for affiliation and 252 against. The vote made the position of James O'Grady even more difficult, though a nine per cent vote in total and a five per cent vote in favour was hardly impressive. [13] O'Grady himself could not understand the point of view of the conscientious objector, either from a religious or a social standpoint. 'I have tried earnestly to do so, and have to confess that I cannot yet see or appreciate his views. I do not intend to put the argument from my point of view but I repeat the view of Lord Hugh Cecil - a supporter of conscientious objectors - 'if the conscientious objector refuses to help the State, in its hour of need and danger, by refusing to perform work of a character that does not involve the taking of life, and which is allocated to him by representatives of the State, then he ought either to be interned or deported''. 'That' declared O'Grady, 'is a Socialist doctrine which I venture to assert few Socialists can logically controvert. The solution to the problem is near at hand and the genuine conscientious objector will be dealt with by the Civil Courts and Civil

Authorities'.

O'Grady returned to the attack on pacifism in his report to the membership on the Dardanelles campaign. 'This was a gross blunder and the Mesoptamia campaign a hell. Yet I would say to my pacifist friends. These men fought from no lust for bloodshed, suffered for no vain glory of conquest, died for no personal vanity that their deeds may be recorded in the pages of history. They fought, suffered and died for an idea'. O'Grady had been on the Commission of Enquiry into the Mesopotamia Campaign but 'was jockeyed out of the appointment by the Mandarins of his own Party'. He seems to have been no more popular in the Party than in the union.

The union and its officers took an active part in the Anti-War demonstration in London in April of 1917. No.1 Branch (Central London) sent to the EC a strong protest 'against the cowardly and brutal attacks upon the demonstrators' by some elements of the crowd - 'the police doing nothing to prevent this hooliganism'. Alex Gossip and the EC participated in the demonstration and were subjected to these physical assaults. 'They are not evil', he reported, 'but poor dupes misled by the gutter press'. Nevertheless, the matter was pressed by the National Council for Civil Liberties and raised in the House of Commons and at the London County Council. [14]

An interesting comment on the issue of conscientious objection arose at a Conference on Education attended by the General Secretary. Alex Gossip obtained the passage of a resolution against military drill in schools and on the question of the shortage of school teachers suggested; 'open the prison doors of the many school teachers incarcerated in gaols at present for conscience sake'. The fate of the working class conscientious objector could be appalling. G.E.H. (full name not given) was a wood carver and a member of the union. He was arrested in April 1916, sent to Harwick Circular Redoubt, lodged in a dark cell, put in leg and arm irons, fed on bread and water and on 8th May 1916, his resolve unbroken, was sent to France, court martialled at Boulogne on 19th May, 1916 and sentenced to death by shooting. He refused to abjure his principles and sentence was commuted to ten years penal servitude. He was transferred to Dumfries in the South of Scotland to serve his sentence 'beyond the reach of visits from friends and relatives. [15]

The EC took up the case, writing to the Prime Minister strongly protesting against the repeated imprisonment, and pointing out 'that this is a violation of the Military Service Act intended to safeguard the historic right of individual freedom of conscience and opinion, and further demands that in all cases where there is evidence of genuineness of conviction, such conscientious objectors be set at liberty'. Sadly there was no response to its pleas; nor to the others made in the latter years of the war by various branches to the EC and to the government relating to individual cases. The treatment of working class conscientious objectors continued to be different from that meted out to the middle and upper classes. The treatment of the Bloomsbury set was the most obvious example. [16]

Perhaps the final word on pacifism should be that of Alex Gossip at the 1918 Conference of the National Council for Civil Liberties. 'We view with a considerable amount of alarm, for the safety of real democracy, the various insidious attempts which are being made to perpetuate this hideous thing (militarism) and to foster and develop it amongst the children attending our public schools'[17]. A resolution passed by the Conferenc at his instigation read as follows: 'This Conference declares its opposition to the military training of children under the age of eighteen, to the introduction into schools of special lessons on the authoritative view of patriotism and other political matters, and to the application of any political or religious test whatsoever for teachers. We demand such revision of political histories used in our schools as will eliminate the undue influence given to wars, and enlighten our children on the extent to which cooperation between groups and nations has been the greatest factor in the development of civilised communities. This Conference further holds that children in all schools shall be trained in independent thought on public questions, national and international and in the exercise of their capacities as future voters in local and Parliamentary elections'. [18]

Throughout the war Alex Gossip kept the vision of workers' internationalism alive with NAFTA, constantly bringing events on the international trade union stage to the attention of the membership. As the year 1915 came to an end he informed his members of the conditions of the trade unionist in other countries involved in the war, in particular those of the German Woodworkers' Trade Union which had some 80,000 men fighting on various fronts and had sustained losses of 4,000 members killed in action. 'We note the intense desire for peace expressed by the various unions [affiliated to the International Woodworkers Association] and trust the time will soon come when the organised workers, the world over, will be powerful enough to prevent war'.[19] Two years later he drew the attention of the membership and the Parliamentary Committee of the TUC to the banning of trade unions in the British West Indies. Appalled at this and the penalties allowable under the ban he exhorted the PC to take action on the matter. [20]

The EC records show the general secretary sending protests to the American government against 'the grossly unfair decision of the American courts in sentencing trade unionists in San Francisco, one to death and the other to life imprisonment, for an alleged bomb incident with which they clearly had nothing to do'. He comments in the *Monthly Report* 'The capitalists of western America have been moving heaven and earth to destroy the forces of organised labour'[21]. Internationism was as important in time of war as in time of peace. 'The industrial workers in all nations must be linked together if ever we are going to get rid of the slavery and oppression of our class. The property and the power which came from conquest always find their way into the hands of the few. A continent may be added to the Empire tomorrow, and the worker and his fellows will remain homeless - and will remain the slaves of Capitalism until they become its master. The Capitalist fears nothing so much as the very idea that workers and toilers of all countries may come together and discuss their own affairs, Heaven and earth are being moved to keep them separate and apart, and if it suits for the moment, they are flung at each other throats. To teach the workers of the various countries of the world that the workers in countries other than their own are their enemies is the deliberate policy of plutocracy.....to perpetuate the enslavement of the toilers of the earth'. [22]

NAFTA, as already noted, observed the initial industrial truce. As the war progressed, however, and the government did nothing to control the cost of living or war profiteering, proceeded with 'dilution' and 'direction' of the labour force, so did the unions' disenchantment with the government grow. It quickly focussed on the new Munitions of War Bill which became the subject of discussion between Lloyd George and trade union leaders in June 1915. NAFTA summarised the provisions of the Bill for the members as: government control of munition factories; limitation of profits on war work; the suspension of trade union rules restricting output of munitions; the enrolment of volunteers for a mobile corps of munitions workers; the creation of special courts to deal with refractory workmen. The NAFTA delegates voted against all these proposals. Fred Bramley reported; 'The rush and absolute careless haste to support the government in this matter, regardless of the consequences involved, made one wish to see, in some trade union leaders, the recovery of their ordinary reasoning powers'. And how, questioned Alex Gossip, was the post-war employment of the man who left a job to undertake war work elsewhere to be safeguarded?. Lloyd George replied, 'such cases could be safely left to the force of public opinion'. 'We venture', noted Gossip, ' to express a doubt on this reply!'.

The effect of the Munitions Bill was to compound the problems of dilution which NAFTA had suffered from the earliest days of the war - dilution by women workers but initially by Belgian refugees. The furniture trade was notorious for the number of employers willing to find any excuse for reducing wage levels; Belgian refugees and women workers did not improve the situation. As early as December 1914 Alex Gossip was warning the membership that 'attempts are being made by so-called patriotic employers to take advantage of Belgian refugees and to employ them at rates far below those paid in the district. These people should be treated as guests and not used to displace Britishers and reduce wages'. Fred Bramley had found some such employers, and had sent reports to the War Office proving 'without a doubt that several of the most notorious sweaters in the East End are using Belgian labour, are engaged in government work and in every way violating the fair contracts clauses'. A.A. Purcell, the union's other Trade Organiser, reported the situation in Manchester; 'Here refugees are put up in a shop, none of them knowing what they will be paid. In Sheffield refugees in one of our shops are paid £1.00 and £1.50 less than the weekly rate for the district'.

At this stage of the war the tide of opinion was unsympathetic to such views. The *Manchester Guardian* noted 'If Belgian refugees were paid below the trade union rate, it would be undesirable, but it would not be a very crying evil' [23]. The War Refugee Committee made a clear statement to the contrary; 'There is no charity in taking work from an Englishman and giving it to a refugee, if the refugee accepts lower wages. Such employment is selfishness masquerading as charity'. It was, however, in High Wycombe that the problem of exploitation of refugee and women workers was most acute. The Belgians were being paid twopence per hour below the rates established after the 1914 lock-out and the women just over twopence farthing per hour for work for which men would have had to be paid eightpence or eightpence halfpenny.

The High Wycombe Polishers Branch had 170 men enlisted in the colours. During their absence the employers made an effort to fill their places with cheap labour, 'with the probable result' noted Fred Bramley, 'that on their return they will be met with the cry 'not wanted' '. The Munitions Act had become a tool of the unscrupulous employer to break unionism and reduce wage levels. There were numbers of reports in 1915/1916 of unemployed craftsmen being rejected for munitions work whilst women and boys were 'readily taken on'. When these matters were raised at Tribunals they were brushed aside as being of 'no moment'. Not surprisingly NAFTA leadership and, for example, that of the Engineers adopted an aggressive stance on dilution. Alex Gossip warned the membership; 'You will be approached by government officials with a view to holding joint local conferences with employers to discuss the introduction of women into the trade. You are asked, if such a conference is held, not to commit yourself to anything, but to report proposals to the EC at once. We are endeavouring to get a conference with the Home Office, with our kindred trades, with a view to discussing the matter nationally, and securing a uniform policy as to safeguards, etc.'. [24]

The conference was called at the Home Office in January, 1916 between the Employers' Federation and the trade unions in the furnishing trades on the subject of the employment of women. The attitude of the NAFTA was protective. It was summarised in the statement of Fred Bramley the Trade Organiser. 'We must act with caution, in the interests of our men, in the interests of the nation, and also in the interests of women, to prevent the sweaters of our trade using the war period, and the plea of patriotism to further their own ulterior motives to secure cheap female labour, to the detriment of the trade, the men employed in it, and the thousands of our members fighting their country's battles in all parts of the world. One doesn't want these men to come back and find their places taken by women at one-half of the rate. Innovation may be necessary; women may have to be employed; but to secure proper safeguards is a duty imposed on us all'. By the standards of today the eventual agreement does allow a charge of sexism to be levelled at the furniture trade unions. 'If it is found necessary to employ female labour, this be permitted, provided that a suitable agreement is entered into between the Employers' Assocation and the Operative Union in the district' [25]. This was an important move in making such negotiations at a local level mandatory between the two sides of the industry. It paved the way for better working relationships and consultation on issues other than female labour. However, it fixed women's rates at two-thirds of the men's rate for comparable work, a proportion which was to remain until equal pay legislation of later years. The agreement went on to specify that no piecework was permissible for female labour. Further, and more far-reaching, all females introduced into a factory were required to join the appropriate trade union. By the end of the war period NAFTA had 3,000 women members, and women's wages and conditions became part and parcel of any trade agreement from this time onward.

The amended Munitions Bill went through Parliament early in 1916. The union's Parliamentary Secretary, James O'Grady, was responsible for an amendment to the Bill which had a useful bearing on the question of dilution in the post-war period. In the original proposals union men were prohibited from striking against the introduction of non-union labour. As amended the Act provided that the introduction of non-union labour in a shop during the war would be considered a change in working conditions and subject to restoration to the original situation at the termination of hostilities. After the war non-union labour would have to go or join the union, so ensuring that unscrupulous employers could no longer use dilution to break the union in a workplace.

Attitudes to women workers were, however, far from liberal. In a trade plagued with recurrent unemployment and substantial seasonal variation, it would have been astonishing if some of the membership at least, was not apprehensive about the post-war situation. A.A. Purcell, Trade Organiser, wrote: 'To prevent the introduction of female labour, unless we have men unemployed, is out of the question; however, as men return from the war, first preference should be extended to the men who were previously employed'. He went on to urge members to ensure that the return of furniture workers from the war should not be used as an excuse by firms to reduce the quality of the terms and conditions established with such difficulty over the years. 'A thirty hour week with all our members in work will be preferable to a fifty hour week with a third of our members out of work and incurring unemployment benefit. If you spill your blood to defend the life of a nation, then a just share of the work (and the wealth) at all times renders the nation worth the fight at any time'. [26] A similar point is still being made seventy years later!

Anxiety over the introduction of female labour was justified by future events. Nor did management make any bones about its attitudes at the time. Alex Gossip quoted the following from the trade magazine *Engineer:* 'The introduction of female labour might be used so as to lead to a lowering of the rate of payment for services. The fact of the matter is, not that women are paid too little, but that men are paid too much for work which can be done without previous training. It is only the trade unions which, after the war, will stand in the way of our realising the anticipation that we might be able to reduce our workshop costs by the employment of women. Much depends upon the attitude of the women themselves. If they can be brought to see the economic advantages to the country, to recognise the facts we have put forward, and to agree to accept a lower scale of wages than skilled men, they may, by their preponderance of numbers, be in a position to defy the unions'. [27]

It was precisely to counter this possibility and to take into account the new role of women in the furniture industry that NAFTA changed its rules. The normal work for women in the trade had been in polishing and upholstery. Now they were being recruited as drivers (horse drawn), packers, labourers, timber yard workers and the like. NAFTA rules at this time limited women membership of the union to those tasks which had traditionally been women's work. The EC now asked the membership to change the rules to allow these women into emergency membership for the duration of the war. This was agreed by 770 votes to 305, a majority in favour of 465. [28] The exploitation of refugees as well as women workers was not confined to British employers. In High Wycombe the union had to battle with a Belgian employer who had set up a factory employing his own countrymen and women who had fled from the war on the continent of Europe. The employer had imposed an 84 hour week without overtime payment, and paid his workforce at 7d. per hour for men and 3d. per hour for women, using the threat of military service to keep his labour force in line. Happily, local and union pressure brought the matter to a swift and satisfactory conclusion. It provided a salutory reminder of the excesses possible without the vigilance and activity of the union officials.

Despite the Munitions Act, pressure for improvements in wage rates grew as the war continued. With this pressure came demands from the membership for trade movements. A substantial advance in making trade movements more effective was taken by the signing of a joint agreement in December 1915 by NAFTA, the Amalgamated Union of Cabinetmakers, the Amalgamated Union of Upholsterers, and the

Amalgamated Society of Woodcutting Machinists which contained the follow provisions:

1.  That in the event of any section of the Furnishing Industry contemplating trade action [trade movements], notice shall at once be given to the parties to this agreement, locally, and where members of more than one society are involved, or likely to be involved, no dispute shall take place prior to the Executive Committee being consulted and have opportunity of discussing the full situation in the district affected;

2.  When a joint movement is agreed upon, each society shall pay its share of the joint expenses in proportion to the number of members either brought out on strike, or employed in shops dealt with under the auspices of the Joint Committee, and working under the Rules and Conditions dealt with during the dispute where a Society has no members so involved or effected no claims for joint expenses to be made;

3.  Each society to be responsible for the payment of dispute support to its own members, and a joint understanding to be arrived at in the direction of adopting a uniform policy of dealing with new members of the respective Unions;

4.  Should any dispute take place in a shop where less than the whole of the section is involved in the first instance, and no satisfactory settlement can be arrived at after endeavours have been made to do so, the various societies shall agree to withdraw all other members if necessary, with the consent of the Executive Committee concerned;

5.  A weekly detailed statement of Joint Income and Expenditure shall be supplied to each Executive Committee during times of joint dispute;

6.  The question of the apportionment of the expenses of the official or officials in charge, shall be raised and dealt with at the termination of the joint dispute'.

An agreement of this kind had been under consideration for some time. It became a practical proposition after the help given to NAFTA by the other unions during the High Wycombe lock-out. Just as the Scottish lock-out had brought the English and Scottish unions together, so the dispute at High Wycombe provided the catalyst for the joint action agreement of 1915. Essentially, therefore, there was to be a joint approach on trade movements and a separate funding of members in dispute. A 'one out all out' policy was adopted to give strength to sectional interests. The funding and expenses of disputes were to be closely controlled and discussed to avoid premature, forced return to work by the less affluent member unions, and full-time officials were to be used on a joint basis.

This agreement was a most important step along the road to eventual amalgamation. While it was at times shaken by accusations of poaching

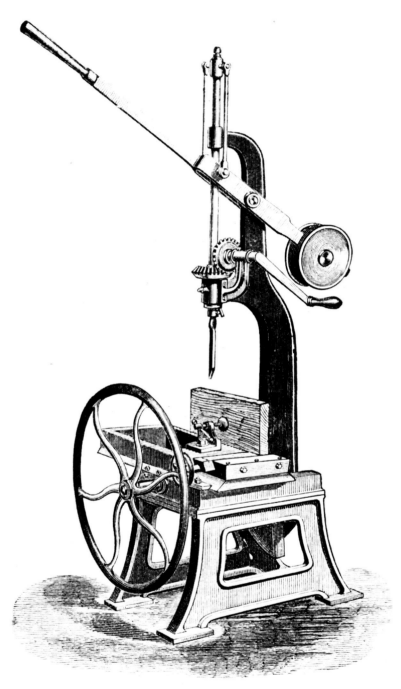

HAND-POWER MORTISING AND BORING MACHINE

HAND OR STEAM POWER SAW BENCH AND BAND SAWING
MACHINE COMBINED

CONTINUOUS ROLLER-FEED CIRCULAR SAW BENCH

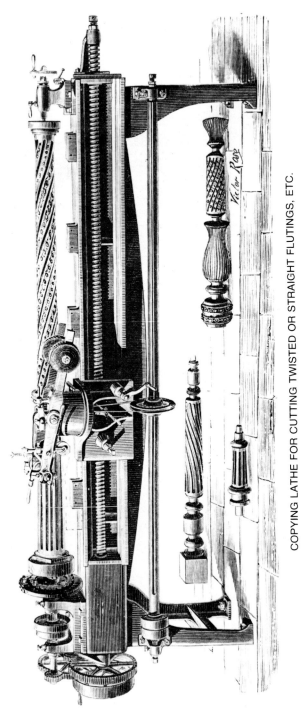

COPYING LATHE FOR CUTTING TWISTED OR STRAIGHT FLUTINGS, ETC.

## FURNISHING WORKERS WANT

BOSSES wont give it, TALK wont get it -

A C T I O N will!

Let's get ready now!

Demand that the Shop
Stewards  invite all
Shops to a meeting
to set up that

ALL-LONDON  COMMITTEE  of  ACTION

and

show the Employers we mean business
by deciding in YOUR  shop

to    STOP  OVERTIME !

Issued by the Furnishing Trades Minority Movement
38, Gt. Ormond Street, London, W.C.1.
No. 2.  Sept.1929

Let your mate see this

# National Amalgamated Furnishing Trades' Association

---

# ARE YOU FULLY RATED

## In accordance with the Wycombe Agreement?

Is the firm at which you work NON-FEDERATED?
If it is, you are still entitled to demand Wycombe's
agreed Wages and Conditions

You are entitled to the **RATE** when your efficiency
attains adult experience, no matter on what process
you may be working

**THE RATE** is that minimum wage which has been
agreed to between Employers and Employees of the
Furniture Trade in Wycombe and District

Discuss these matters with your shop mates.

## JOIN THE TRADE UNION AT ONCE

If you work at a Firm not a member of the Employers
Federation demand at once the conditions of the High
Wycombe Agreement, Section 1, as between High
Wycombe Furniture Manufacturers' Federation and
the National Amalgamated Furnishing Trades' Association

**Minimum Wage 1s. 5½d. per hour**
**Wycombe Section 1s. 5d. per hour**

The *pro. tem.* Organiser is always available to prospective members
**COUNCILLOR EDWARD ROLPH,**
**260 Bowerdean Road, High Wycombe, Bucks.**

*Freer & Hayter, Printers, High Wycombe*

# Coronation, 1937

# N. A. F. T. A.

#### High Wycombe Joint Committee.

Your Trade Union applied to the Employers Federation and non-federated Employers for

### Coronation Holiday with pay.

The Federation has left it to the individual Employers.

Some **will pay**.     The Majority **will not**.

Why ?    Because you are not organised in Your Union.

Patriotism does not mean forfeiture of your pay.

Make your Employer prove his patriotism by not making Coronation day a lock out.

Yours fraternally,

C. F. HAWKINS,

*Organiser.*

All holidays should be paid for.

## JOIN YOUR TRADE UNION AT ONCE!

Freer & Hayter, Printers, High Wycombe.

# HIGH Wycombe
# LOW Wages!!!

### The *Lowest* within
### GT. BRITAIN for

## FURNITURE WORKERS.

N.A.F.T.A. Members have voted solidly to end the Local Wages Agreement and now demand the

## 4-POINT CHARTER.

* ★ **3/- per hour for Journeymen**

* ★ **Proportionate increase to all other Sections.**

* ★ **40-hour Working Week.**

* ★ **Better Conditions of Employment.**

**Every Furniture Worker**
 **a *N.A.F.T.A. Member.***

**Every Furniture Factory**
 **a " *N.A.F.T.A. Shop.*"**

The few non-Unionists in the district should apply for Membership of N.A.F.T.A. to any Branch Office or by writing to : N.A F.T.A.
District Management Committee,
7/8, Queen's Square, High Wycombe.

New Goswell Printing Co. (T.U. throughout), 220, Goswell Road, London, E.C. 1

WHEN the decisions on WAGES, HOURS, HOLIDAYS WITH PAY of the FURNITURE MANUFACTURING TRADE BOARD operate in Factories where TRADE UNION WAGES and CONDITIONS are not observed

# Non-Union Workers

## will require the assistance of

# N·A·F·T·A

## THE FURNITURE WORKERS' TRADE UNION

### by which

## All Trades and Sections are Efficiently Represented

UNITY IS **!**     PREPARE NOW BY **!**
STRENGTH **.**     JOINING THE UNION **.**

### CONTRIBUTIONS :

TRADE SECTION (Men)    **9d.** per week
SECTION 3 (Women)    **6d.** per week
Juniors    ..    from **1d.** to **6d.** per week
(Higher Contributions and Benefits optional)

*Fill in this Form and post to—*

| | | |
|---|---|---|
| **N.A.F.T.A. Head Office** (Trade Board Dept.) 219 Golders Green Road London, N.W.11 | OR, | **High Wycombe District Office** N.A.F.T.A. 7-8 Queen's Square |

*Name*............................................................    *Address*....................................................................

*Trade* .........................................................................................................................................

London Caledonian Press Ltd. (T.U. all Depts.), 74 Swinton Street, W.C.1.— w 7315

The Production Speed-up has brought prosperity
to the Employer

*but*

the reward for the Worker
has been

# S H O R T    T I M E

## &

# U N E M P L O Y M E N T

---

# N U F T O
# FURNITURE  WORKERS
# HAVE  CLAIMED
# A
# Shorter  Working  Week

---

On  the  FACTS  the  TWO  CLAIMS  are  fair
and  reasonable

UNITY  under  N.U.F.T.O.
will  win  a  fair  deal  for
FURNITURE  WORKERS

*Issued by the General Executive Council of the National Union of Furniture Trade
Operatives, " Fairfields," Roe Green, London, N.W.9.
Printed by New Goswell Printing Co. Ltd. (T.U.) 220 Goswell Road, E.C.1*

# First Delegate Meeting of Upholsterers

*Central Hotel, Ranelagh Street, Liverpool, March 21st, 1891*

Object : AMALGAMATION

A. MUGGOCH     M. THOMPSON     R. TISDALL
J. BOWIE     A. SALTER     H. TIPLADY     S. BECKLEY
J. COSSAR     J. FLEWITT     W. WATSON
J. HALL     J. RYAN

*Manchester Society :*
STEPHEN BECKLEY & ALFRED SALTER

*Glasgow Society :*
JAMES BOWIE & ADAM MUGGOCH

*Edinburgh Society :*
MARTIN THOMPSON & JOHN COSSAR

*Dublin Society :*
RICHARD TISDALL

*Belfast Society :*
JOHN HALL & JOSEPH RYAN

*Liverpool Society :*
HERBERT TIPLADY & WILLIAM WATSON

*Liverpool Association :*
President : JOHN FLEWITT
Secretary : HENRY WILLIAMS

# ALEX GOSSIP

The President
Vice-President
General Secretary
and the two
Assistant General
Secretaries
at the
Celebration
1st May, 1947

Gen. Sec.
A. G. TOMKINS

Vice-Pres.
W. POPE

Pres.
R. S. SHUBE

Asst. Gen. Secs.
J. R. SHANLEY   A. J. BICKELL

BOB SHUBE AND BEN RUBNER

and by differences in interpretation, it provided a basis for a concerted union policy in the furnishing trades for the future. Despite a steeply rising cost of living, attempts were made throughout 1916 to keep a lid on workers demands by the issuing of authoritative statements from establishment figures. Alex Gossip brought a typical example to the notice of the members. The Bishop of London wrote; 'There should be an industrial truce for the next five years and the Church should teach the working men that they are to do a fair day's work, and that we have to produce more and more in this country to enrich all classes'. [29]

The realities of working life were to be found not in such insensitive statements but in the East End of his own bishopric. Fred Bramley was at that very moment attempting to organise the West End in conjunction with the General Secretary of the United Furnishing Trades Society, Jack Cohen. The aim was to raise the basic rate by 1d. an hour. There were enormous difficulties. Piecework was rife and rates varied between 6d. an hour and 1/7d. an hour dependent upon speed and type of work. Bramley and Cohen succeeded in their task without need to revert to the strike weapon. Typical of the relationship between the owners of these businesses and the trade union officials was this reported exchange. In one case the employer in resisting the union's demands claimed that the advance would put 5/- increase on a bedroom suite. 'Said he, 'My customers have refused to pay it. What shall I do?' 'Well' said we, 'What they refuse to pay for, they cannot have. Knock it out of the job'. 'Oh', said this particular employer 'that sounds alright, but I assure you we could not make our stuff any worse than we make it now'.' [30]

The East End of London furniture trade was a running sore in the standards of the industry as a whole. As Fred Bramley reported: 'Perhaps some time we shall have our men on strike for sanitary conditions in the workshop, for more air, more light, and the opportunity of being able to breathe whilst getting a living. After the war we shall have to do something big in the East End of London. A revolution in the furnishing trade is needed. The sweater must be driven out. Our industry needs purifying. The comparatively decent employer suffers, our men and women suffer, and the community is left to deal with the evil effects of a bad system'.

The ground swell for improvement in wages built up during 1916. 'The shackling of the powers of organised labour have prevented us from forcing up the wages of our members to meet the ever-increasing cost of living.....our only consolation is that as far as we were concerned we had no hand in this shackling ....the standards of comfort of our members generally has been reduced, whilst the profiteers have been allowed to ride rough shod over the workers'. In Bristol the workers not on government contract work and not covered by the Munitions Bill struck for a 12 per cent increase after negotiations had failed and after four weeks achieved their aim. [31]

By 1917, however, the pressure mounted on the EC to support trade movements in High Wycombe, Liverpool, Manchester, Hull, Leeds and at many other places. These improvements were, in the main, achieved by negotiations alone without even token stoppages. However, in August, the Swansea Employers refused to give way and were supported by the Employers' Federation. NAFTA fought the dispute with the aid of the Upholsterers' Union and the Women's Trade Union Federation. It affected only the firms not on government contract work in the area and was not settled until October, when the firms in dispute settled on the terms accepted by the other employers on contract work who had resolved their situation by arbitration. In Manchester a trade movement had achieved a twelve and a half per cent increase in wages in the early part of the year. By the end of the year the Manchester workers had struck for a forty-eight hour week also. The dispute was settled in three weeks and was of particular importance. For the first time the rates of pay of unskilled and ancillary workers to the furniture making trades was part of the package of demands. The group which constituted the Partial Benefit Section of pre-war years and the war time emergency membership were now organised. As a consequence their wages and terms and conditions of employment became part of the negotiation unit. [32]

A.A. Purcell noted in his report on the dispute; 'I cannot stress the importance of the shop stewards in this dispute. They collected subscriptions from those shops with members still working (having settled separately or on government work) to such good effect that dispute pay was never less than 15/- per week for those on strike'. [33] This was the first use, in January 1918, of the title 'shop steward'. Up to this point the elected leader in a department or small workshop had been referred to as 'shop secretary' or 'shop leader'.

The furniture makers struck on two further occasions in 1918. In Redhill in Ireland the workers were working 56 hours a week for 25s. to 30s. There was 'no electricity or gas in the town so the workers were compelled to pay for the oil for the lamps and for the polishing materials, rags, spirits, wadding, brushes, varnishes and glass paper used'. All that the town produced was exported to Liverpool and one hundred and twenty workpeople were involved. The strike lasted 24 weeks before victory was won and the full demands of the workforce met – one hundred per cent increase in wages. High Wycombe workers came out in November, 1918. On this occasion only one week of picketing was required before the dispute was settled with an increase of twelve and one half per cent across the board. [34]

Despite the benefits gained by the union through the war period the *Largest Furniture Manufacturing Factory in the World* remained unorganised, that of Lebus in Tottenham. Not only was it the largest; it was 'as bad as the worst in this country' wrote C.F. Hawkins, the Trade

Organiser who had taken on the task of organising this group. The union opened a branch in Tottenham but despite its best endeavours Lebus remained unorganised for many years to come. [35]

The General Officials of the union also benefited from the upward movement in wages. On an EC proposal to increase their salaries the membership voted by 2,247 votes to 40 for an increase. At the end of 1918 the General Secretary received £5.10s.0d. per week and Trade Organisers, Organising Secretaries and Assistant General Secretary £5.0s.0d. per week.

The most important development on the industrial relations front for NAFTA during the war years related to the work of the Whitley Committee set up to 'make and consider suggestions for securing a permanent improvement in the relations between employers and workmen'. This resulted in a conference on 13th February 1918, held at the Ministry of Labour with both employers and unions on the advisability of setting up a Joint Industrial Council for the Furniture Industry. Alex Gossip, who represented NAFTA, declared that he 'had reservations in this matter, but equally had no mandate from the membership to agree or disagree'.[36]

In essence the JIC for the Furnishing Industries would, as outlined in a brief submitted by the Ministry of Labour, consider wages and hours in the industry as a whole, the regulation of production and employment, consideration of the existing machinery for the settlement of differences, the collection of statistics and information on materials and the distribution of timber, markets, costs, and average profit or turnover. It would also study processes and design, health matters, education and press statements on matters affecting the industry and make such representations as were necessary to government departments. [37]

In placing the matter before the membership the General Secretary wrote: 'In submitting this matter to the members for their consideration and keeping in view the type of some of the firms represented on the employers' side, the EC and the General Officials desire it to be clearly understood that on no account could they have dealings with those employers who do not employ trade unionists and do not observe and pay the proper conditions and rates'. His statement was curiously peripheral to the main objectives of the Joint Industrial Councils and the objections to them. Roberts suggests; 'For the left-wing elements (in the unions) Whitleyism appeared to be an attempt to wean the workers away from demands for real workers' control, and to fob them off with insubstantial schemes of joint consultation'. [38] Whether this was so in the case of Alex Gossip we do not know. He was, however, 'extremely surprised at the result, when a vote of the membership produced a majority of 1,343 to 803 votes in favour of the union assisting in the establishment of a JIC and remained skeptical. He and C.F. Hawkins of the EC nevertheless attended a conference in May 1918, to set up the JIC for the Furnishing Industry. 'We are not sanguine'; wrote Alex Gossip to the membership 'as to the beneficial results and already have crossed swords over such matters as refusing to recognise employers who do not observe trade union conditions or employ trade unionists. We successfully opposed, even in the teeth of the opposition of some on our own side of the table, an attempt to get us to assist with the organisation of the employers, even though it was accompanied by a similar proposal that the employers should help in making trade unionists. Frankly it is not part of our business to aid in organising those we have to be continually opposing, and it is our business in organising workers to deal with those in our own class who do not care about paying their contributions, though they are always prepared to accept all benefits'. [39]

At the first formal meeting of the JIC in December, 1918, the union tabled the following resolution; 'In view of the end of the war and demobilisation, that a 44 hour week be established from 1st. January, 1919 throughout the Furnishing Trades without reduction in wages from the standard rate, and should it be found that after three months there are still men available for employment a further reduction in the hours to 40 per week shall take place'. The post-war battle lines were being drawn up by NAFTA and the Employers. [40]

For the leaders and membership of NAFTA the event of the war years which captured the imagination in those dark days was the Russian revolution. Alex Gossip wrote: '1917 has been a year of gloom.....the Russian Revolution was the one bright spot'. He went on to commend to the membership the Russian Charter of Freedom produced by the Provisional Government after the first Russian Revolution. It proclaimed:—

1.  Immediate amnesty for Political and Religious offences;
2.  Freedom of speech, press, association and labour organisations, with freedom to strike even in the Army;
3.  Abolition of all Social, Religious and National distinctions;
4.  Universal suffrage

'Compare that with what has taken, and is taking place here', he challenged.

James O'Grady, MP, Parliamentary Secretary, informed the membership that with Will Thorne, MP, he had been chosen to visit Russia as part of an Anglo-French delegation and to convey the congratulations of the British Parliament to the government at Petrograd. 'Though my views on the war and my support for the Government are at variance with some members, they will all be with me, I am sure, in my congratulations of the Russian people. It is significant and indicative of the changes in attitude of politicians and government at Westminster when two Socialists are appointed on such a mission'. [41]

It was not the officials of the union only who welcomed the Revolution, but also the membership. Typical of the many branch resolutions sent *via* the EC to the new Government was that from No.18 (Birmingham). 'Hearty congratulations to our Russian fellow workers and comrades, the leaders and the Members of the Russian Social Democratic Parties, on their accomplishment of the first steps in the overthrow of their tyrannical governing class, and we wish them "God Speed" in the establishment of a truly free and democratic system of society and hope – also that all countries will soon secure the fullest measure of freedom and that all international barriers are swept away'. [42] At the Scottish Trades Union Congress the NAFTA delegate William Leonard was one of the prime movers of the message of congratulations sent to the Provisional Government and, more important, to the Council of Workers and Soldiers Delegates.

The Russian visit of O'Grady and Thorne is relatively ill-documented. Apparently there was a third man involved, W.S Sanders, who is never referred to by O'Grady, for Arthur Henderson, now a member of the War Cabinet, was instructed to get 'a suitably composed British Labour Deputation [to] accompany the French party with the same object'. The party of French Socialists referred to were in England *en route* to Petrograd 'to persuade the Russian socialist party to do all in its power to bring the war to a satisfactory conclusion' and 'W.S. Sanders, Will Thorne and James O'Grady agreed to go and the two deputations proceeded to Russia'. [43] The real purpose of the British visit was, it seems, to persuade the Russian government to stay in the war. Insofar as this was known and understood from the outset O'Grady and Thorne were open to charges of duplicity. O'Grady complained of 'others who in Congress and at the Annual Conference of Socialist Parties (ILP) passing resolutions declaring Will Thorne and myself to be renegade Socialists'. [44] In his defence he declared that 'the second purpose of my visit was to urge on the Workmen's and Soldiers' Council to save their revolution from reaction and counter-revolution by participating in the government of Russia. Can anyone in these islands except those who cry 'Peace, peace, where there is no peace' find fault with our mission? The only persons in Russia who used the resolution of the ILP and the speeches of former comrades, against us, were the physical force anarchists and the extremists of one political party (the Bolsheviks)'.

'True it is', he went on, 'and I admit it, we did in the course of addressing the Workmen's and Soldiers' Council at Petrograd, Moscow, Minsk, Devinsk and Psor, and when addressing the troops on the North and West battlefronts, urge them to take care that having got rid of the despotism of the House of Romanoff, that of Hohenzollern did not fasten its shackles on their new won liberty. This also may be accounted to our mission as a crime. If so, I shall be proud of the appellation. Did our mission do any good it may be asked, in particular by the pacifist? It is not for me to say. I simply point out facts. The Workmen's and Soldiers' Councils have sent six Socialist members of their body into the Provisional Government which now, let it be said, is known in Russia as the Coalition Government. The result is to save their country from anarchy and to inspire their armies in this war of liberation until the only military despotism in Europe is defeated'.

O'Grady's anger was directed to the Parliamentary Labour Party and to the officials of NAFTA who had throughout the war taken a consistently pacifist line. 'Some of my Parliamentary colleagues, have been spluttering on platforms and writing kind, brotherly articles to a certain type of weekly newspaper decrying our mission. However, these do not count, except with those hitherto enemies of labour now pacifists'.

The statement marked the parting of the ways between NAFTA and James O'Grady. A measure of patching up would occur over the next few years, but with the Russian mission he isolated himself from the Executive and the membership in a manner which made reconciliation ultimately impossible. Yet, in defence of O'Grady, his position and his attitudes were honestly consistent with his pro-war stance. James O'Grady believed the war had to be fought. This meant the prosecution of the war by the maximum means available to ensure a speedy and satisfactory conclusion. There was very good reason for the British government to attempt to keep the Russian army in the field. Facing it were eighty Divisions of the Central Powers. Their removal from the Russian front and subsequent transfer to the Western front before the American army could be assembled and trained, swung the balance heavily in their favour in terms of manpower in the early months of 1918 [45]

NAFTA was represented by Alex Gossip at the Convention held in Leeds on the 3rd June to congratulate the Russian workers on their revolution. Some 1,150 delegates were present and 'one left that vast conference with renewed faith in the glorious ideals of Internationalism'. The recognition of the solidarity of labour of all lands and its oneness of interest was the dominant feature of the vast assembly.....and amply repaid us for all the abuse which has been hurled at those who all along have opposed the forces of Capitalism masquerading in the guise of so-called patriotism. The vituperative language of the Gutter Press and of some Labour men is sufficient to convince us, if that is necessary, that we are on the right path. The fear and trembling of the Government at the mere idea of the soldiers and workers forming a joint committe shows clearly how they realise the true inward feelings of those who are in the Army, and are afraid of them'. [46]

The general secretary, with C.F. Hawkins of the EC, were the NAFTA delegates at the resultant District Conference for London and

Home Counties of the Workers' and Soldiers' Council held in Hoxton on the 28th July. Seven branches sent delegates, but as Alex Gossip reported; 'the meeting was broken up and many of the delegates injured by an organised mob of hooligans, well primed with drink, and incited to passion by a lying and misleading circular spread broadcast through all the pubs in Hoxton by a party which is well-known to us under a high sounding Labour name! [Fisher/National Socialist Party].....Some of our personal friends were brutally kicked and injured severely by the very people they have worked so hard for all their lives. These poor misguided dupes and tools of the Capitalists had not the slightest idea that they were being used by the enemies of their own class. One can feel sympathy for them but not towards those who knowing better, have deliberately espoused the cause of the exploiters and oppressors of the poor and have vilely misrepresented the only movement in the interests of the people, both in Parliament and out of it'. [47]

The present author was not allowed access to the Home Office and Metropolitan Police files on the Meetings of the Worker's and Soldiers' Societies but the reports in *The Times* are illuminating. 'The meeting to form the Workers' and Soldiers' Societies was prevented by the activities of an angry crowd. The church premises in which the meeting was held was wrecked and some of the conference delegates injured. The speakers were expected to be Mr W.C. Anderson, Mr John MacLean, Mr J. Finchley and Mrs Snowden. Miss Sylvia Pankhurst also attended. The meeting was broken up by men and women including Australian and New Zealand troops with extreme violence and without the interference of the police. The attack occurred at 3 o'clock and about half past four the police were able to draw a cordon round the premises and hold the people in check. One arrest was made of a railway porter, charged with a breach of the peace. This action was repeated in Newcastle where again Colonial troops were at the forefront of the attacks on the delegates present. In Swansea the meeting was broken up and the delegates chased from the building'. In a final broadside aimed among others at James O'Grady, Alex Gossip wrote: '*We* absolutely refuse to be bought, either with money, praise, flattery or any other method adopted by the Capitalist class'. [48]

The October Revolution was greeted by the NAFTA 'with enthusiasm'. Fred Bramley as delegate to the Trades Union Congress moved the following resolution: 'This Congress welcomes the declaration of the Russian workers in repudiating all proposals for Imperialistic conquest and aggrandishment. We also send to the workers of Russia our wholehearted congratulations on their magnificent achievement in securing the downfall of official tyranny, persecution, and despotism of an autocratic Government, expressing the hope that the Russian Revolution will hasten the coming of a peace based upon, not a dominance of tyrannical monarchs, militarists and diplomats, but on the principles of nationality, democracy and justice maintained by a League of Nations'. [49]

The Russian Revolution continued to be an area of contention between O'Grady and the union. When Maxim Litvinoff, the Ambassador of the Bolshevik Goverment of Russia attended the Labour Party Conference, O'Grady wrote, 'His speech would have been a success had it not been that he went out of his way to speak in terms of contempt of Kerensky and of the elected constituent assembly in Russia'. [50] Reporting on the special conference of the Labour Party held in London on 26th. June, 1918, he added: 'some of the delegates and members of the public in the gallery made a demonstration against our Russian comrade Kerensky. I felt the matter very keenly, knowing the man's great work in the revolution and how heroically he tried to save his country from a relapse into anarchy and despotism'.

Not only was this a frontal assault on the views of the officers and members of the union of which he was Parliamentary Secretary; it also disregarded the fact that Kerensky was in the United Kingdom as an enemy of Soviet Rule in Russia and in favour of continuation of an imperialist war. Notwithstanding, O'Grady went on: 'his [Kerensky's] mission to Western Europe cannot fail of good results. Its purpose has no other motive than a resurrection of the ideals that brought the great and wondrous change to Russia, buried in centuries of oppression'. With his support of the anti-Soviet movement the final parting of the ways between NAFTA and O'Grady was further advanced. A relationship between the union and its Parliamentary Secretary remained for the time being, but it was conducted in an atmosphere of icy formality and often of disdain.

Typical of such an exchange between them occurred in 1917 when O'Grady supported Lloyd George and 'his most effective choice of the labour members who have been given Government posts'. 'Those Labour MP's like G.H. Robert', commented Alex Gossip drily, 'who are doing their best to bewilder the workers in the interests of the capitalists'. This particular exchange opened the door to public criticism of O'Grady within the *Monthly Reports*. The Scottish branches questioned the sum of £40 spent by the union each year in O'Grady's East Leeds constituency. He explained this by advising them of the need to retain an agent on registration work also noting that as Member of Parliament for East Leeds he disbursed at least £1 per week from his MP's salary for travel etc. 'I am tired of the bounders in our movement ever seeking to pull down to the ground one of their own class'. [51]

O'Grady, decided, however, at this point to protect himself for the future. 'I am glad to inform the membership [of NAFTA] that on 17th. July, 1917 I was elected as General Secretary of the National Federation of General Workers. This is a new Federation of Labourers' Unions and is a salaried post. I shall have the support of a membership of 500,000.

The salary will keep the roof over the wife and kiddies heads should anything happen politically. I mention this because I have been attacked bitterly and unscrupulously by a small section of our members, and life as a consequence since 1914 has been a rougher journey than one should expect, even in wartimes. I have tried to do my duty as I saw it, but persecution knows nothing of obligations or of the humanities. One of my foremost persecutors has taken a Government job, another has been after such a job for years. Hail to consistency'. [52] This last remark was taken by those inside and outside the union to be an attack upon Fred Bramley whose only government connection was as a member of the National Service Committee on the Aircraft Industry for which he received no salary. O'Grady had, in consequence, to publish a fulsome retraction of this implied slur in the next *Monthly Report*.

James O'Grady was the 1917/18 Chairman of the General Federation of Trade Unions. Such was his lack of popularity within NAFTA that in the election of delegates to the GFTU Conference, he lost his seat to C.F. Hawkins of the EC The subsequent conference was an open conflict between the NAFTA delegate and O'Grady. As Chairman, O'Grady opened the attack with a speech which ended; 'I declare in the name of the Federation our determination to carry on the war, and I condemn those pacifists who would seek to disrupt the Labour movement'. Public battle was joined when at the election of the Management Committee it was stated that O'Grady was representing the Dockers' Union. Hawkins objected that O'Grady was not a *bona fide* delegate and ineligible to be Chairman since Ben Tillett of the Dockers was already on the Management Committee. There followed a long and acrimonious complaint by O'Grady against NAFTA for not electing him as delegate. Eventually the issue was put to the vote. The delegates endorsed O'Grady's position and so avoided a further scandal.

The row spilled over into the *Monthly Reports* with O'Grady describing Hawkins' report of the GFTU Conference as 'contemptible'. 'I do not complain', he declared, 'about not being elected by the members but against the methods that were adopted in the matter of the election' (i.e. lobbying against him whilst he was in Russia).

The battle then moved to the vote for a NAFTA delegate to the Labour Party Conference to be held in January 1918 in Nottingham. O'Grady received 1,020 votes and Hawkins 774. The immediate situation was effectively defused, but there was between O'Grady and NAFTA too much bitterness for any opportunity of scoring points to be missed. When in the *Monthly Report*, O'Grady thanked the membership for electing him as delegate to the Labour Party Conference, he pointed out; 'In that position I cannot, of course, hope to represent the views of the minority except, perhaps, in one particular of political activities. This was the need for the governments of the Allies to make a clear and simple declaration of their war aims which he defined as Restitution,

Reparations, the Right of people to live their own national lives and the establishment of a League of Nations'. It should be noted in his inclusion of Reparations he was adopting a stance quite contrary to the policy of the Labour Party which was strongly against any indemnities. 'Whilst I was in Russia', he continued, 'I considered their aims of no annexations, no contributions and the rights of people to National Self Assertion to be too vague and I and my fellow delegates to Russia tried earnestly and repeatedly to persuade them to change these to Restitution and Reparations. I futher consider the statement of war aims issued by the Joint Committee of the Labour Party and TUC as too academic and verbose, as all academic expressions of view must be [echoing the ouvrierism of Fisher]. In answer to my pacificist friends – I protest with all my soul against their assumption that I wish to continue this war an hour longer than is necessary to safeguard the future'.

His union opponents saw nothing here but O'Grady's ambivalence, bankrupt idealism and hyperbole and confirmed their view by contrasting his January speech with his next statement to the union on the War. 'Not until the German military Idol is destroyed can the world rest in security', he declared. And referring to a visit as part of an MPs' delegation to Verdun 'a journey to the depths of Hell' – in which 500,000 German and 300,000 Frenchmen died – 'God!, that men should be so insane'. O'Grady then went on to state that the reported speech of the German Minister for Foreign Affairs, Von Kuhlman, setting out peace terms 'was unacceptable'. 'Those of us supporting the government are resolute that there shall be no German dictation of peace terms, but will watch ceaselessly and keenly for opportunites to end this terrible war by the establishment of a 'clean peace' '.

The end of the relationship between NAFTA and O'Grady was imminent. He was finally and utterly discredited in the eyes of his union foes when at the 'Coupon Election' of December 1918 he was returned unopposed by the Coalition as a 'National Democratic' Labour candidate. NAFTA had put forward for that election Fred Bramley who came second in the ballot behind the coalition candidate and in front of the Liberal candidate. 'I did, however', he said, 'keep the Labour Standard clear of the intrigue which secured success in other places'. [53]
Fred Bramley had, however, left his position as a Trade Organiser for the union (though retaining his union membership) since, when the TUC moved into new office premises in Eccleston Square, it appointed him as full-time Assistant Secretary – the first full- time official to be appointed. His correct and full title was 'Assistant Secretary to the Parliamentary Committee of the Trades Union Congress', since the term 'TUC' still referred to the annual conference rather to a central trades union organisation. The Parliamentary Committee maintained this continuity from one Congress year to another and was composed of union officials who devoted part of their time only to TUC business;

indeed the PC Secretary combined his work with that of Member of Parliament.

Fred Bramley wrote that, 'In accepting this position I am inspired by a desire to take part in dealing with questions of a general nature affecting all trades unions alike and having had an opportunity of realising the potentialities of more effective national action, I have decided to take some responsibility for the development of the Parliamentary Committee and its function, with that object in view. I am not leaving the trade union movement. I am getting more completely involved in it. I shall still be serving you in another capacity'. Bramley's view of the task before him had been summed up in a speech which he made at the Bristol TUC of 1915. 'After this war is over, there will be greater events in the industrial field, the problems of re-adjustment, the increased necessity of preventing the rich from imposing the burden of war consequences upon the poor, and the vital necessity of increasing industrial solidarity will command our special attention'.

Fred Bramley's departure left a gap in the organisation. His place was taken up by C.F. Hawkins, Polisher, No.20 Branch (London Polishers), a long serving member of the EC, an avowed pacifist, socialist and long-time antagonist of James O'Grady. The union had earlier elected D. Thorn, a cabinetmaker from No.23 (Glasgow) Branch, as their Scottish Trade Organiser, and as a result of an amalgamation Jack Cohen, cabinetmaker, joined the full-time officials as Organising Secretary.

Amalgamations were not a major feature of the war years as they had been prior to the conflict. However, some progress was made. In 1916 the old West End Cabinetmakers Society joined NAFTA. Its days of glory were long since past. It had 28 members only, seven of them on the retired list. This small society joined No.2 Branch West End Cabinet-makers as individuals, thus avoiding a vote on the 'merger'. A vote was, however, required on the amalgamation with the United Furnishing Trades Union (sometimes referred to as the Independent Hebrew Society). Fred Bramley and Jack Cohen (General Secretary of the UFTU) had, as we have seen, worked together to 'improve the East End Trade' and a vote was taken in favour of amalgamation by 2,178 votes to 38. Out of a total membership of 16,000, of which nearly 5,000 was in the armed forces, this was judged to be insufficient. The Registrar of Friendly Societies objected to the amalgamation and a re-vote was called for. In December, 1917 the membership voted in favour by 6,610 to 85. This was still not sufficient to satisfy the Registrar who demanded a total vote of 50 per cent of the membership. In a wartime situation this was extremely difficult to achieve but with the assistance of C.W. Bowerman, MP, Secretary of the Parliamentary Committee of Trades Union Congress, the amalgamation was eventually allowed and came into effect in April 1918.

Another group of workers who joined NAFTA in 1918 were the

London Piano Workers. C.F. Hawkins and Jack Cohen had devoted a considerable effort to organising this group and by December, 1918 had enrolled 1,375 members in two new branches, No.62 Holloway and No.113, Barnbury N.7. These efforts were capped in December by the signing of a comprehensive Working Agreement on wages, hours and conditions of employment, including the abandonment of piecework and sub-contracted work. The potentially most important amalgamation negotiations of the war period, however, took place between NAFTA and the Amalgamated Joiners. The two EC's met on 28th February, 1918 and agreed a basis for merging which was to be put before the respective membership after it had been cleared by the General Council of the Amalgamated Joiners. The Joiners decided that they wished there to be a favourable vote of NAFTA before going to their General Coucil. This was duly taken in June, 1918 with 8,747 voting for amalgamation and 251 against. The Joiners were slow to take further action on the matter . At the end of 1918 their General Council had still not met to consider the amalgamation, which never took place. It remained an indication of the belief of the officials and the membership of NAFTA in industrial unionism that they were prepared to dissolve their own association and join up with another society to achieve this end.

NAFTA regarded the post-war world with some disquiet. There were 'too many barriers of self-interest in the way of progress', declared Alex Gossip who quoted from a pamphlet circulated to all trade union officials by Sir John Pilter, President of the British Chamber of Commerce in Paris. [54] 'Labour must learn to look upon Capital not only as a necessity, but also as his best friend; further, Labour must rid its mind of the thought that Capital finds life easier than it does. Labour is freed of all anxiety as to bad seasons, bad debts, errors of judgement, which give Capital many a sleepless night'. [55] Alex Gossip noted, 'the grammar is also Sir J. Pilter's'. The General Secretary also brought to the attention of the membership the statement of the Chairman of Cunard Shipping who at its Annual General Meeting predicted 'stormy days ahead', principally arising from 'Labour unrest due to the false hopes held out of a new heaven and a new earth after the war. The disillusionment would be very bitter when it came'.

One piece of legislation which promised, if not a new heaven, then at least a better Britain in post-war years, was the Fisher Education Act of 1918. The NAFTA attitude to Fisher was enthusiastic. He 'promised to be the most sympathetic and practical educationalist that has occupied the office for a number of years, wisely carrying out a policy of going to meetings of trade unionists with a view not only of trying to understand the workpeople's claims to education, but of persuading them to back up his efforts in the House of Commons'.[56]

On this point at least, Gossip's enthusiasm was shared by James

O'Grady. Writing to the membership on the second reading of the
Education Bill he noted; 'The opposition centred on the raising of
compulsory education from twelve to fourteen years. The arguments
centred round the extra costs and the fact that the abolition of the half-
timer will ruin the cotton trade. Mr Fisher has done what no other
Minister of Education has done. He has come to the workers at their
conferences and meetings, found their point of view and their desires in
the matter of their children's education, and attends the discussions in
the House of Commons fortified with his experience and strengthened to
resist any attempt to destroy the purpose of the Bill. He loves children
and glorifies education, in that it will develop in the child all the latent
genius and beatitudes which we as a nation in our race for wealth and
power have foolishly overlooked'.

The war had produced thousands of disabled servicemen who were by
reason of their injuries unable to return to the war or to their former
employment. A number of solutions to this problem were put forward
including that of introducing them into the furniture industry. The
initial reaction of the union and its leadership to this idea was hostile, as
is evidenced by the report made by Alex Gossip to the Board of Trade
enquiry into the 'Training and Employment of Disabled Servicemen'.
'The furniture trades have had one of the highest records for
unemployment of all trades.....whilst the union has great sympathy for
the victims of the war.....one in every four of the union's members was in
the armed forces and the work of furniture making is becoming highly
sub-divided, which as a union we are opposed to; it will be impossible to
train a man quickly in this trade. The NAFTA would also bring to the
attention of the Board the problems of noise, dust and fumes which are a
part of the furniture making process and which we cannot but feel will be
injurious to the disabled'. [57]

Handcraft industries and, specifically the furniture industry, have
suffered periodically from the attention of those who would place the
handicapped or disabled in such employment. They have been seen as
'anyone can do it' industries. Moreover, the splitting down of the
production of furniture into elemental tasks was opposed by the union
right up until the Second World War. As used in factories in the East
End of London and in the largest firms it was regarded as the de-skilling
or de-humanising of an essentially skilled trade. In a period when craft
was on the defensive and when the prospect in the post-war period of a
return to pre-war unemployment loomed large, the introduction of
elemental task working for the disabled in factory production was
unacceptable. Fred Bramley, commenting upon the inquiry in the
*Monthly Report*, stated: 'Pensioned labour is dangerous. It must not be
used to lower the standard wages and conditions in our industry which is
the approach which will be used by the unscrupulous employer in our
industry'. [58]

In January of 1918, however, NAFTA decided that it would cooperate in the setting up of committees, known as Local Technical Advisory Committees, for the selection and training of disabled ex-servicemen for the furniture industry. The union had made its points well at the discussions at the Board of Trade and the new Committees gave them the power to avoid dilution and wage cutting by the dishonest employer's use of the disabled. It also ensured that those who entered the industry in this fashion were properly trained to earn their living. No-one would be selected for training without the consent of the local branch of the union. The instruction and training given was to follow an agreed schedule. The standards to be achieved in the training were to be established by the trade union, and the trade union branch was required to have a knowledge and control of the wages paid to those in sheltered employment and training. [59]

On the face of it this was a highly protective and effective measure of control over the employment of the disabled. In practice this was not the case, since comparatively few of the disabled who were unable to take up their pre-war employment because of their disability were capable of entering the furniture industry because of its high demands on manual dexterity. It was still a machine-assisted hand-production industry. The unexpected benefit was that the terms of the instruction required the setting up of technical training centres with schematic and progressive training programmes. These very rapidly became technical training establishments which took on the role of apprentice training. The technical college courses in High Wycombe, Bristol, Manchester, Liverpool, Leeds and London owe their genesis, at least in part, to this legislation.

The war years were over. Over 4,600 members had served in the armed forces and 272 had died in action. The union had grown wealthy in membership and capital. Organisation was strong and its officials were amongst the finest in the country. Yet it was with pessimism rather than hope that NAFTA viewed the approaching post-war years. 'As far as one can judge there would appear to be every probability of the usual Capitalist Peace being introduced with its inevitable evil consequences for the future. Whether the final result of the war will be that the world has been made safe *for* Democracy or safe *from* Democracy depends on the working class in all the countries concerned. Let us remember that if poverty and misery, long hours of toil and a more firmly established capitalist system are to be the reward of the workers of this country, then we the workers will have, indeed, lost the war with a vengeance'. [60] [61]

# CHAPTER VI

# *1919 – 1926*
# *— from Optimism to Defeat*

The immediate post war years were for NAFTA a period of 'defiance not defence'. With membership rising to nearly 33,000 in 1920 the union fought and won against a national lock-out imposed by the Cabinet Manufacturers Federation and was successful in a strike against the Piano Manufacturers Federation. Working hours were reduced to 47 per week from 51 hours, wages rose to an average of 1/11d. per hour and a national ban on overtime to absorb returned servicemen into the industry was imposed and sustained.

The collapse of the post war boom in 1921/22 brought massive unemployment to the furniture industry and the union was forced to accept a sliding scale of wages tied to the cost of living index. The remaining years of the period to the General Strike of 1926 were highly defensive, yet neither the union's executive nor its officials were cowed by the situation. Their stance was one of maintaining the offensive on all possible occasions. Using the JIC, NAFTA had proposed a national 44 hour week for the furniture industry at the meetings in 1918. By February 1919 the employers responded with an offer of 48 hours. The union side replied with a proposal for forty-six and a half hours which the employers agreed to consider, whilst in the meantime the union side placed an immediate ban on all overtime. The employers' response was to renew the offer of a 48 hour week with the addition of a set of national working rules and conditions, and with wage rates to be set on a regional basis but related on a national basis to a sliding scale tied to the cost of living. All these points were acceptable to the unions except for the 48 hour week and at the March JIC meeting it was agreed to put this question to a National Conciliation Board which was set up with five representatives from each side. [1]

In an effort to precipitate action in these very slow negotiations the union took matters into its own hands by signing a separate agreement with the Liverpool employers for a forty six and a half hour week and 2/-

per hour. It then turned its attention to Manchester and here it met resistance. To encourage the employers to settle, NAFTA called out 1,000 members in the Manchester area but this was countered by the National Wholesale Employers Federation which locked out some 4,500 union members on July 1st, 1919. The lock-out, though referred to as 'National' was effective only in Manchester and High Wycombe. In London, Liverpool and Scotland the manufacturers did not respond to the Federation's call, so allowing NAFTA to levy 4/- per working member to finance the dispute.

This lock-out was serious for the union but it lacked the basis for the crusading fervour of the Scottish and High Wycombe disputes of earlier years. This was not a movement to improve inhuman working conditions and starvation wages; it was a trial of strength between the union and the employers fought against a background of high demand for furniture from the domestic consumer. The determination of Alf Purcell, the organiser in charge of the dispute, to discredit the employers in the eyes of the public reflected this new situation. 'To fight back is our game. The lying and filthy dogs who form the great part of the Employers' Federation must be exposed. We must say openly and avowedly how they are daily fleecing the public with furniture rubbish; say how the public is buying oak which was never near an oak tree. Then there is the great Jacobean and antique furniture swindle...', i.e. the manufacture of instant antiques.

The dispute was finally settled on the September 22nd, 1919 with an agreement on a 47 hour week, 1/11d. to 2/- per hour, and no payment by results. The end of the struggle was untidy and acrimonious. The agreement between the Employers' Federation and the EC of the union was arrived at in London without reference to Alf Purcell and the strike committees in Manchester and High Wycombe. Alf Purcell was rightly incensed at this apparent backing down on the part of the union and at the lack of consultation. He would have adopted quite different tactics. 'We should call out all our members up and down the country - that would solve it in days'. The reality was that the union was effectively under siege from other quarters as well as the National Federation and its first priority was to get this particular dispute settled on the best terms it could in order to meet the new challenge from elsewhere. [3]

This challenge was from the London Piano Manufacturers' Federation. The Federation had taken advantage of the furniture trades dispute and threatened to lock out its employees, including 4,500 NAFTA members, on August 20th unless they accepted non-union working and payment by results. 'This notice gave your EC and General Officials a harassing time since it would have brought the membership out of work to over 10,000' at a time when its finances were already at a low ebb. Alex Gossip played for time calling meetings with the Piano Employers and securing the temporary withdrawal of the lock-out notice. Alf Purcell's crusade in Manchester and High Wycombe had to be settled to allow the union to fight the new battle when it was ready and financially able.

By April of 1920 NAFTA was ready for the fight with the Piano Employers to commence. A demand for improvement of wages and the abolition of payment by results where it existed was turned down by the employers and on April 10th. NAFTA withdrew its membership from all factories. The recruitment of members in the piano trade had been very successful and 6,500 men and women representing 95 per cent of the workforce were called out. They remained out for thirteen weeks before the Employers conceded to the union terms and the victory was complete. Hours were regularised at 47 per week, wages were increased by fourpence halfpenny per hour, a complete code of working rules and conditions was accepted. Shop stewards were established in every department of every factory and recruitment of labour for the Piano Industry was placed in the hands of the union, branch offices becoming in effect the labour exchanges for piano workers and employers. It was a magnificent result achieved by the careful planning of men and finances and backed by a loyal and organised membership. It was, however, a 'good times' agreement and with the return of poor trade the piano industry once again became a constant source of anxiety for NAFTA.

The rejection of payment by results remained a central tenet of the NAFTA philosophy at this time and cost it dear in disputes and in members who were expelled for accepting the practice. A letter to Alex Gossip from the Secretary of London Cabinetmakers and Upholstery Trades Federation explained the position so far as his union was concerned. 'We cannot dare to ignore nature's law of the survival of the fittest. Provided the rates are fairly fixed in joint agreement and the slowest man can make sure of a minimum wage so long as he does a fair average week's work, and provided the employer has guaranteed that an improvement in effort shall never again only result in a cutting of the rate, I do not think Labour will wish to deny a keen man the fierce joy of doing his best for a fair pecuniary advantage as a reward. Pious expressions of opinion and beliefs that men are working or normally work their hardest are not a sufficiently stable basis on which to run a business. Statistics both general and individual exist to show that output per man per hour has decreased enormously until it is hardly too much to assert that under the hourly system, the more money a man gets the less he does'. [4]

In refuting this argument Alex Gossip clarified and defined his union's stance against PBR. 'What the employer wants from a workman is more and more hard work, more and still more output of goods during a time of abnormal demand, but this is no new thing, and the same doctrine has been preached time and time again during periods of booms in trade, and the inevitable glut in the world's markets after a time, with all that means for the worker thrown out on the streets, after he has produced more than there is an effective market for. While thoroughly agreeing with the demoralising effects of the work shirker (and we can see its evil effects in the so-called upper classes every day of our lives) and always having advocated that those who are physically and mentally fit ought to do their fair share of the necessary world's work, what is needed is not more work but rather more real leisure for the real worker and more real work from those who live off other people's labour'.

Another dispute which occurred in this early post-war period was particularly important in its effect upon the thinking of Alf Purcell. He spent the early months of 1919 in Belfast helping with the general strike in that city. 'My memory ranges right back to the London Dock Strike of 1889 and I can see that many episodes right up to the great Liverpool hold up of 1911, but these were not so complete as the solidarity of Belfast in the early weeks of February. No trams, no electricity, no gas. The town shops in all branches of industry at a positive standstill. the Strike Committee's *Daily Bulletin* is the only official city newspaper. A General Strike Committee is absolutley united and determined to be loyal to every section rendering support. The Lord Mayor hawking for the military, and the workers' pickets supplement the policing of the city in its darkened hours. Everyone is urging the 44 hour week since it would minimise unemployment. As a movement it has admitted of no side issue, it has kept to the reduction of hours every time and all the time. This dispute had won before it started. It had won complete Working Class Solidarity in Belfast and as such it contributed an illuminating page in the history of the world's greatest industrial struggle. If twenty big cities in the United Kingdom would do simultaneously and with Belfast completeness a similar act of solidarity, the final emancipation of the working class would be within a year's distance of accomplishment'.
5

It was easy to make such a wish father to the deed. The fulfilment of that deed was another matter. Alf Purcell shared with other trade unionists the inability to recognise that a major strike in one industrial town does not, no matter how complete in its effect, necessarily constitute a threat to the power of the State as a whole. The failure to think through the consequences of a General Strike in the United Kingdom and this tendency to escape into rhetoric and to avoid the reality of what might be implied by the emancipation of the working classes, suggest that the seeds of the defeat of 1926 were sown in Belfast in February, 1919.

1919 and 1920 were prosperous years for the furniture industry but the seasonal downturn in trade normally associated with January and February was particularly marked in 1921. As the year progressed trade did not pick up but stayed at a 'poor and dull' level. The JIC for the furniture industry had been abandoned by the unions in February, 1920 and with it the associated National Conciliation Board. As demand grew from the employers' side for cuts in wages and changes in working conditions, and with short time working affecting almost all furniture workers, the union recognised it was in no position to defend itself against a concerted attack from the employers.

The dramatic fall in prices can be illustrated from Harrods catalogues in 1920 and 1921.

Table

The Fall in Furniture Price, 1920 & 1921

|  | May 1920 | May 1921 |  |
|---|---|---|---|
|  | £ | £ |  |
| Oak Dining Table | £15 | £8.15s.0d. |  |
| Oak Chest of Drawers | £12.10s.0d. | £6.15s.0d. |  |
| Oak Bedroom Suite | £35—£50 | £22—£39 |  |
| Oak Sideboard 5 ft. | £22—£40 | £12.15s.0d. | to |
|  |  | £18.18s.0d. |  |
| Three Piece Suite | £38—£45 | £29—£36 |  |
| Easy Chairs | £7—£16 | £4.15s.0d. to £14 |  |

6

The National Conciliation Board was resurrected at the union's request and after a series of meetings, the union was forced to accept a 5 per cent cut in wages and a subsequent fixing of wages according to a sliding scale based upon the cost of living index. For every six and a half points change from an index figure of 128 on September 1st 1921, wages were to rise or fall by one halfpenny per hour, with a monthly revision until January 1922, when the revision became quarterly. The union held on to the 47 hour week but with short time working the rule, this was no more than a nominal achievement. It did, however, contrive to have 'no PBR' written into the agreement, at least as far as NAFTA members were concerned.

The National Conciliation Board settlement effectively took wages and working conditions out of collective bargaining for the foreseeable future and problems of unemployment and resistance to PBR became NAFTA's main industrial concerns. This gave the organisation an opportunity to look to its own organisational structure, and give its officials time to look outside the industrial scene for solutions to the economic ills that beset its members.

NAFTA's self-examination was prompted by two events. The national lock-out in the Cabinet Trade of 1919 had revealed strong resentment of the centralised, London dominated nature of the Executive Committee and its apparent failure to communicate with and respond to the needs of the regions. Not all the criticism levelled by Alf Purcell and others at this time was completely justified but it had sufficient merit to be considered. The second catalyst for change was the failure to conclude the long running amalgamation negotiations with the Carpenters and Joiners solely on a failure of that society to agree to merge. The disappointment that accompanied the reversal was grasped by the advocates of change and turned to their own use. [7]

Once again it was Alf Purcell who took the centre of the stage. 'We have failed to bring about the amalgamation that we all had hoped for. Since this is not to be we must take this opportunity to re-model our own Association to make it stronger, more representative and able to face the future. I propose: 1.  to open the Association to all furniture workers whether skilled or unskilled; [8]
2.  to adopt a National Executive Committee elected by districts rather than on a national base;
3.  to adopt a system of District organisers and so recognise officially the *de facto* specialisation of organisers by areas already in existence;
4.  to adopt a uniform rate of contributions at a higher rate to avoid too frequent levies;
5.  to allow districts automomy within the national structure;
6.  to call annual or biannual conferences of district elected delegates;
7.  to abolish the branch fund and establish a scale of branch officers salaries'. [9]

The proposals were discussed in the EC and at Branches for some months and a delegate conference called in October, 1921. This rules revision conference met in London and agreed to divide the United Kingdom into eight districts. Each district was to have its own organiser elected for a three year term of office and paid £10 per week. The General Secretary and the Assistant General Secretary were to be employed on the same basis. Each district was to elect one representative to the EC except London which was allowed two. Branches wre to hold back for their own expenses 2d. per member per week from the new scales of contributions, viz.,
Section 1. 1/6d. per week with 18/- out of work and 36/- dispute pay per week;
. Section 2. 1/- per week with 12/- out of work and
24/- dispute pay per week;
Section 3. 6d. per week with 8/- out of work and
18/- dispute pay per week.
Benefits were to be paid for twelve weeks in any fifty-two weeks period.
Levies of 6d., 4d. and 2d. per week per section for a maximum of twelve

weeks could be authorised to the EC when necessary.

There had clearly been a broad and general acceptance of Alf Purcell's ideas, and though the call for a wider membership from the unskilled was apparently ignored, such members could be organised in Section 3 with its reduced levels of contributions. Constitutional details settled, the membership then set about the task of appointing organisers for each district and after some months the following were elected.

| | | |
|---|---|---|
| District No.1 | London | C.F. Hawkins |
| District No.2 | Glasgow | William Leonard |
| District No.3 | Dublin | Jack Collins |
| District No.4 | Manchester | Alf Purcell |
| District No.5 | Birmingham | H. Parsons |
| District No.6 | Bristol | A. Rowe |
| District No.7 | High Wycombe | Ted Walton |
| District No.8 | Sheffield | R.F. Robinson |

A dispute quickly blew up about their payment and the maintenance of the 'equal pay for all officers' principle. In September 1919, Alf Purcell objected to the increases then being mooted as inequitable in that Alex Gossip as General Secretary was being offered an additional £1 and the organisers only 10/- per week extra. 'If an advance is to be given at all, it should be equal to all. This is just what we demand in the workshop - equal treatment to all and no favouritism'. A highly embarrassed EC put the issue to the vote of the membership which endorsed Alf Purcell's sentiments by 2,337 votes to 953 - a majority in favour of 1,384. [10]

The union had re-established its organisation, modernised its functions and in doing so contained its dissident sons. In an adverse economic climate this served effectively to hold the membership together at around the 21,000 after a fall from a peak of 33,000. What these changes did not do, nor organised labour achieve, was to an improvement in the economic situation in which this and other unions fought to survive.

NAFTA had in the early years of the century looked for reforms through Parliamentary representation of the working classes and at considerable cost and effort played its part in this movement with its own sponsored MP from 1906. Disenchantment with the performance of its own member and with the Parliamentary Labour Party had set in during the Great War. NAFTA therefore sought solutions to the apparently intractable problem of the improvement of the conditions of the working classes through other organisations as well as through the more obvious vehicle of parliamentary representation. That it continued to sustain and support the idea of parliamentary candidates in view of its disenchantment with O'Grady is perhaps a comment upon the inate conservatism of the working classes on the one hand and upon the strength of the received view of the democratic process on the other.

The final rift with O'Grady took place after his unopposed canditature in 1919 which finally sealed his reputation as a turncoat among sections of the membership. His own Branch No.1 Central London, refused to accept his weekly membership contribution after this election, despite instructions to do so from the EC. The matter was put to a vote of the whole membership of NAFTA and Jim O'Grady's letter to the membership in his own defence was both bitter and controversial. 'I have ever paid my own expenses as an MP, at a cost of £36 per year....I venture to state you will find a strong Hebrew vote against myself...If an employer treated his employees as I have been treated during these past four years by a minority of members I would have told that employer to go to hell and claimed victimisation pay'. [11]

Whether or not any Semitic consideration entered into the question has never been established. However, the membership upheld the EC's decision that O'Grady should be allowed to retain his membership by 1,819 votes to 1,014. No.1 Branch showed its dissatisfaction in a counter proposal that MP's, whether prospective or sitting members, should submit themselves to the re-selection process each year. The membership agreed this proposal by a large majority. O'Grady then resigned as Parliamentary Secretary and from all subsequent contact with the union. [12]

O'Grady was MP for East Leeds. It is an indication of the fragile state of the Labour Party's finances that following this split the local party approached NAFTA cap in hand and pleaded with the union to continue its financial support for the local party despite the O'Grady split. NAFTA membership agreed this by 1,586 votes to 605, and continued to give support to the East Leeds party until the end of that Parliament at a cost of £60 per year.

This money came from the Labour Fund. NAFTA's record of internal support for this fund was not good. Some commentators on the furniture unions have suggested that this was indicative of a politically conscious leadership and a politically apathetic membership. While this may seems to be so it disregards a number of relevant factors: the seasonal nature of the employment of furniture workers, the spectre of unemployment with which they lived, the numbers of members lapsing each year through arrears of contributions and above all the union's prominent role in the parliamentary and political developments of these years, all of which were enthusiastically supported by the membership by voting and by participation, seem to tell a different story. [13]

There were, however, some dissenting voices within the union. When the EC proposed and the membership voted to transfer £2,000 from the General Funds to the Labour Fund by 4,572 to 1,626, a member from Dublin wrote a letter of complaint to the Registrar of Friendly Societies. In 1910 judgement given in a case brought by W.V. Osborne in a similar complaint against his union, the Amalgamated Society of Railway Servants, had resulted in the Trade Union Act of 1913, which prevented trades unions from using any funds other than those subscribed for political purposes into a separate Political Fund. Alex Gossip commented, 'We have another Osborne in our midst'. Be that as it may no such transfer was legally permissible. [14]

The post-war years of labour's offensive on the industrial front came to an end in 1921 with the return of trade depression. Though nationally 85.9 million working days were lost in disputes there were 2,000,000 workers without jobs. This led to the setting up of the National Unemployed Workers Committee Movement at a conference of some eighty unemployed workers committees in London in April of 1921. Alex Gossip was initially National Secretary of this movement. All committee members took an oath 'Never to cease from active strife until capitalism is demolished; this alone will end the horrors of unemployment'. It very rapidly became a Communist led organisation, particularly after Wal Hannington was appointed national organiser at the conference in Manchester in November, 1921. Indeed, by the Fourth Congress of the Communist Party in March, 1922, the executive committee reported that the leadership of the unemployed was firmly in the hands of the Party. (Except in Scotland where the ILP was for the time in command). Alex Gossip continued to be a supporter of the Movement but when by 1923 the Red International of Labour Unions British Bureau had become responsible to the British Communist Party for its control, his support became verbal and moral rather than participative.

Another left-wing movement actively supported by NAFTA during these years led to the setting up of Socialist Furniture Guilds. Guild Socialism had its origins in the pages of New Age, a weekly review edited by A.R. Orage. In 1912 S.G. Hobson wrote a series of articles in the magazine in which he advocated the replacement of the wages system by the organisation of the country's industries into a series of self-governing guilds. These ideas attracted a number of intellectuals led by G.D.H. Cole who founded the National Guilds League in 1915 with William Mellor as Secretary. Their aim was the application of syndicalist and industrial unionist conceptions to British conditions. The revolutionary strike of syndicalist theory was to be abandoned and capitalism was to be gradually replaced by encroaching on the functions of the capitalist, thus giving an ideological framework to the conceptions of workshop control developed on the Clyde and elsewhere during the war. Industrial Guilds would gradually become industrial unions. [15] [16]

By 1920 the Guilds movement had attracted considerable Communist Party membership and with it intense discussion on the role which they might be expected to play. This caused a split of opinion into those who saw it as necessary to overthrow capitalism before setting up the Guilds and those who saw the Guilds as an alternative to capitalist society. This latter view was the one which attracted NAFTA, and in particular, Alf Purcell. More important, other officials with Communist sympathies thought otherwise, but it became clear that the argument would affirm that the Guilds were a purely Socialist movement. William Mellor, by this time a prominent member of the Communist Party, writing in *Labour Monthly* noted: 'The National Guilds League has failed to give a clear answer to the question posed by the Russian Revolution, of how to bring about the change to the new Society' [this despite the fact that the policy of the Guild League had been drawn up by leading communists in the League after consultation with the Communist Party] and in the League elections of 1922 no Communist candidate stood for the executive. 'The Communist Party' he concluded 'has dropped the League'. [17]

NAFTA put theory into practice in Manchester in 1922. In the February Alf Purcell asked the membership to support the concept of a Furniture Guild 'pledged to make furniture on a basis of no profit and no interest'. The Manchester branches raised £200 by local levy and NAFTA raised a further £500 by general levy. A warehouse was rented from the AEU, fitted out, and 30 unemployed furniture makers set on, initially doing repair work; soon the Guild was tendering for new work and within three months over £1,000 of furniture had been produced.

The success of the venture led to the setting up of a London Guild but the EC could only grant £30 for this development and asked the London Branches to carry out their own local levy for further funds. Moves were also made in Warrington and Bristol to set up Guilds but no monies were forthcoming from the union's general funds. As a result a National Loan was organised calling for some £10,000 as working capital for the furniture guilds. There is no record of the actual amount subscribed by the membership to this loan. However, NAFTA did make a significant contribution to the future of the Guilds by seconding Alf Purcell for three months, June to September 1922, on full pay to help organise the Manchester Guild.

Unfortunately the Guilds were desperately under-capitalised and by November of 1922 both the London and Manchester Guilds were in difficulties. The cause of the financial problems lay in the close ties between the Furniture and Building Guilds. The failure to obtain sufficient working capital from the union caused the Furniture Guild to borrow from the Building Guild. When this latter group ran into difficulties it pulled down the Manchester Furniture Guild with it. [19] S.G. Hobson writing in the Guild Socialist makes it clear that the problems of the Building Guild stemmed from a basis of inexperience: 'labour costs have got out of hand; mismanagement on some sites ruined the others'; men are being paid for doing nothing, in one instance payment being authorised for all to attend a race meeting'. He summed up with the understatement: 'The Guild structure, while good, had some flaws of organisation'.

The membership refused on a national vote to levy for more funds and in January of 1923 the Manchester Guild failed leaving only £43 after payment of debts to be returned to NAFTA funds. London failed later in the year and the only modest success story was the Piano Guild which struggled on for nearly three years before finally fading away. It would be easy to discuss these efforts as nive. The attempt was brave, the workers were unemployed; the losses incurred were substantially less than the sums which would have had to be paid out in unemployment support and for a short time at least working class solidarity and socialist concepts had achieved a tangible result.

The wish to strike out in a new direction, to formulate a new working situation for furniture workers was encouraged by the growth of large firms in the industry. NAFTA found itself at odds with these firms over their attitudes to working conditions and PBR. Meredew was the first firm to clash with NAFTA over its refusal to recognise the union, to observe any reasonable set of working conditions and to pay overtime. A running battle dragged on intermittently from 1920 to 1925. This culminated in a Mr. Hard, the owner, posting notices increasing hours to fifty four and a half per week. The three members of the union who protested were sacked. The factory was picketed from March to June, 1925 but to no avail. Success came in July from an unexpected source. The Employers' Federation objected to the 'unfair conditions' being applied in Meredew's factory and required the owner to reduce the hours to forty seven per week in line with the rest of the industry. Interestingly, the three sacked cabinetmakers were reinstated, but Meredew's resolutely refused to recognise the union in any way. [20]

This was not the only instance of joint action. In Liverpool NAFTA, AUU and the Liverpool group of the National Federation of Furnishing Trades all agreed to 'black' chairs and frames made by the firm of Christopherson. The Federation reported to its members: 'conditions exist in Messrs. Christopherson's shop, such as to allow them to enter into unfair competition with the chairmaker members of the Federation'. [21]

The most significant battle that NAFTA fought with a large firm during this period was, however, that with Lebus. The largest furniture factory in the United Kingdom (and later in the world) had presented a direct challenge to the union for many years. Prior to the First World

War the Lebus factory had operated a payment by results scheme. During the war and for some years after, it adopted day work with no incentive bonus. By 1922 the company was finding this method of payment unsatisfactory and, taking advantage of the high local unemployment in the Tottenham, Edmonton and Ponders End area took the decision to return to payment by results. 'For the past 4 years since we re-started furniture making after the war', stated the Works Manager, 'we have been working on plain time at the dictation of the union (NAFTA) who would accept nothing else. Restriction of output has been so appalling in all departments that we have come to the conclusion that the only way in which we can carry on business is by introducing a system of payment by results or piece work. Of a workforce of 3,500 some 600 have withdrawn their labour'. The union spokesman, Mr. G. Bracken, was reported as saying: 'There is a working agreement between the employers and the union. Last Thursday the management told the cabinetmakers that payment by results was to be introduced. We objected that this was contrary to our agreement. The firm replied 'either accept PBR or seek work elsewhere'. The paper goes on to note: 'We understand from Messrs. Lebus that they have been inundated with applications for employment and that all vacancies are filled'. [22] [23]

The situation was a stalemate. With the 600 men out, including the works' secretary (convener) and 4 shop stewards, NAFTA picketed the factory. The *Tottenham and Edmonton Weekly Herald* reported: 'The Labour troubles at Messrs. Lebus, Tottenham continue....the premises having been continually under observation by pickets....the vacancies have now all been filled by new hands....there are some reports of intimidation being directed towards some who have been taken on'. The local Trades Council held a protest meeting in the Municipal Hall, Tottenham 'at which the 1,200 present unanimously supported the strikers'. A notice was also read from a number of Cooperative Societies who promised to boycott Lebus goods. A further attempt to force Lebus to negotiate the problem was made by way of a court action. 'At Edmonton County Court an action was taken by Mr. Samuel Hart, a member of NAFTA, against Lebus and Co., over wrongful dismissal and one hour's wages of 1/9d. The applicant had worked for the company for 22 years as a cabinetmaker, working piece-work before the war and time work since'. In the event, the claim failed and costs were awarded to the company. [24] NAFTA found itself isolated in this dispute since the upholsterers refused to fight over PBR which they had always accepted as a wage system, and so with 300 still out, the others being employed elsewhere, the dispute had to be closed down in September. This was a major and humiliating defeat which soured inter-union relationships and hardened NAFTA's stand against PBR at a time when a modification of this stance would have been both judicious and far-sighted.

It must not be thought that large factories and heavy capital investment in the 1920's were always necessary for profitability. The industry was still at a transitional state and would remain so till the Second World War. Those who failed to recognise this were doomed to failure. C.F. Hawkins reported: 'I visited a large firm in our trade the other day. It was run by a financial corporation with directors on full-time fees and was complete with up-to-date machinery, power produced on the premises, jig systems, staffs of engineers, draughtsmen, elaborate offices, time cards, clocks, and every known device for mass production, increased output and all that. They were involved in all kinds of 'on costs', overheads and expenses. They were discharging a number of men because in their plan they had overlooked the fact that there were not sufficient customers for the goods they were making. They were trying to get fresh work but were concerend with the difficulty of high wages. After examining the details closely we were able to show that even without any wage costs at all, their 'on costs' were such that they were 2/- in the pound too high to get any work'. [25]

The opportunity for the working classes to record their disillusionment with the post-war world came with the General Election of 1923. NAFTA gave financial support to three candidates; a nominal support for O'Grady in its financial commitment to the constituency party and a small financial and membership support for J.P. Gardner in North Hammersmith (Gardner was a stone mason and as such was a member of NAFTA but out of the main stream of union activity). The main thrust of the union support was for Alf Purcell in Coventry. As many full-time officers as could be spared, including the General Secretary, were drafted in to the constituency. Alf Purcell himself is recorded as addressing 83 meetings in 18 days.

It was not a clean fight. In a Tory seat the word was spread that to elect a Labour Member of Parliament would double unemployment, but if a Conservative were returned, one employer at least would start another 500 men in a new factory. Alf Purcell reports, 'The mystery of it! How so many factories on short time for months, went on to full-time for the four weeks before the election!' [26]

All three candidates were elected (O'Grady included) and took their place in a Parliamentary Labour Party with 191 seats. The Conservatives with 258 seats had secured the highest poll and the Liberals 158 seats. 'The Liberals could either keep the Conservatives in power or turn them out, thus offering Labour as the single second largest party the chance, if it would, of forming a minority Government. The Liberals opted for the second course, and the Labour Party under Ramsay MacDonald decided to accept office, though they realised that they would be liable to be turned out whenever the Liberal Party felt minded to vote against them'.

The election was seen by the establishment as apocalyptic. Wrote the English Review: 'We stand now at a moment when the sun of England seems menaced with final eclipse. For the first time in her history the party of Revolution approach their hands to the helm of state, not only as in the seventeenth century for the purposes of ovethrowing the Crown, or of altering the Constitution, but with the design of destroying the very basis of civilised life'. [28]

NAFTA was much more restrained. The District officers expressed their pleasure at Alf Purcell's win in Coventry. Alex Gossip took an even more sanguine view, noting the death of a great leader in Russia rather than the advent of a minority government at home, albeit with three members of the union within that Government He wrote; 'Lenin is dead; that great Russian leader. We put on record our deep and sincere sympathy with the relatives of Nicolai Lenin, as also with the nation as a whole and not only the Russian Republic but the world as a whole'. [29]

This lack of enthusiasm arose from the disillusionment that beset Alf Purcell when he entered Parliament with such great hopes and found it smothering them. 'I am bound to say that neither the show part or what is termed the business part impresses me, except in a very depressing way. The processions are childish in the extreme and the foolish proceedings of listening to someone (the King) read what someone else has written belong to a past age. Similarly, the awful parade of pomp and jewels is a frightful and disgusting mockery when taken and compared with the terrible conditions now prevalent amongst so many of our fellow workers'. Similarly, with the debates - 'they are so rural. It is all a case of what have we said, not let us do. There are too few fully fledged trade unionists and really well tried working class represent-ations for my liking in the ministries'. Nevertheless, Alf Purcell persisted in Parliament and NAFTA voted him an extra £200 per year to support himself, the constituency and his position as Parliamentary Secretary to the union.

For NAFTA in 1924 the brightest light shone from its involvement in the hierarchy of the trade union movement. Fred Bramley was General Secretary of the TUC, with Alf Purcell as President, while William Leonard was President Elect of the Scottish TUC. The Congress of the former held in Hull from the 1st to 6th September, 1924 was a triumph for the union. The resolutions empowering the General Council to press for an amalgamation of the two existing trade union Internationals was agreed, as was the reorganisation of the trades union movement on an industrial basis - Industrial Unionism - a long held objective of NAFTA. In relation to the events to come, the NAFTA resolution - in composite form, giving more power to the General Council of the TUC to mobilise all available forces in any industrial struggle proved to be of fundamental importance. NAFTA supported and lost a motion to re-admit the trades councils to the TUC and also a motion to accept the affiliation of the National Unemployed Workers Committee Movement.

On balance, however, it was a good Congress for NAFTA. The Labour Party Conference of October 1924 was not as satisfactory. Alex Gossip was the NAFTA delegate and the whole of his report concerns the question of the affiliation of the Communist Party. 'Your delegate spoke and voted against all three separate proposals aimed against the Communist Party and individual members, believing as I do in one common united front against the common enemy. It is quite true there are differences in opinion, but if we can work with warmongers and imperialists, half-baked Liberals and Tories etc., who have joined the Labour Party, possibly in all good faith, it is incomprehensible to me why we should refuse to work with those, who, whatever may be said about them, by some, have proved their loyalty and devotion to their class, which is also ours'.

The Conference was closed a day earlier than scheduled due to the dissolution of Parliament and in the election that followed Alf Purcell lost Coventry, polling 17,888 votes to the Conservatives' 22,712, and the Liberals' 12,953. J.P. Gardner lost Hammersmith in a straight fight with a Conservative by 10,970 votes to 12,925. James O'Grady did not contest East Leeds as he had been knighted and appointed Governor of Tasmania.

The minority Labour Government had been hamstrung throughout its short life. Labour supporters had hoped for a radical government, prepared to grasp the problems of unemployment and poverty, a government on the offensive. The realities of political life as a minority Administration and as the first Labour Administration at that, suggested that its uninspiring record was partly the result of caution, and the desire to create confidence at home in Labour's moderation; and partly of the old difficulty, a lack of time in ten crowded months, to develop bold new initiatives.

Labour lost the 1924 General Election. If it was a case of 'great opportunities wantonly and recklessly thrown away by the most incompetent leadership which ever brought a Government to ruin', as Philip Snowdon wrote to F.W. Jowitt, then it did, indeed, deserve to fail. Yet the critics of the first Labour government with their reliance on socialist clichés, could offer no other viable course of action. Alex Gossip and Alf Purcell must be seen to have been in this group. The suggestion that the party could have taken office, formulated a truly socialist manifesto, and gone to the country to have it accepted at the ballot box was not only an avoidance of responsibility but assumed that the British public thirsted for a social and economic revolution. This was patently not so. Union leaders such as Alex Gossip and Alf Purcell knew this, yet maintained the illusion to the end. Alf Purcell's comments upon the government indicate the lack of any practical proposals. 'A bold policy will win them miles and miles of support. Hesitation will let them down. Attack should be the watchword. To dare to do should be the attitude. The Government must assert themselves as a working class Government. Anything less will bring them down'. Such rhetoric was not enough.

The change of government, however, intensified the dilemma of trade union leaders such as Gossip and Purcell. Since they were no longer represented in Parliament their vehicles for pressure and change had once again to be external. External pressure groups were mainly Communist dominated or inspired. If trade unionists joined them, this was rather a comment upon the vitality of that party than an indication of the underlying political allegiance of those who joined. NAFTA's leadership had always been on the political left of the socialist movement and it was natural that Alex Gossip saw 'the Russian Revolution is the one bright spot' in the first quarter of the twentieth century. It was equally appropriate that as pacifists and left wing socialists it should be prominent in the formation of the 1919 'Hands off Russia' movement, with Alf Purcell as President and Alex Gossip on the executive. [31]

Alf Purcell visited Russia in 1920 as a member of the TUC delegation. 'It will enable a working class judgement to be formed of the situation in Russia'. He returned enormously enthusiastic over Soviet achievements and wrote at length to the membership about his visit. Three years later Alex Gossip made a similar visit as a fraternal delegate to the All Russia Woodworkers Federation Conference in Moscow. His invitation had come as a result of his strong plea for the inclusion of the Russian delegates at the 1922 International Conference of Woodworkers in Vienna. He was defeated by 54 votes to 19 but from this time was regarded by the Russians as a sympathetic trade union leader. He wrote of his visit more briefly but referred to it on numerous occasions over the years, lectured to Branches on conditions in Russia and for many years held up to the membership the vision of Russia as an example upon which to model itself. Gossip knew that NAFTA was not a revolutionary union with revolutionary members. Looking for change through pressure groups and the raising of the workers' consciousness, he inevitably became involved with many organisations that were later to be proscribed by the increasingly middle-of-the-road Labour Party.

Alex Gossip was a prominent member of the Minority Movement formed in August, 1924 on the instructions of the Executive Committee of the Communist International and seen by the Communist Party as a means of gaining control over the trades union movement. This was to be achieved by drawing in the large number of left wing trade union militants who were dissatisfied with the existing cautious leadership. Militant trade unionists in the Minority Movement were to act through minority movement groups at union branch level to direct policy along lines determined by the Communist leaders of the movement. How effectively the movement achieved this is difficult to discern as far as NAFTA was concerned, but Minority Movement policy on international-ism, whereby the movement was to exert pressure for international trade union unity, was quite in line with exisiting NAFTA policy. As a proponent of this philosophy the Furniture Workers' Union was an honoured member of the Minority Movement. [32]

Alex Gossip wrote in defence of the Minority Movement: 'Its function is one of trying to link up all left wing elements so that the opinions of thousands of organised workers may have the influence they deserve to have in the shaping of the policy of other bodies'. This appears to place Gossip and NAFTA in too prominent a position in the Minority Movement. Roderick Martin puts the position succinctly; 'Harry Pollitt was the lynch pin of the Minority Movement. Although prominent supporters like Arthur Cook, Alex Gossip and Sam Elsbury were important in winning union support, they played only a marginal role in the internal development of the movement'. [33]

Alex Gossip was more specifically involved with the Greater London Left Wing Committee - later renamed the National Left Wing Movement. Communist dominated, it nevertheless matched in its ideals Alex Gossip's political philosophy. It was set up by the South West Bethnal Green party on 21st November 1925 with the aim of 'Bringing the Labour Party back to the idealism and fighting spirit of Kier Hardie and the host of unremembered'. The initial leaders of the movement were James Maxton MP, Alex Gossip and William Paul, editor of the *Sunday Worker*. Their first pamphlet *The Left Wing and Its Programme* referred to the ever-growing concern of active workers in the labour movement at the drift of the right wing labour leaders towards Liberalism. [34] Imperialism was another target for the Left Wing Movement. It saw imperialism as the source of the troubles of British workers. In a programme of action clearly edited by Alex Gossip it demanded 'the transformation of the League of Nations - now a weapon of imperialism, into a real League of People recognising rights of full and free self-determination for subject races'. It called upon the Labour Party to hold periodic conferences of representatives of peasants' and workers' organisations throughout the Empire and to assist native peoples in their struggles for freedom and independence.

The main vehicle for propaganda used by Alex Gossip and Alf Purcell other than the union journal was the *Sunday Worker*. This newspaper was launched by the Communist Party, was under CP control and dependent for funds on the Communist International from which it received an annual subsidy of £4,000. Its most prominent contributors were not exclusively Communist but drawn from the whole of the left wing of the Labour movement. [35] In May 1925, the *Sunday Worker* pulled off a considerable coup in the campaign for Labour Party affilation of CP members by bringing together at a meeting, A.B. Swales, the Chairman of TUC, Alf Purcell, the Vice Chairman TUC, Ben Tillett, John Jagger, Ben Turner, John Wheatley MP, James Maxton MP, David Kirkwood, MP, Ellen Wilkinson MP, George Buchanan, MP, J. Campbell Stephen MP, S. Saklatrala, MP, Tom Mann, Willie Gallacher, and Mrs Helen Crawford. Letters of support came from A.J. Cook, John Bromley and Alex Gossip. '*The Sunday Worker*, it declared, 'is understandably proud that it has successfully brought together the advance group of both the Parliamentary and industrial organisation with the members of the Communist Party'. No statement was published after the meeting but it was assumed that some sort of basis was found for a united platform of left wing action. [36]

Such hopes were, however, dashed by the failure to influence the 1925 Labour Party Conference to allow Communist party members to affiliate. The failure was particularly serious in that the left wing leaders so carefully cultivated failed to speak out in favour of the motion. The *Sunday Worker* group had evidently decided to support the executive on rejection. This leaves as an open question why this course of action was adopted by the individuals involved. MacFarlane suggests that it was cowardice in the face of a largely hostile party conference. This is to disregard the character of the members of this group about whom such a suggestion is out of the question. Postgate takes a more acceptable view that the executive line was adopted in the absence of a tenable alternative policy. [37]

Problems of direction and the fight for ascendancy between the right and left wings of the labour movement left a policy vacuum at a critical period in the history of the Labour movement. The need to fill the vacuum was made all the more pressing by the knowledge that after Red Friday the Tory Government was inevitably committed to a trial of strength with organised labour.

The return to the Gold Standard in May, 1925 by the Chancellor of the Exchequer, Winston Churchill, formed the basis of the build- up to the General Strike of the following year. By returning to the old parity of the pound sterling, the export of goods was restricted by the high value of the pound against other currencies. Exports could only be sustained by forcing down prices and it was implicit in the move that the effect would be to force down wages, and though all sectors of the economy would suffer, that the coal industry would be more affected than most.

The invasion of the Ruhr in 1923/24 had reduced German coal production and export and British coal mining had temporarily prospered in this artificial situation. The evacuation of the Ruhr, subsequent substantial increases in German coal exports to pay the reparations due under the Dawes Plan,and a general world recession, coupled with falling demand for steam coal, resulted in a subsantial slump in British coal exports.

The coal owners saw the solution to this problem in longer hours and lower wages; the miners thought otherwise. Faced with an ultimatum they responded by rallying support through the trade union movement and the General Council of the TUC was empowered to call a strike on any scale deemed requisite in the event of a continuation of the deadlock. The subsequent climb down by the government and agreement to a nine months subsidy was greeted with rejoicing as the 'Victory of Red Friday'. Alex Gossip warned his members; 'The Prime Minister has just told the Miners' representatives that not only must their wages come down, but those of all other workers in all other industries, so we know what is in store for us if we do not all stand together'. [38] [39] The government was playing for time and in the ensuing months, through both official and unofficial bodies, especially the Organisation for the Maintenance of Supplies, it prepared to meet the threat of a General Strike.

The trade union movement was not unaware of these moves and strengthened its own organisation by giving much wider power than ever before to the General Council of the TUC and its Industrial Committee. By contrast with the government, however, the preparations made for the conduct of such a strike were quite inadequate, despite warnings and pleas from within the labour movement.

The National Left Wing Movement called for a Labour-Co-operative Commissariat for the Maintenance of Supplies in anticipation of interference from the OMS and other organisations of a fascist character. It called a conference, a special National Conference of Action, at Latchmere Baths, Battersea, on 21st. March, 1926, attended by 1,500 delegates. With Tom Mann in the chair Alex Gossip moved the resolution on the defence and maintenance of trade union rights. Among other things he urged the formation of 'a workers' defence corps in order to protect working class speakers from bourgeois terrorism, to protect trade union headquarters from fascist incendiarism, to defend strike pickets against police interference and to act as a powerful working class force, capable of defending the political and industrial rights of the workers'. This appeal harked back to a time when industrial conflict was for industrial ends. The implications of such a workers' fighting force were ignored, as were the relationships with the apparatus of the state and the workers' relationship to it.

In 1919 Alex Gossip had written: 'Organised workers in this country need a plan of campaign, carefully thought out beforehand and the weapons of industrial warfare ready at hand, before we go over the top'. [40] Five years later that call for a carefully orchestrated revolution to bring nearer the workers' state was no more than a pipe dream. The reality was now of defence; this was no call for a workers' and soldiers' corps to take over the role of policing the new order. It was a statement advocating a defensive corps, an Anti-Violence Brigade, to protect trade unionists in an industrial dispute. Alex Gossip was refusing to recognise that a general strike could ever be a revolutionary and evolutionary weapon. In such a strike there had to be a winning side. If it was the trade union and socialist movement, with what sort of world, with what sort of structure, would they replace the existing order?

As to the imminence of a general strike the membership of NAFTA was well and truly warned. As early as November, 1925, Alex Gossip wrote to the members: 'The press is full of the desires of the capitalist and governing class to organise a force of scabs and blacklegs with which to defeat the workers should those employed in vital industries be forced at any time to strike. We sincerely trust that no member of our Association will have anything to do with any OMS or Fascist movement. The same applies to Special Police or similar bodies which may be got up. Let us stick to our own class, the working class, and refuse to be led away by any specious promises to play the traitor to organised labour'. [41]

In July, 1925, Alf Purcell stood for Parliament at the by-election for the Forest of Dean. It was a difficult campaign, not helped by the refusal of Ramsay Macdonald to support his canditature, but with the assistance of most of the full-time officials of the union and Labour MP's and 98 speeches in 14 days by Purcell himself, he won an unexpected victory. The losing Tory commented bitterly at the declaration of the result: 'This result convinces me of the need for a restriction of the franchise'. As Vice-Chairman of the TUC, General Council member, and member of Parliament for a mining community, Alf Purcell of NAFTA was to be at the centre of events in the coming year. [42]

On 29th. April 1926, a Conference of Trade Union Executives met at Farringdon Hill in London. The Government subsidy for the miners ran out on April 30th, and the mine owners had posted notices in most pits to end existing employment contracts on the same day. All parties felt that somehow the situation of confrontation would be avoided and that a settlement would be reached. Indeed, so strong was this feeling that the first TUC plans for a national strike were only made that very week when a plan of campaign was drawn up by Purcell and Bevin. 'Even this was a tentative draft plan since no-one knew what the attitude of the various unions would be, and because of the lack of enthusiasm amongst the majority of the General Council for any militant action'. [43]

The strike plans were produced by a General Council torn by conflicting objectives. The Council wanted to make it effective but it also wanted to make sure that control did not pass into the hands of revolutionary agitators; and so it became in plan, at least, a *partial* general strike with the electricity workers and woodworkers held back as a second line of attack if necessary. [44]

Symons' comments upon this confusion is echoed by Phillips; 'On 5th May, in the face of mounting confusion and frustration, the original committee arrangements at TUC Headquarters were dissolved and a new apparatus for the conduct of the strike set up. This was to be named the Strike Organising Committee and was dominated by Ernest Bevin and Alf Purcell (Chairman). From this time on the General Council became increasingly less and less concerned with the running of the strike and more and more absorbed with the negotiation of prospective terms of settlement with Sir Herbert Samuel'. [45]

In the event the mine owners offered a 13 per cent cut in wages and an 8 hour day. The offer was refused, the miners locked out and the individual unions agreed to hand over their autonomy to the General Council for the emergency period. The Baldwin Government forced the issue to a strike on the refusal of the *Daily Mail* printers to allow a reactionary anti-miners' article to be printed, and the General Strike had begun.

What, perhaps, more than any other factor, caused the failure of the General Strike, was the realisation of the General Council, that it had unleashed a political and revolutionary weapon. Faced with the enormity of such a step, it drew back mentally and materially in its prosecution of the strike and in so doing created a situation of inevitable failure. The resultant sense of betrayal among the strike activists was overwhelming. It has been argued by Symons that at a local level the strikers were over-optimistic, that they 'interpreted their own solidarity as a portent of victory, whereas it was merely a foundation on which victory might be built. Such local and partial pictures were wholly misleading and took no account of the government's activities'.

Yet it is difficult not to feel that the workers were indeed betrayed; not wittingly, but betrayed nevertheless. They were led to the barricades by a leadership which failed to recognise that once the barricades were manned they were in a political and revolutionary situation. When they saw what this required the leaders retreated and the workers were lost.

The furniture workers' experience of the General Strike was a frustrating one; in the place of organisation they found confusion. It was the avowed intention that they, in common with many others organised, should be held back as a second line of attack and should be heavily levied to support those actually out on strike. In the event these instructions were either never received or were misinterpreted. All members of NAFTA joined the strike on the first day, and the confusion resulting from union orders to return to work and local orders to stay out was demoralising. Nationally, the furniture workers were controlled by a special Action Committee consisting of the General Secretary and the EC taking instructions from the TUC, but the difficulties of communication and the overlap with unions such as the Amalgamated Union of Upholsterers and the Woodcutting Machinists who were acting on local initiatives caused bitterness and recrimination.

In the event, all furniture workers returned to work at the end of the strike in remarkably good order and with little victimisation. Waring & Gillow in Lancaster threatened to sue NAFTA for breach of contract

but did not pursue the claim. The West of England Employers'
Federation and the London Cabinet Trades Employers demanded an
apology from NAFTA for breaking its agreements by coming out on
strike and further demanded a guarantee that it would never again call
out its members as part of a general strike. The EC refused to give such
an undertaking and these demands were dropped. [46]

A more insidious move was combatted in Middlesborough. The
employment exchange in this town required the unemployed to sign a
document: 'I hereby declare I did not leave work in accordance with
TUC instructions or in sympathy with those who did, and I would have
continued work after May 4th, if work had been available'. Without
such a declaration it refused to pay any benefit, and a number of
NAFTA members were affected. Alex Gossip himself dealt with this
matter and forced the withdrawal of the document. The final accolade to
the NAFTA membership for its stand was that the Russian Woodworkers Trades Union sent a congratulatory telegram to NAFTA
commending it on its solidarity during the strike and on its refusal to
apologise for its actions. [47]

Perhaps the strangest aspect of the General Strike as far as the
furniture unions are concerned, was the silence of Alf Purcell on the
failure of the strike. The General Council, of which he was a member,
was bitterly attacked in the union journal by Alex Gossip and by the
District Organisers, yet Alf Purcell did not reply in the journal but rather
in the *Sunday Worker*. Alex Gossip had already written a bitter article of
recrimination in this newspaper. 'Why did it fail - why was the second
line of strikers not called out on May 7th.? Why was defeat accepted
without the miners? This was a betrayal!' Alf Purcell replied to what was
seen as a direct attack; 'The recent General Strike must be regarded as
being in the nature of a preliminary encounter and more as a
demonstrtation than anything else. It had never been tried before in this
country. It was something new. We were all moving in a new and wide
field of activity. It was only natural that the weapon should prove
difficult and unwieldy under the circumstances. Whether we like it or
not, the class struggle itself, the inexorable urge of economic forces is
going to create the conditions for other and more formidable General
Strikes'. Following such generalisations he then tried to cloud the real
issue with hyperbole; 'The workers of Britain have learnt to fight as a
class and that, in itself, is the greatest advance the workers have made in
this country. Those who talk about the failure of the General Strike are
mentally a generation behind the times in which we live, and those who
imagine that this, the first general strike, is the last, can have no real
understanding of the conditions that brought it about'. [48]

The appropriate comment upon such a statement came in an
anonymous letter in the following week's correspondence column. 'I fail
to find anything in the article by A.A. Purcell that will convince honest

minded labour people that their [the General Council's] policy of retreat was a magnificent victory. I say unhesitatingly that the workers state quite frankly that they were sold'. An ominous portent for the political future of Alf Purcell came in an unsigned article in the *Sunday Worker* some months later. 'The Biggest Bubble that has been pricked is the leftness of Messrs. Purcell, Hicks, Bramley & Co. The moment they were required to put their left phrases into action, that moment saw them scurrying behind Mr. J.H. Thomas' skirts for safety'.

It was left to Alex Gossip to spell out to the membership what consequences would follow the strike. 'The Government is to bring in legislation that will restrict our ability to strike unless a majority of members in a secret ballot vote for such a strike. They will restrict and restrain our right to picket. They will require a Fighting Fund to be separate from the Benefit Funds and this Fighting Fund will be liable to action for damages. Finally they will require us to 'contract in' to a Political Fund not contract out as now. Members should note that nothing has been said about Employers locking out their workers, about Employers refusing work to certain workers, nor how Employers shall use their funds nor to which political party they shall give them'.

Despite such initially pessimistic predictions Alex Gossip and Alf Purcell were more optimistic by the end of the year. Alex Gossip wrote: 'The General Strike should have opened the eyes of even the most blind and apathetic, and made them determined to hasten the day when this present wicked and unrighteous system will be cast overboard and a righteous system established in its place'. [51] Alf Purcell shared this sentiment. 'This is by no means the last General Strike. It is the first general strike. You will get it, all in good time. The stress under which the working class is suffering will compel a general strike. As soon as the millions who have been side-tracked by the Tory Party get back on to the proper line, this is the side upon which they will be found. When that happens it will be goodbye to general strikes. These will be finished with, but so will the Tory Party and the capitalist class'. In the years that followed the General Strike the leadership of NAFTA was to return again and again to the theme of direct action, but in reality trade union organisation in the aftermath of this event was to become defence in the face, not so much of organised capitalism, but of unemployment.

Before leaving the period 1919-1926, however, it should be noted that while ending in defeat, it witnessed also a flowering of the enormous talent and vitality within the union. NAFTA gave the labour movement three MP's, the General Secretary of the TUC, the President of the Scottish TUC and President of the British TUC. It was deeply involved in the major left-wing movements of the time - in the Unemployed Workers Movement, the National Minority Movement and the National Left Wing Movement. Men of the stature of Alex Gossip, Fred Bramley, Alf Purcell, William Leonard, Jim O'Grady, J.P. Gardner and

Alf Tomkins were all drawn from this small union - a group of leaders of an importance and in numbers quite disproportionate to the size of NAFTA itself.

It can be argued that the process by which the union drew in, developed and projected such men, stemmed from the industrial conditions of furniture making in the late nineteenth century. The art and craft of furniture making in terms of cabinetmaking, upholstery and polishing was a quiet group activity. To be a good craftsman required technical knowledge, manual dexterity, a working knowledge of calculations and an ability to plan ahead. Day working, as opposed to payment by results and its associated elemental task working, brought men together in groups in a relatively quiet industrial situation and required relatively little instrusive supervision of its participants.

Talk, argument and discussion were not only possible within such working groups but a necessary condition to making and moving large pieces of furniture around a workshop. The hours of work might be long, the availability of employment uncertain, but the opportunities for self-improvement, both at work and in the branches, with their extensive libraries, and the very nature of the work itself attracted the type of craftsmen who were both intelligent and perceptive and who developed in the workplace a working class bond of strength paralleled in only a few other industries. The traditions that stemmed from William Lovett in the nineteenth century found their full flowering in the earliest decades of the twentieth. The union would continue to be led by exceptional men but with the advent of PBR and the pressure for higher production, they would be different men, honed on a different wheel, products of a different age.

# CHAPTER VII

# All Hail the Advance Guard — NAFTA 1926 – 1931

In the immediate wake of the defeat in the General Strike of 1926, the whole of the trade union movement was put on the defensive by the Trades Disputes and Trades Union Bill brought in by the Conservative government. NAFTA had also to contend with an unfounded attack from within the labour movement by J.H. Thomas and his supporters. Politically NAFTA found itself in a difficult position. It was at odds with the Mond-Turner talks which sought to reconcile the interests of labour and capital, and among the few unions to support the Cook-Maxton response. It became more and more isolated as the Labour Party seemed to drift more and more to the right. The second minority Labour Government seemed to justify the NAFTA position. The subsequent move of MacDonald, Snowden and Thomas into the so-called National Government with Liberals and Tories, while further vindicating its position was also a matter of some despair for the union.

It was the struggle with unemployment which above all occupied the energies of NAFTA during this period. The state of trade had been poor after the General Strike, but by the beginning of the 1930's it had become so bad that 25 per cent of the membership was out of work and a majority of the rest were on short time. Membership was declining and benefit funds were exhausted. The very existence of the union in its provident benefit aspect was under threat.

By the end of 1926 NAFTA membership had fallen to 19,700. At the beginning of 1927 matters seemed to be improving and the small Liverpool Union of Picture Frame Makers joined the Association. Moves towards amalgamation were boosted by the General Council of the TUC which wrote to all furniture unions calling upon them to meet to discuss the possibility of mergers. The call was ignored by the Wood Cutting Machinists, the Progressive Cabinetmakers and the Progressive Polishers (the latter very small London societies) but NAFTA did meet the Amalgamated Upholsterers and the United Polishers Society.

Unfortunately, the discussions, though useful in establishing and reinforcing links, did not produce a basis for amalgamation, the Upholsterers and Polishers acceptance of PBR and the different rates of benefit paid being the most important obstacles to further talks. [1]

May 1927 brought the introduction of the Trades Disputes and Trades Union Act described by Alex Gossip as 'ridiculous and fantastic in its terms and outrageous and unjustifiable in its effects'. The EC warned the members that 'the right to strike, organise picketing, political action, and freedom of association are all to be drastically curtailed' and the General Council of the TUC circularised unions asking members 'to fall into line in readiness to play his or her part in the great fight which the present Government in a reckless and partisan spirit is forcing upon the British Working Class movement'. [2] Reality could not match rhetoric. The unions and labour movement were too close to a resounding defeat to put up any sort of fight and to the dismay of the left wing the Bill was enacted with comparatively little opposition. Alex Gossip commented: 'In our opinion, the general Council of the Trades Union Congress, and the Executive of the Labour Party did not approach the question in the militant spirit which is so necessary to success, but confined themselves to a series of more or less weak demonstrations in the various districts and gentle babbling in the House of Commons, and there was nothing done to rouse any real enthusiasm against the obnoxious Bill and no fighting lead given'. [3]

No one could ever have accused NAFTA of lacking fighting spirit, and when J.H. Thomas produced his extraordinary smear on Alex Gosip and NAFTA at the Blackpool Labour Party Conference of October 1927, he was subjected to the full fury of righteous socialist indignation. Thomas was the favourite 'whipping boy' of the left and had been the target of a long campaign of vilification by the *Sunday Worker* in a series of unsigned articles, some of which were undoubtedly in the style of Alex Gossip, particularly with regard to his friendship with wealthy Tories such as Lord Inchcape with whom he stayed during Cowes week. [4]

At the Conference Thomas publicly accused Alex Gossip of applying to the General Council Strike Committee for permission for his members to build huts in Hyde Park during the General Strike. These huts, which were undoubtedly built, were intended, he claimed, to accommodate Special Constables and strike blacklegs. Alex Gossip emphatically denied the charge and called for a full investigation of the accusation by the General Council of the TUC. This was agreed to. The charge, amounting to infamous conduct by a trade union leader, had the effect of rallying support around Alex Gossip. Almost every branch of the union wrote to him expressing its support and condemning Thomas's statement.

That the charge was at best mischievous and unsubstantiated is borne out by Alf Purcell's comment in the *Monthly Report*. As a member of the General Council Strike Committee during those ten days he was able to report, 'I have no hesitation in stating that no such application was received by the Strike Committee during the General or National Strike period of May 1926. I have never then or since heard a word about this incident until I saw a report of the Labour Party Meeting at Blackpool. I would wish members to know that I was Chairman of the sub-committee dealing with the issue of licenses for work during the General Strike'. [5]

The Committee of Enquiry met at the TUC on 17th and 24th November, 1927, and was composed of Ben Turner (Chairman), H. Boothman, G. Hicks, J.W. Ogden, Rt.Hon. F.O. Roberts MP, Miss J. Varley, W.M. Citrine, A.S. Firth, J.H. Thomas MP, J. Bromley MP, A. Couley, A.G. Walkden, A. Gossip, B. Rockman, A. Tomkins, and A.H. Urie. Thomas stated that as all documents relating to the charge had been destroyed he would be relying on the evidence of three witnesses to prove his charges. Walter Citrine, General Secretary TUC, responded by stating quite categorically that no documents relating to the National Strike had been destroyed. Thomas's evidence before the Committee was, to say the least, confused. He admitted that he did not know exactly who had written the letter to the Strike Committee asking for the license for NAFTA. He called his witnesses. The first could not, under questioning, recall whether such a letter had ever been received. The second thought he had heard a report of such a request from someone. The third stated that he heard from someone else that the union had asked for permission but he could not remember who that person was.

At the second meeting of the Committee on the 24th November, Citrine informed the meeting that an extensive search of the documents relating to the National Strike had been undertaken. No letter had been found nor could anyone who might have been concerned with the matter recall such a letter. The meeting ended with the promise that a full and public report of its findings would be published by the General Council. Patently Thomas's charge was unproven and this was confirmed at an internal (TUC) meeting of the Committee on 11th January 1928, when Ernest Bevin refuted absolutely the Thomas allegations against the Furniture Workers and at which Citrine also declared NAFTA innocent of the charge. [6] Subsequent investigation of the unpublished documents available has established that temporary wooden latrines were built in Hyde Park prior to the General Strike by the London building firm of J. Mowlem.

Unfortunately, NAFTA decided to publish a report of the TUC proceedings in the *Monthly Report* for October, 1927, and in so doing provided the Committee of Enquiry with an excuse to avoid the publication of its findings and an inevitable condemnation of Thomas. In the *Daily Herald* of 26th January it stated, 'The General Council of the TUC declines to publish a report of its findings in this matter as

NAFTA has dealt with the matter in its journal — to all intents and purposes, publicly finding Mr. J.H. Thomas guilty without the full evidence being taken into consideration'. There is no evidence at the TUC, in an otherwise well-documented file, as to how this last decision was arrived at, and the accusation against NAFTA was, as far as the Committee of Enquiry was concerned, no longer a matter of concern. Alex Gossip responded in the *Daily Herald* on the following day: 'Anything more contemptible is difficult to imagine. This is a manufactured excuse to save the face of Mr. Thomas, and if it had not been one excuse it would have been another'.[7]

Alf Purcell was the one man who might have avoided these public recriminations and who might also have ensured a public vindication of Alex Gossip. He was absent in India on a TUC delegation at the time. Without a friend at court NAFTA was unable to persuade the General Council to change its mind. NAFTA EC wrote to Thomas asking him if he was prepared to withdraw his accusation and apologise but he refused to answer and it is an indication of the isolation of the left wing that the union was quite unable to force him to retract his claims; nor could it influence the TUC to utter a public denial of the charge, and had to rely for vindication on the publication of a pamphlet to make its case. [8] NAFTA had to let the matter rest, and though the whole episode had been most unsatisfactory, the union was, by the early months of 1928, more concerned over the fundamental issues raised by the Mond-Turner talks and the Cook-Maxton response.

In November of 1927 Sir Alfred Mond of ICI and a group of employers from a variety of industries, informally approached the General Council of the TUC with a proposal to meet and discuss methods of improving industrial relations. The then Chairman of the General Council, Ben Turner, accepted the invitation and a series of meetings were held.

The left wing of the trade unions and of the Labour Party was astonished and dismayed at this turn of events and, bearing in mind the events of previous years and the vindictiveness shown to the workshop leaders of the labour movement after the General Strike, saw this as a complete sell-out by the right wing of the movement. Alex Gosip wrote: 'In view of the deep antagonism shown by many organised workers against the so-called Industrial Peace Conference, those representatives of the workers who are responsible should ask themselves how is it that the capitalist press and class are describing them in such loving terms. We welcome peace as much as anyone but this can only come with the complete destruction of the hateful and iniquitous system of society under which we exist at present'. [9]

Gossip returned to the attack some weeks later. 'Let me remind the membership as to who Sir Alfred Mond is and what he stands for....In his recent visit to Italy he is reported as stating 'I admire Fascism because it is successful in bringing about social peace....Fascism is tending towards the realisation of my political ideals, namely, to make all classes collaborate loyally'.[10]

The interim agreement resulting from the Mond-Turnr talks was published in July, 1928, and had proposals dealing with unemployment, recommendations in favour of recognising the trade unions as bargaining agents, the encouragement by employers of trade union membership, and proposals for the setting up of joint consultative machinery between the TUC, the Federation of British Industries and the National Confederation of Employers' Organisations.

The left wing response of the Miners' Federation and James Maxton, Chairman of the ILP, became known as the Cook-Maxton Manifesto. It vigorously denounced 'class collaboration', recorded 'serious disturbance at the direction in which the British labour movement was being led', called for an 'increasing war against capitalism' and protested that 'much of the energy which should be expended in fighting capitalism is now expended in crushing everybody who dares to remain true to the ideals of the movement'.

Cook took the battle, which he had been fighting alone on the General Council of the TUC, to Congress in September 1928, but was heavily defeated. Rubbing salt in the wounds, Congress instructed the General Council to make a special investigation of the activities of disruptive elements in the trade unions and to take action against those which it considered to be following policies 'hostile to the general interests of the labour movement'. [11]

In the final analysis the Mond-Turner talks were of little value to the trade union movement, and of no value at all to NAFTA and the furniture workers. Alex Gossip pointed out; 'We have heard a great deal of late of the wonderful achievements of the General Council of the TUC as a result of the Mond-Turner conferences, and of how recognition of the unions has been established. Lord Melchett (Sir Alfred Mond as was) is of a different opinion and he has knocked the idea on the head in several speeches. I ask the members to note the speech reported in the *Morning Post* of 28th September. 'We were never asked and we would never have conceded for a moment, that we should in any way be compelled only to employ union labour. We were never asked and we would never have conceded, and nobody could possibly interpret it into any form of words that I have set my hand to, that there should be any differentiation in my works between union and non-union labour'. [12]

These concerns at a national political level did not pre-occupy the leadership of NAFTA to the exclusion of the routine of union work. The twenties had seen the substantial introduction of the spray gun and nitrocellulose lacquer as a means of finishing furniture. Prior to that time the french polisher, working by hand with shellac and varnishes, had been the normal medium for decoration and protection of the finished article. In the wake of this production change the polishers fell victim to dermatitis. Traditional french polishing materials had never presented this problem. Now the needs of higher levels of polishing output to match spraying had led to their adulteration. Quite what the actively irritant elements were was never established, but the problem was clearly related to the solvents and ingredients used to cut down the drying time for the polishing stage, to give quickly the results which would in times past have taken many hours of work. The reaction of employers who did not introduce spray equipment was to purchase french polishing materials which gave the same output as the spray guns but without the capital outlay.

The original spray guns were crude and their operation little understood. Initially they produced as many problems for the workers as the adulterated materials themselves. Mechanisms to extract the solvent vapour were non-existent, masks and protective clothing were unknown and men using the equipment were severely affected by respiratory problems. The initial appraoch of the employers was to man the spray equipment with untrained boys and learners, but in January 1928 NAFTA signed an agreement with the London Cabinet Trades Employers Federation permitting only fully qualified polishers to use these new sprayiung machines. The polishers did not altogether welcome this agreement and the *Monthly Reports* of the period record rejection and distaste for the new equipment from the members. It became obvious that in everyone's interests a measure of compulsion had to be introduced, and in 1930 NAFTA was able to get an amendment to Section 79 of the Factories and Workshops Act dealing with the spraying of volatile solutions. No sprayed material was to include benzene; no sprayer was to be under the age of eighteen; a separate room was to be set aside for spraying and the vapour mechanically removed and fresh air be let in. The air in the spray room was to be changed every two minutes and the sprayers provided with protective clothing. The mess room for the sprayers was to be separate from the spray room and also washing and toilet facilities. [13] The early introduction of these regulations was a tribute to the sterling and persistent work of Alex Gossip and the General Officials of NAFTA.

Another major document from this period was the Joint Agreement of Co-operation and Mutual Aid between NAFTA and the Wood-workers Union of the USSR. This was the product of years of championing the cause of internationalism and co-operation between unions in a world-wide context and with Soviet Russia in particular. The agreement was enthusiastically endorsed by the EC and by a vote of the membership. Its aims were to:

1.  Set up an Anglo-Russian Committee of Co-operation with one representative of each union;

2.  Give moral and material assistance during stikes and lockouts;
3.  To assist the woodworkers of other countries in their struggles;
4.  To fight against the splitting of the Trade Union Movement of the Woodworkers;
5.  To strive for the creation of a real International of Woodworkers;
6.  To resist the breaking out of new imperialist wars;
7.  To provide regular exchange of information, reports, etc., and the regular mutual exchange of delegates to conferences, congresses, etc.

There appears to be no evidence of the agreement being called into action during the period relevant to this Chapter, despite the strains to which the Union was being subjected; but as a moral and financial pact it suggested that even when the union reached a financial crisis point it had no reason to lose faith in its future; there was always a friend to whom to turn in time of need. Nevertheless the union nearly foundered upon the rock of unemployment which remained distressingly high. One method of easing the burden on the industry is described by C.F. Hawkins, the Organiser for High Wycombe in 1928. 'There are 1,500 of our members out of work nationally, but only 17 in High Wycombe. This is not to say there is a lot of work available in the town but rather that we use work sharing. Short-time working is and has been normal for the last year or so but when an employer is 'busy' he 'borrows' employees from those that are slack and this is arranged through the local Federation of Employers and our union. Both the members and the employers like the system since it avoids involvement with the Employment Exchange and any chance of being disqualified for benefit'.[14]

Work sharing and wage rates tied to the cost of living had their problems as C.F. Hawkins explained: 'Apathy is the bugbear in this district. There are two special contributory factors to this. First, we average less than 1 per cent wholly unemployed in the Wycombe district though at the moment there are more than 50 per cent of the furniture workers on short time. Second, wages are varied automatically on the issue of the cost of living index. This leaves us with a position where workers have little fear of total unemployment and they think that the wages are settled for ever. Both these provisions have their value but they do have a doping effect upon the workers, tending to reduce their interest in organisation'.

Problems of the tied wage structure and work sharing were to be examined again before the period was out but it was the political scene which occupied the stage from mid-1929 onwards. Alf Purcell was the Parliamentary Secretary of the union and MP for the Forest of Dean, and J.P. Gardner was a NAFTA sponsored MP for North Hammersmith. This apparently stable state of affairs was disturbed in April 1929 by Alf Purcell's decision not to fight the Forest of Dean constituency in the next election. He wrote to the members: 'Due to certain personal and domestic causes it has become necessary for me to change from the

Forest of Dean to Moss Side, Manchester, which latter division I hope
to succeed in securing for the Labour Party at the forthcoming General
Election.[15]

No further explanation was given, nor is there any evidence to
supplement this comment except that Alf Purcell's home was in
Manchester and that he might reasonably have wished to spend more
time with his family as he grew older. No mention of his resignation is
made in the *Monmouthshire Beacon* or the *Gloucester Journal* for the
period and the *Gloucester Echo* merely notes the reselection meeting.
'The executive of the Forest of Dean Labour Party chose a short list of 4,
Frank Hodges, ex-Secretary Miners' Federation of GB, F.W. Gold-
stone, Gen.Sec.NUT, Mr Potter, editor of *The Miner* , John Alpass,
Labour member Gloucestershire C.C. Mr A.A. Purcell, the present
member for the division is not standing'. The EC of the union were
concerned by this change of plan but loyally supported the move and
granted Alf Purcell £400 towards his candidature and £50 to J.P.
Gardner. [16].

In the event Alf Purcell lost the fight at Moss Side. 'The Catholic end
of the constituency let us down over Labour policy on public
expenditure on sites and repairs to their schools'. The final result was
Conservative 11,625 votes, Labour 9,522 and Liberal 8,191. The union
gave all the support it could with district organisers and Alex Gossip was
in good voice. Their efforts were supplemented by a 'team of students
from Manchester University'.

The loss of his Parliamentary seat led Alf Purcell to resign as
Parliamentary Secretary to the Union and J.P. Gardner, MP, took his
place. There was, however, no other suitable post within the union for
Alf Purcell and he accepted an appointment as Secretary to the
Manchester and Salford Trades and Labour Council. 'I have no excuse
to offer, except a desire to keep working inside the trade union
movement. Maybe the work I am undertaking will give me more and
better opportunities than is the case at the moment. Naturally I would
have wished to remain inside the Association but there is little or no
room under existing circumstances and I am bound to find work
elsewhere. There is nothing less than horse sense in that'. [17]

A sidelight on this affair concerns Alf Purcell's seat on the General
Council of the TUC. In February 1928 nominations were called for for
delegates to the TUC Conference of 1928. Alf Purcell was nominated
and was opposed by Alf Tomkins. In a straight fight Tomkins received
the nomination by 683 to 348 votes (5 per cent of the membership). A
variety of reliable sources within the retired membershiup of the union
have stated in private that the Organising Committee for the Furnishing
Trades of the Communist Party had not forgiven Alf Purcell for what it
saw as 'his betrayal of the working classes during the General Strike' and
taking the opportunity of his (A.A.P.'s) absence in India on a TUC

delegation 'decided to put their own man (Tomkins) in as a delegate'. It is further suggested that 'by organising the right branches to vote heavily in a situation which resulted in a notoriously low poll, they would achieve these ends'. [18]

Alf Purcell was lost to the union but not to the trade union movement. He continued as Secretary to the Trades Council until his death in 1935. He was a vigorous crusading figure, in the forefront of all union activity in the city and is remembered to this day as the most influential and effective official ever to hold that post.

The election which brought the second Labour Government to power ensured that it was in trouble from the start. It was dependent upon Liberal support and entered office as the depression struck. In the King's Speech that opened Parliament there was a promise to deal effectively with unemployment which stood at 1,163,000 or 9.6 per cent but by the end of the year it had risen to 2,500,000 or 20 per cent. Britain was still on the Gold Standard and the Chancellor of the Exchequer, Philip Snowden, was a fanatical believer in this economic measure. By July, 1931 unemployment had reached 2,750,000.

The depression and its consequential unemployment hit the furniture industry very hard indeed. Unemployment was running at over 3,000 for the autumn months of 1930, that is, over 16 per cent, a figure much reduced by work sharing below its true level. Financiallly the union was worse off than these figures might seem to indicate. Because most of the members were on short time they were paying reduced contributions.

The depression deepened even further in 1931, the industry failing to emerge from the post Christmas lull, and by March 4,600 members were out of work, some 22 per cent of membership. Funds were running low and the contribution rate was raised by 6d. per member per week in an effort to balance the outflow of funds. This availed the union little and by the end of June, with 25 per cent of members wholly unemployed, the financial situation became critical. Alex Gossip wrote to the members in July to tell them just how desperate the crisis had become: 'Our sick fund is £100 overdrawn and the general fund is £3,500 overdrawn. If our losses continue at this rate and if account is taken of the loss of contribtions of those out of work, then this fund could be requird to pay out £60,000 in this year alone, which it would be totally unable to do.[19]

Even the hard times practice of work sharing had broken down. C.F. Hawkins wrote: 'There is just not enough work to share. In Wycombe we have 800 members out of work and the rest have been on short time for over a year. Branch secretaries, knowing the circumstances which prevent members meeting their branch dues are heartbroken at the prospect of scratching them off the books. The question of how long the Association can continue the brave struggle to pay out-of-work pay without jeopardising the organisation for wage bargaining and fighting purposes is now being seriously discussed by a number of branches in the area'.[20] In September, with 4,300 unemployed, the worst fears of the Association were realised. NAFTA's London members were locked out.

The background to the dispute dated from 1929. Trade in London at least had been reasonably bright that year and by consultation the union had been able to persuade the employers to abandon the sliding scale arrangement in favour of a fixed rate subject to revision by negotiation. The rate had been fixed at 1/9d. per hour and while elsewhere it fell over the next two years to 1/6d. or 1/7d. per hour London workers retained their premium rate. The London employers now demanded a 2d. per hour reduction in the rate and gave one month's notice of this change.

NAFTA was, despite its financial situation, prepared to fight this demand. The ground was cut from under its feet by the AUU who, with funds as low as those of NAFTA, agreed the reduction without a fight. Potentially, NAFTA could have had 4,000 members out on the streets. In the event only 761 were locked out for refusing the new working rates. The men and women concerned were out for two weeks when the employers offered to phase the reductions in wages in two stages, 1d. immediately and 1d. in the spring of 1932. Mass meetings were held of all London members. In each case the members refused to accept the compromise. They also refused to accept an additional levy of 1/- per week on those working (there was a 4/- per week levy on London members who were still in employment). In the light of this con-tradictory response and with an eye on its depleted funds the Association had no alternative but to close the dispute down and accept the employers' terms. As Alf Tomkins, London Organiser, stated: 'The response to the 4/- per week strike levy has been simply awful'.

At a national level the economic situation was a cause for grave concern. A run on gold by foreign investors in the spring had allowed Snowden to appoint the May Commission to investigate the nation's finances. This was even more dire in its predictions than he had hoped for and in its report in July 1931 proposed savings of £96 million, of which £65 million was to come from cutting unemployment benefit by 20 per cent, raising contributions and applying a means test, £13 million from cutting teachers salaries and £8 million from cutting public works expenditure for the maintenance of employment.

Not only was this series of cuts abhorrent to Snowden's Parliamen-tary Labour Party colleagues. The very dire nature of its pronostications started a further run on the pound and £50 million borrowed to stop the run was soon swallowed up. The Government attempted to borrow a further £80 million which the international bankers would only make available on condition of the acceptance of the May Plan.

The Government was now at a crisis point. Ramsay MacDonald went to the King ostensibly to resign the Premiership. In fact he returned to Downing Street charged with the task of forming a National Government, including Stanley Baldwin and other Conservatives and

Liberals under his leadership. Unrepentant in his betrayal of his socialist principles he is quoted as having remarked to Snowden: 'Tomorrow every Duchess in London will be wanting to kiss me'.[21] Alex Gossip, in common with all socialists, was appalled, 'The present political situation is enough to break the hearts of all those who have worked so long to make a real socialist government possible'.

In August, Snowden introduced his emergency Budget cutting unemployment benefit by 10 per cent and public sector wages by the same amount. On 21st September, this arch-devotee of orthodox finance had to introduce a Bill suspending the Gold Standard. Thus ended the artificial basis of the financial crisis, though the crisis itself remained. The Tories now pressed for Tariffs and a General Election. Parliament was dissolved on October 7th.

In the election that followed the Labour Party was heavily defeated. Its representation in the House fell from 289 seats to 52 (46 Labour, 5 ILP, and 1 Independent) whilst the Coalition candidates polled 14,500,000 votes and won a total of 558 seats of which 471 were Tory members.

J.P. Gardner was one of the victims of this defeat. One NAFTA Member of Parliament did, however, remain; William Leonard, the Scottish Organiser and Vice President of the Scottish TUC who had fought the St. Rollox division of Glasgow at a by-election in June 1931, and who retained his seat in the 1931 debacle.

G.D.H. Cole wrote: 'The Labour Government of 1929-31 had never attempted to apply a constructive socialist policy. Caught in entanglements with the other parties which were in a position to turn it out at any moment, led by a Prime Minister set on retaining office at any price and by a Chancellor of the Exchequer who was utterly determined to resist the only measures which could have enabled it to confront the crisis, without surrendering its principles, and consisting mainly of men who had no understanding of the nature of the crisis or of the forces that were arranged to defeat them, the second Labour Government floundered from mistake to mistake'. [22]

The crisis in the nation and within the Labour Party was reflected in the financial crisis which now faced NAFTA in 1931. Unemployment had not fallen even in the buying seasons of spring and autumn and remained stubbornly stuck at 25 per cent of the membership. The High Wycombe branches proposed to the EC that NAFTA should become a 'dispute pay' only union since out-of-work support now represented such a drain on funds that it frustrated its wage bargaining functions, pointing to the failure of the London dispute as evidence to support their case. Whilst agreeing with this stance, the EC argued that the provision of Provident Benefits stablilised the union membership since members had a lot to lose by leaving the union. The French Woodworkers Union was a 'dispute only' union and was now in the process of becoming a

Provident Union only because its members 'flit in and out of the union on the eve of any trouble and leave after settlement as there are no other benefits accruing'. [23]

The nettle was grasped and the membership agreed to a swinging cut in the benefits paid by the union in an effort to save the situation.

|  | Section 1 | Section 2 | Section 3 |
|---|---|---|---|
| Out of work pay became | 10/- | 6/- and | 4/- per week |
| Dispute pay became | 20/- | 12/- and | 8/- per week |
| Contributions stayed at | 2/6d. | 1/8d. and | 10d. per week, |
| the rates having been : | | | |
| Out-of-work pay | 18/- | 12/- | 8/- |
| Dispute pay | 36/- | 24/- | 18/- |
| Contributions | 1/6d. | 1/- | 6d. |

An era had come to an end. Alex Gossip was now 69 years old but was still an ardent and effective orator and organiser. Many of the old colleagues who had fought with him to build the Association were gone and the membership had dropped to only 17,000 but the old fires of optimism and socialism were still alive to guide the union through the dark days ahead. As 1931 ended he wrote to the members: 'The year just gone has been packed full of strenuous and worrying times for all concerned and if we can read the signs of the times aright, these will undoubtedly increase and become more severe, as the Captitalist system is entering on its last lap, and we are really in the transitional period, passing from one system to another. We are the custodians of the future welfare of our class and it behoves all of us to do all we can to help the movement along. The old pioneers of progress did not trouble over what was thought of them by reactionaries, and neither should we. "All Hail the Advance Guard".'

# CHAPTER VIII

# *1932 – 1939 — Through the Dark Day*

From 1932 to 1939 the embattled situation of NAFTA continued. Its fight was less against employers than against its post-war bogey unemployment to which was added the twin evil of Fascism. As a left wing socialist organisation, it had under Alex Gossip's leadership recognised as early as 1924 the danger of Fascism to working class organisations and to democracy. From then on it fought an unremitting struggle to counter the threat at home and in Spain, and to raise trade union consciousness of the danger it represented. The equally insidious evil of unemployment reduced NAFTA in this period to its lowest membership since 1916. By careful management, dedication from within the membership and support from the 'fair' employer, the period ended with the association strong, organised and ready to enrol the many who remained unorganised in the furniture industry.

NAFTA started 1932 with a membership of just over 18,000 of whom 4,869 or 26.3 per cent were out of work. By February, notoriously the worst month for unemployment in this still highly seasonal trade, the figure for the workless had risen to 5,653 or 30.44 per cent of membership and hovered just below this figure for the remainder of the year. It is a commonly held belief in the furniture trade that it was NAFTA's strict adherance to a policy of 'no payment by results' for any furniture worker who wished to be a member of the union which brought the Association to such a low membership in the '30s. It is certainly true that the membership had become very conservative by this period in its attitudes to those workers in the so-called 'mass production factories'. That membership resisted a number of attempts to organise a Trade Section until 1938. But an equally cogent argument can be put that, in a period of such appalling unemployment, the prospect of a trade section, formed to fight the 'unfair employer' implied no more than a fruitless struggle and a loss of funds. Any further reduction in the funds of the union would effectively have crippled it to such an extent that the full members would have lost even the low out-of-work benefit that the union was able to pay.

As to the 'no PBR' aspect of the argument, by 1933 the union was in practice organising PBR workers wherever it could. The operative clause of the rules allowing this read that 'such workers must try to secure proper conditions, namely day rate payment, as soon as possible'. Indeed a a great many of the furniture workers in High Wycombe who were members of the union were working in factories in which the take-home pay was PBR related. [1]

One of the strongest proponents of the argument that non-acceptance of PBR held back the growth of NAFTA, was Jock Shanley, then organiser of the Amalgamated Union of Upholsterers, later General Secretary of AUU and subsequently Assistant Secretary of NUFTO. As Jock Shanley explained: 'The growth of the machine dominated furniture making concerns in the East and North London was considerable from the mid to late 1930's. These were not the sweated sections of the trade (which undoubtedly did exist) but rather highly organised, well capitalised concerns, in which the worker on PBR enjoyed conditions and hours comparable with those in the 'fair' firms, but in which the workers earned 2/6d. per hour or more compared to the 1/9d. per hour paid for day work. How could NAFTA organise a man to take a wage reduction! There was a sweated section of the industry and this had to be tackled eventually. In those firms the employee was truly exploited and this sector was a threat to the selling base of the PBR firms just as they threatened the selling base of the day rate firms'. [2]

This argument is generally accepted by many commentators on the furniture industry but it has to be treated with some caution. The firms referred to employed no more than 7,500 workers and came to their peak in the late 30's when NAFTA was regaining its membership. Moreover, it disregards the effect of unemployment and short time working which in the early 30's reached unprecedented levels for the furniture industry. 'No PBR' was *a* causal factor but it is not proven that it was *the* causal factor. One feature, however, within the overall context of unemployment in the 30's is the apparent disparity between the official statistics for unemployment in the furniture trade and the levels of unemployment amongst NAFTA members, as can be seen in the following table:—

Percentage Unemployment in All Trades, Among Furniture Workers
and among NAFTA members, 1939 [3]

| Year | Unemployment all Trades | Unemployment Furniture Workers | Unemployment NAFTA Members |
|------|------------------------|-------------------------------|----------------------------|
| 1930 | 14.6 | 10.0 | 16.0 |
| 1931 | 21.5 | 19.0 | 25.0 |
| 1932 | 22.5 | 21.7 | 28.1 |
| 1933 | 21.3 | 20.6 | 29.3 |
| 1934 | 17.7 | 15.4 | 22 |
| 1935 | 16.4 | 13.9 | 18.32 |
| 1936 | 14.3 | 11.6 | 15.0 |
| 1937 | 11.3 | 9.8 | 12.7 |
| 1938 | 13.3 | 13.4 | 13.2 |
| 1939 | 11.7 | 12.8 | 15.9 |

The answer to this riddle lies in the nature of the furniture industry and its output. NAFTA membership in the nineteen thirties was concentrated by and large in those firms who were at the 'better 'end of the trade. In these firms the employee was paid at a day rate for a skilled output destined for a customer who bought on quality rather than on price. In the depressed years of the thirties such customers were rarer and the financial constraint on all classes made purchasing decisions much more dependent on price. The 'quality trade' suffered more severely in the downturn in retail activity than the 'volume trade'. The volume trade as far as furniture was concerned was almost totally composed of firms who paid their employees on PBR. Insofar as the pursuit of the purity associated with day rate payments led to a membership which suffered a high level of unemployment, the case made by Shanley and others is well founded; in all other respects the arguments are not substantiated.

A further consideration which contradicts the general 'no PBR' line is revealed in the membership figures [4]. In the 1932-1939 period annual recruitment to the union was as high as at any time after the first world war and reached a peak of 5,000 new members in 1937 alone. This was the period in which advocates of the line would have suggested that NAFTA was failing to recruit from the 'mas production' factories. Such high recruitment was, however, not reflected in overall membership since it was matched by equally high turnover of membership arising from arrears of union dues. Losses of members due to the unemployment and short time working of the period must surely lay heavy emphasis on these factors as of prime importance in the low membership of the union at this time.

The foregoing arguments should not be taken to imply that NAFTA was in any way complacent during this period. The contrary is true. In an effort to resolve the problem of unorganised workers and declining membership, NAFTA held a rules revision conference in Leeds in August 1932. The main result was a proposal to create two trade sections, in addition to the three normal membership grades, with contributions of 9d. and 5d. per week respectively, with dispute benefit only payments of 18/- and 10/- per week. Despite this national conference decision the membership rejected the proposal on a ballot by 2,483 votes to 925. [5]

C.F. Hawkins, writing in the journal after this vote, explained that as far as High Wycombe was concerned, this was a very short sighted decision. 'In Wycombe employers state 'they are all trade unionists when there is any trouble on'. For these workers the unemployment benefit does not appeal to them, the compulsory insurance scheme has dished us of that inducement to membership. Up to now there are no other unions functioning for furniture workers, but some scheme must be evolved to attach to our union those thousands of workers for purely trade organising purposes, before a new trade section appeal from another union steps in and complicates our control of working conditions'. C.F. Hawkins was not being particularly prophetic or alarmist in making this statment. He was, as an organiser, only too well aware that with the substantial majority of the workers in the trade unorganised, this threat did exist. It was, in a year or so, to materialise in the form of the Transport and General Workers Union. [6]

Concerned as it was over employment and unemployment, the refusal of NAFTA to participate in the TUC demonstration on unemployment in the spring of 1933 does at first appear to be out of character. This was not the case; 'The EC could not, and has no intention of trying to place any obstacle in the way of members taking part in the TUC and Labour Party Joint Demonstration re unemployment, but so far as the EC are concerned, as an executive it is not taking part. These joint bodies are debarring the organised unemployed, i.e. the National Unemployed Workers Committee Movement, from participating and have declared openly they will use the police to prevent those who try'.

NAFTA was an outcast so far as its relationships with the TUC and the Labour Party were concerned. It had moved from being an influence at the very centre of the Labour Party and TUC organisation, together with other left wing organisations, to the outer fringes. Such a position was not without its perils, but at least it could be said that the leadership, through this dark period of labour history, kept faith with the ideals and principles of socialism, whilst all around were compromising theirs.

By February 1933, however, unemployment had risen to 32.6 per cent of a membership now down to 15,800, and by March there were 5,363 members out of work, some 34 per cent. [7] For the rest of the year these dreadful figures remained nearly constant and the cost of this situation in terms of human misery coupled as it was with the application of the notorious means test, can only be contemplated with dismay. The leadership, impotent to change the situation, nevertheless looked to the formation of a Trade Section as a long term answer to the problem, if not in whole, then at least in part. Alex Gossip wrote 'Our membership is now down to about 15,000 and 5,000 of these are out of work, 5,000 are on short time, working 28 hours per week or less, and so are only paying half contributions. This only leaves 5,000 mnembers paying full contributions. In the light of these facts the membership should recognise the utter impossibility of being able to continue paying even the present very much reduced out of work benefit (10/-, 6/- and 4/- per week). The EC has been reluctantly compelled to face the fact that it might be in the best interests of all concerned if this undertaking to pay unemployment benefit was abandoned altogether. [8]

'Efforts must be made', he went on, 'to gain control of all factories and workshops working under conditions other than covered by our agreement, and this applies to all workers even though they be on piecework or other systems other than plain time work. It must be recognised that such workers so organised must try to secure the proper conditions as soon as possible, and having secured trade union rates and conditions, must not revert to their previous conditions. If we are to maintain and improve what we have already secured, we must have a thoroughly organised industry in which no non-unionist will be allowed to participate.' The statement went on to ask the membership to vote again on the setting up of a Trade Section, but the proposal was again rejected, this time by 2,187 votes to 1,070.

A final attempt was made by the Association in 1934 to change the situation. 'The Executive has had under consideration the present position of the union and the difficulties which have to be faced in securing new members and retaining those who have been erased for arrears particularly in High Wycombe. There has also been a very serious reduction in funds due to the fact that the unemployed members need not pay General Fund contributions, and that those on 28 hours or less pay only half contributions. This has caused a reduction of £10,000 in funds in 1933 as compared to 1932. Even with the benefits cut, the debt of the General Fund to the Tool Insurance Fund has increased to £4,878 at the end of 1933, with no prospect of any real improvement in the trade. You are asked to vote for the setting up of a Trade Section with contributions of 10d. per week, with the benefits confined to Dispute Pay, General Benefit and Legal Aid where necessary'. The vote was again against the EC by 2,329 votes to 984. With this final rejection the EC left the question until trade improved and turned to other equally pressing problems.

One of these was that Irish nationalism was entering the area of trade union organisation. A newly formed Irish Union of Woodworkers, based on Dublin, was recruiting members from the wood achinists, the joiners and from NAFTA 'by beating the nationalist drum, which should never be allowed to interfere with trade union solidarity and is essentially reactionary in outlook', wrote Alex Gossip, The threat as far as NAFTA was concerned was not too great and the eventual total loss to the new union was less than one thousand members.[9]

In London the fight to maintain wages and conditions was built round the concept of the 'fair firm' which complied with the local agreements and in consequence was able to bid for the very important cooperative trade. In this connection Alf Tomkins invented a new phrase to describe the firm applying unfair working conditions. 'Yet another 'Rat Shop' has been discovered supplying bedroom suites to the London Cooperative Society. This shop is paying 1/1d. per hour as top rate on a 54 hour week'. The London rate at the time was 1/7d. per hour for a 47 hour week.

In 1934 it was the declining internal strength of the union in the furniture trade which gave it more concern than any other issue. With only 14,900 members the worst fears of C.F. Hawkins were realised when the Transport and General Workers Union recruited the workforce in the factory of Everest Upholsterers of Long Eaton near Nottingham. This action did not go unchallenged. NAFTA, the Machinists, and the Upholsterers took the TGWU before a special committee of the TUC. The TGWU was represented by Arthur Deakin 'who showed himself in a very bad light, and attempted to act the dictator, and if all officers of that union are like this, we can readily understand the deep discontent which exists amongst so many of his members'. The TUC Chairman, Arthur Shaw, ruled in favour of the furniture workers and the TGWU was ordered to desist from all future attempts to recruit from this trade 'since it is already well represented and organised'. [10]

To make matters worse, the unemployment situation in the trade, previously brightened by regions where the out-of-work were relatively few, began in 1933 to show that the situation was almost equally bad everywhere. The following table for August 1933 shows how widespread and evenly distributed unemployment in furniture making had become.

Furniture Trades

Regional Breakdown of Unemployment

| Number of Branches Reporting | of Which Branch Membership | Number of Members Unemployed | % of Members Unemployed |
|---|---|---|---|
| 29(11) | 3,959 | 1,356 | 31.7 |
| 17(2) | 1,952 | 588 | 30.1 |
| 6(5) | 720 | 198 | 27.5 |
| 29(7) | 2,419 | 658 | 27.2 |
| 13(3) | 1,121 | 253 | 22.6 |
| 9(4) | 1,021 | 351 | 34.4* |
| 10(4) | 662 | 162 | 24.5 |
| 19(3) | 1,730 | 420 | 24.2 |

* includes Barnstaple Branch with 58.7% unemployed.
() branches not reporting

While NAFTA did not support the TUC/Labour Party unemployment demonstration of 1933 it actively endorsed the National Hunger March of 1934. 'The EC commends to the membership the following document. 'This Congress and March shall lead the working class fight against the Unemployment Bill, the Means Test and the Anomilies Act....it will lead the fight for the restoration of the 10 per cent economy cuts and for all increases in wages and a 40 hour week.

Unity against the starvation attacks of the National Government

Unity against the growing threat of Fascism

Unity against the sharpening threat of war'

signed: Alex Gossip, Wal Hannington, John Jagger, W. Locker, James Maxton MP, Harry Pollitt, Jack Tanner'.

The March and Congress were an unqualified success in bringing the problems of the unemployed to the attention of the southern areas of the country. Moreover it was done in such a way as to avoid the accusation of political bias. C.F. Hawkins writes; 'The unemployed workers passed through Wycombe, and, as advised, no stress was given to the viewpoints of any political party in the propaganda opportunities created by the interest in the marchers' passage through the town. Concentration was focused on the distress of the unemployed and their families, the protest against the new unemployment Bill and the appeal to the Government to extend the benefits. There was undivided support for this which assisted the solidarity committee and other comrades to collect and distribute funds for food etc., the church authorities providing the halls for sleeping accommodation'.

Alex Gossip wrote; 'The Great Hunger March and Congress has been a complete success and has drawn attention to the question of unemployment as nothing else could possibly do, and there was no mistaking the burning desire for all united efforts to force this matter to the forefront. The Capitalist press tried to belittle the great turn out in Hyde Park which, notwithstanding the better weather, was some 100,000. Some of the papers gave the figure of 50,000 and the notorious *Glasgow Bulletin* even went down to 10,000.

The end of 1934 saw unemployment in the industry down to 2,863 members or 19.1 per cent but this upturn in the economy was not to be taken as an improvement for all. Only 655 of those unemployed were in benefit. The remainder were long term unemployed who had run out of the twelve weeks benefit allowed in any one calendar year. [11] A similar pattern of unemployment remained a problem throughout the pre-war period as these November figures show:—

| Year | Unemployed | % | In Benefit | |
|------|-----------|------|-----------|---|
| 1935 | 2,280 | 14.1 | 631 | |
| 1936 | 2,016 | 11.7 | 609 | |
| 1937 | 2,261 | 11.2 | 718 | |
| 1938 | 3,058 | 13.8 | 835 | |
| 1939 | 3,767 | 17.8 | 1,113 | (start of war) |
| 1940 | 1,953 | 8.5 | 566 | |

Yet cheerful news broke through. East End United Branch 15, had started the '15 Sports Club' and this had been extended to the organisation of camping holidays for the members of the branch. Alf Tomkins reported on a visit to the Club's holiday camping site in North Devon. 'Over 100 campers in a glorious setting. The organisation seemed to run with pleasureable ease, a real example of comradeship, each taking his turn at the work required to be done, and the spectacle of staid and soberly minded furniture workers disporting themselves in the sunshine, in shorts and bathing costumes, made me proud of the example which had been set by this branch of our union'.

Annual holidays with pay were the exception rather than the rule at this time. Indeed two weeks holiday with pay did not arrive for all the furniture workers until 1946, though some employers did give at least one week's paid holiday. The leadership of NAFTA began to press for holiday with pay for all workers in 1935 and was particularly active in pursuit of this aim by 1937. It received help in its campaign from an unexpected source, the employers' magazine of the furniture industry The *Furniture Record*. In an editorial it stated; 'Being convinced that the time must come when every employee will receive a holiday with pay the *Furniture Record* intends as part of a strong and unhesitating editorial policy to advocate the adoption of this reform throughout the furniture industry, believing that its institution will react to the ultimate good of employers and employed alike. It must react to the ultimate good of employers and employed alike. It must be remembered that legislation to enforce holidays with pay is by no means outside the bounds of possibility, and in this as in so many other directions, it is preferable for reforms to be made voluntarily than to have them forced upon one by government action, with its natural sequel of forms to fill up and inspectors to ensure compliance.[12]

Self interest was clearly mixed with altruism and an evident aversion to the government officials invading the premises of furniture manufacturers. Such an antipathy to officialdom could be harnessed at a local as well as national level, and in the town of High Wycombe, Charlie Hawkin, Ted Rolfe, and other union officers of the district produced a duplicated paper - *The Furniture Worker* - from 1933 until 1936. Priced 1d. and issued monthly it offered information, promoted solidarity within NAFTA and fought campaigns of an essentially local nature. It was, however, not adverse to a little backhanded blackmail as the following extract illustrates:-

'There is a furniture factory not far from Abercrombie Avenue where to tell the truth one would never believe a factory inspector had ever entered....Fancy, just fancy, 130 men use two dilapidated lavatories, whilst the others are unusable....as for the drains, they and carbolic have never met....what is amazing is the dampness of the place, fire insurance premiums must be very low here as the place would never burn, for when tools rust, and glue won't dry, it's time something was done by the factory inspector and such places condemned or renovated....'
and the article winds up:-

'We don't want to jolt the factory inspector. We don't want to come out publicly with the firm's name but we do intend the above items to be seen into'.
They were seen to and the firm not named; nor for that matter was employment lost by the imposition of a closure order. The situation was improved, which was as important at this time as the improvement themselves.

Improvements, whether they were in unemployment or in factory conditions did not come from the ballot box in 1935. Only 22,000,000 voted out of an electorate of 31,373,000. The Labour Party polled

8,326,000 votes and won 154 seats; the Liberal Nationals took 33 seats, the Independent Liberals 21 and the Tories 387.

Willie Galacher, Communist, won East Fife but Harry Pollitt 'one of the ablest men in this country', as Alex Gossip described him, was beaten in East Rhondda. William Leonard retained his St. Rollox seat but as a Labour Party and Cooperative candidate he was debarred from taking a position as Parliamentary Secretary for the union. J.P. Gardner, the sitting Parliamentary Secretary, had been unable to obtain a constituency and the union was again without members either in Parliament or the General Council of the TUC. Had there been such representation they might perhaps have been embarassed by the fury with which NAFTA greeted the Knighthood granted to Walter Citrine, General Secretary of the TUC in that year's Honours List.

Alex Gossip led the attack; 'We note with strong disapproval, of the acceptance of so-called honours by Mr. Citrine and other Labour representatives from a notoriously anti-Labour-Tory Government. Be it noted, honours of this kind are only given for services rendered against the workers and in favour of capitalist interests. What a betrayal of our class! [13]

The EC minutes note that 'many letters have been received from branches congratulating the General Secretary on his opposition to the acceptance of Mr. Citrine of a Knighthood which can only be construed as being given by a Tory Government for services rendered to capitalism. At the request of those branches, the TUC has been written to by the EC protesting against his acceptance of what is nothing short of a bribe'. [14]

At the Brighton Labour Party Conference that year it must have come as no surprise to Alex Gossip, as delegate for NAFTA, that 'the Labour Party attempted to withold my credentials at first'. The excuse, he claimed, 'that I absolutely refused to bow the knee to the demand that I should cease all connection with the Relief Committee for the Victims of Fascism'. This was yet another organisation banned to Labour Party members. Attempts had been made two years earlier to expel Alex Gossip from the Labour Party for his involvement in proscribed organisations; attempts which failed. Gossip had never been an individual member of the Labour Party but rather a founder member of the ILP, while his attendance at conferences was as representativce of his union. [15]

In their continued reaction to the acceptance of honours from the Tory Government NAFTA were co-proposers of a 'mild composite resolution, as compared to ours, on the acceptance of Knighthoods etc., from a Tory Government which was eventually carried against the platform' and to the undoubted embarassment of the executive of the Party'.

Since so many of the organisations with which Alex Gossip was actively involved were proscribed by the Labour Party because of their Communist domination, it is important to place into perspective the CP of Great Britain in the thirties and the people who were members of the party or associated with it. Some clue to the situation of the time is expressed by John Middleton Murr y. 'To believe think, to pursue, to give oneself to Communism in this country does not mean to become a Communist, it means to devote oneself to the task of making the Labour Party Marxist and revolutionary once more. The English Communist is the man who works with those and for those who aim at a real social revolution. Intellectually, spiritually, ethically, the choice before the conscious Englishman is to be a Communist or nothing'.[16]

As to the proscription of organisations regarded as covers for Communist Party activities Alex Gossip made his position clear in the debate on the subject at the 1933 Labour Party Conference. Emanuel Shinwell referred to them as 'twopenny-halfpenny organisations'. If either of the Labour Governments 'done the job they were elected to do', claimed Gossip, 'then the so-called twopenny-halfpenny organisations would have been absolutely unnecessary'. [17]

The anti-establishment line was continued unabated in the *Monthly Reports* . General Secretary noted 'with deep approval that over 200 members of the Postal Workers Union at their recent conference protested against the General Secretary of the General Council of the TUC being received as a fraternal delegate. When by a small majority he was permitted to speak, the protesters left the hall. [18] They objected, of course, to the acceptance of a Knighthood from a Tory Government which has shown itself as the bitter enemy of the organised workers, and his (Walter Citrine's) pitiful attempts to defend his action only made matters worse'. Such public statements and public displays created many enemies for the Furniture Union in the TUC and it could also be construed as a narrow and vindictive witch-hunt of the very type which the union so much deplored. Gossip would have nothing of this. 'Such bonuses which enamate from a political party which introduced the Trade Union Act of 1927, the Sedition Act, the means test, and which barely veils its support for Fascism are not bestowed for nothing. We heartily applaud our Postal Worker brothers and sisters'.

A similar devotion to principle by the Association is evidenced by its attitude to the Coronation of 1937. 'The EC has decided to return the Coronation Tickets to the TUC. There were several free tickets for standing room and also a few at 15/- each for a seat without any overhead covering. We do not think it is for the trade unions to take part in glorified circus processions, got up in the interests of capitalism'. To the NAFTA leadershp Royalty was synonymous with capitalism and the capitalism of the thirties ensured that never less than one-in-ten of its members were unemployed or that upholsteresses who made the cushions for the coronation chairs were paid £1.19s.2d. per week for 47 hours of work. [19]

The unemployment of the times made strikes for improved wages and conditions impractical. Other than a strike of upholsteresses, there were only two disputes in this period of any size. The first of these was at High Wycombe in 1933. After the Christmas break an employer discharged twelve of his employees on the grounds that he had no work for them. Not only was this in breach of the work sharing agreement; G.R. Hawkins was clear that 'the method of selection of the twelve would bear no other explanation except a conspiracy to break up the shop organisation, as nine of the twelve functioned as shop committee men'. The remaining 100 workers came out in sympathy and all were out of work for three weeks before all were reinstated. 'No blacklegs were obtained, the workers of other factories made weekly collections for the fighting fund in response to our meal time factory gate meetings'. This response to the 'no blacklegging' policy was especially gratifying to the union as there were over 1,000 furniture workers signing on at the Labour Exchange in High Wycombe at the time. Times were hard and the authorities were merciless in their application of the rules of the 'dole', the 'subsidised idleness' as the well-to-do described it. In Wycombe that year 'the child of a furniture worker on Transitional Benefit was run down and killed by a motor car in the morning. It happened that his benefit was being received in the afternoon. The death of the child was known to the Committee and the amount of Transitional Benefit reduced the same day'. [20]

The Scottish Strike of 1936 was larger and more protracted than the Wycombe dispute. It started on May 25th over the refusal of the employers to grant 1d. an hour increase. Initially, it affected some 2,100 workers but this number very quickly fell as firms involved granted the increase, led by the Scottish Cooperative Society factories, on the intervention of Willy Leonard MP, the ex-Scottish organiser. The strike lasted until 17th August by which time only 490 NAFTA members were still out. The strike was won on the basis of an increase of one-halfpenny an hour immediately, with a further halfpenny per hour to be paid from the beginning of the following December.

The upholsteresses' strike in London has been mentioned earlier and affected the women working in the West End workshops of Maples, Heals, Waring & Gillow etc. These women were all on time work. The task of organising was very difficult, particularly in the early thirties where short time working was the rule rather than the exception and victimisation of the organisers within the shops easily accomplished. By 1935 trade was improving. The women had become 100 per cent organised within the AUU and presented their request for an increase from the exisiting rate of 10d. per hour. The employers offered one farthing per hour on a take it or leave it basis and the women struck work. The response was 'magnificent; everyone came out, there was no blacklegging and everybody did their picket duty in the most atrocious weather'. After twelve days and with the assistance of the General Secretary E. Wildson and the Organiser Jock Shanley an increase of 1d. an hour was won. [21]

The poor trading of the thirties precluded any major changes in the tecnhnology of the furniture industry. Innovation and experimentation in a period of depression was regarded as a commercial quicksand. The only area to which this did not apply was in polishing, where the spraying of nitrocellulose became the universal method for finishing the furniture. It was, however, but slowly accepted by the workers, as C.F. Hawkins notices. 'Our polishing members are still not coming to terms with nitro cellulose spraying. There is nothing yet to produce a smooth, bright durable finish equal to pure polishing (French Polishing) but the hire purchase layouts and big buyers of furniture will not pay the cost of it. Art in polishing and skilled handcraft in making is fading out under mass production. We must, therefore, adapt ourselves to the new methods. Any of the firms making finishing products will send a demonstrator anywhere. Why not invite all of them in turn to the branch? However, the work is going to be done, we must fight for the opportunity to do it at our rate'. [22]

At this time, a sideboard which was polished in the traditional French Polishing method took nine and a half hours to finish after staining by the women labourers. When the same sideboard was finished in nitrocellulose spray it took twenty-five minutes, and even that short time was subsequently reduced. [23] The scourge of the polishers, dermatitis, was reduced by the introduction and use of barrier creams. 'At the start of the morning and the afternoon shift, the foreman came round and squeezed some barrier cream on to your hands. You rubbed it in while he was there; not everyone liked it, but it did stop the dermatitis and was much better than the old system of washing your hands in a bucket of washing soda at the end of each shift'.

If the problem of unemployment seemed practically insoluble to the leaders of organised workers in the nineteen thirties, the other evil of the time, Fascism, was one which could be exorcised by 'all militant peoples' provided they presented a united front. [24] As already noted, Alex Gossip had with great perception recognised the evil potential of Fascism and warned his members against it as early as 1924. 'There are two Fascist movements in Great Britain. British Fascisti Ltd. and the British Empire Fascisti. The latter is more secretive but nonetheless dangerous. The British Fascisti are organised into units A, B & C. Each unit (A) consists of seven members under an officer whose duty it is (i) to take active measures against the revolutionary elements in their own districts; (ii) for the purposes of swift mobilisation in the event of a general strike. [25]

These units form a troop, under a troop officer, three troops form a company and three companies a division. Units (B) are comprised of owners and drivers of vehicles of all descriptions; units (C) are used for the purposes of propaganda and publicity. In their publications the Fascisti have openly stated that if the soldiers are not used against the workers in the case of an industrial dispute occurring whilst a Socialist Government is in power, then the value of the British Fascisti would be demonstrated'. Alex Gossip comments 'This appears to mean that they will stop at nothing in their defence of the idle rich'.

It was, however, the arrival of Mussolini and later of Hitler on the international scene which concentrated the minds of left wing leaders on the problem of Fascism. Douglas Hyde comments; 'The shock to the world Communist leaders caused by Hitler's virtual destruction of the mighty German Communist Party was terrific. If this could happen, then anything was possible....The new situation created by the Nazis' successes ended all dissention on the left. It resulted in the tactic of the Popular Front, the decision to enlist the aid of the middle classes, the intellectuals'. John Strachey took the point further; 'This swirling stream of world events is now beginning to have its effect in Great Britain. In less than a year it has set up a remarkably strong current of opinion in favour of the accomplishment of the unity of the British working class by the acceptance of the British Communist Party's recent application for affiliation to the Labour Party'. [26], [27]

Alex Gossip was at the centre of such moves, but his idealism was leavened with pragmatism in his recognition of the dangers of Fascism to his members. 'The Hitler regime in Germany is a distinct menace to the British Trade Unionist, as with their murderous attacks and tortures on political opponents and trade unions, and their determination to cripple the power of the unions and reduce wages to the lowest level, they hope to capture the markets of the world and their competition will make our position as organised British workers much more difficult than it is at present - and that is hard enough. Support the Anti- Fascist Movement'. [28]

He returned to this theme of economic warfare in the following month. 'We equally condemn the murderous followers of Hitler, Hitler himself, and those who are using him as a tool for their own ends in Germany. This is a matter which directly effects the British workers as Fascism aims at reducing the standard of life amongst the workers. They have succeeded in Italy and are attempting the same thing in Germany....In Germany though, just as we know here, in spite of the TUC and the EC of the Labour Party, there is springing up the United Front'. [29]

In 1933, however, the threat of Fascism to workers' organisations and to democracy was as an international rather than a United Kingdom problem. To some extent the threat became a vehicle for the proposals for a United Front and with it the acceptance of the Communist Party and other proscribed organisations into the fold of mainstream Labour Party politics. Indeed, this aspect of the struggle is rather more emphasised in Alex Gossip's messages to the membership than warnings of a distinct and identifiable threat at home. 'We protest against and condemn all those who are attempting at this present time to disrupt the workers and prevent them from showing a United Front against the war mongers and oppressors and exploiters of the people, and we deeply regret that the National Joint Council of the Labour Party Executive and the General Council of the TUC should lend themselves to disruptive tactics. We urge all our members to cooperate with those who through the anti-war and anti-Fascist United Front organisations are playing their part in trying to prevent any further murderous onslaughts on our class'. [30]

The tendency on the left at this time to equate capitalism with Fascism is reflected in the conclusions reached at the European Workers Anti-Fascist Congress held in Paris in June, 1933. Bill Zak and Bernard Rockman were the delegates from the London furnishing trades branches at this meeting of 3,400 delegates from all European countries. The conclusions reached by the Congress were that 'the fight against Fascism was, and meant, the intensification of the fight against capitalism, and for the overthrow of the capitalist system with a united front'.

A year later the problem of Fascism had come much closer to home with the growth of Mosley's Black Shirts. Not only was their whole philosophy utterly abhorrent to the leadership of NAFTA but in particular their obnoxious anti-semitism was a frontal attack on the furniture workers who as a group had one of the highest Jewish memberships of any organised group of workers.

The display of Fascism and the behaviour of the Black Shirts at Mosley's Olympia rally caused Alex Gossip to write to the Home Secretary; 'We have entered our strongest possible protest against the brutalities of the hired bullies of Mosley at Olympia, London. This conduct is typical of Hitler, Mussolini and others of a similar ltype'. He went on to warn the membership; 'Fascism here must be smashed, or it will smash all the organisations built up by the workers for their protection'. [31]

The threat of violence to meet violence was untypical of Gossip's normal reactions as a convinced pacifist and was a clear measure of his concern. That this fear was not shared by all others within the country was itself a concern and he was at pains to point out to the membership that the traditional British right of freedom of speech was a mistaken concept when applied to Fascists. 'If we want to preserve our trade unions, our cooperative societies, our political parties etc., here in Great Britain we must advocate and work for a real United Front of all militant people to combat the enemy and we must not treat this murderous movement as if it were a genuinely sincere one but treat it as we would a gang of blacklegs and scabs'. [32]

The membership saw Fascism as a menace to be fought in positive terms as their attitude to Spain was to show. It did not at this time share the leadership's wholehearted approval of the United Front. 'The EC has had under consideration correspondence from the Communist Party relative to their desire to affiliate to the Labour Party. On the question of War and of Fascism it would appear to be virtually necessary for unity. The EC have decided to submit the matter to those members who pay Political Levy. Are you in favour of supporting the affiliation of the Communist Party of Great Britain with the Labour Party? [33]

The vote was 239 in favour and 193 against - a majority of 46. In 1936 only one-in-ten paid the political levy, i.e. 1,850 members from a total union strength of 17,830. A vote representing only 20 per cent of those paying the political levy was evidently somewhat exiguous. Nevertheless the leadership carried it as a mandate to the Labour Party and Trade Union Congress of that year though in both instances failed to have the resolutions accepted.

Attitudes began to change, however, when in 1936 Spain became the amphitheatre in which democracy and Fascism fought its first battles. Alex Gossip wrote to his members; 'The vile attempt now being made by the aristocratic military clique and the Fascists to obtain power in Spain is being gallantly resisted by the organised workers there, who are receiving support from their comrades in other countries'. 'Branches are collecting money in aid of our Spanish comrades who are resisting the Fascist attacks on their liberties and lives. The Spanish Embassy has been informed of our best wishes for the success of the Government and trust that the Fascist rebels will get what they richly deserve viz; a complete and overwhelming defeat. The Prime Minister has been written to urging him to summon Parliament in order that Great Britain may do all possible to prevent the Spanish Fascists aided as they are by Germany and Italy from securing victory over the Spanish Government'. [34]

This opposition to Fascism earned NAFTA the accolade of an attack in the December 6th issue of *East London Pioneer*, a Fascist newsheet - 'a scurrilous rag' as Alex Gossip described it. In an article by John Beckett an ex-Labour MP, 'now a miserable tool of the Fascists', the article attempted to establish that it was because of the union, of NAFTA and Jewish employers, that long hours and low wages are prevalent in the East End Furniture Trade'. [35] Alex Gossip readily accepted that such conditions did exist, in spite of the unions, and arose among Gentile as well as Jewish employers and affected Gentile as well as Jewish employees. The furniture trade in parts of East London was a 'sweated trade' but it would take more time and powerful allies before the furniture unions were able to tackle this problem successfully.

In 1937 furniture workers were among those who left the country to fight for Republican Spain in the International Brigade. 'We desire to place on record our highest appreciation of the seven members of No.15 Branch (East End United) who have volunteered to go to Spain to help fight the Fascist menace and to protect the Freedom and Liberty, not only of Spanish workers, but of the workers of the world', wrote the EC. And Alex Gossip added, 'They were given a most enthusiastic send off, and the fact that the members in question were amongst the most active and loyal in the branch, made all present more desirous if possible for their safe return when their work in Spain was successfully accomplished'. [36]

There is no record of how many members of the union joined the International Brigade but it is estimated by surviving members of the union that some 35 to 40 were involved. Neil Wood has suggested that what drew these volunteers to Spain was that 'It was the first and last crusade of the British left wing'. Louis McNiece in his poem 'I remember Spain' gives some measure of the idealism which this cause generated:- [37]

'Our blunt ideals would find their whetstones, that our spirit would find its frontier on the Spanish Front
Its body a rag-tag army.' [38]

It was a crusade born and extinguished in flames, symbolised in the bombing of Guernica. The British volunteers in Spain totalled 2,762 and they suffered appalling casualties. 543 were killed and 1,762 wounded. Little training was given nor was much training possible before volunteers were thrust into action. The results were inevitable. Joe Garber of No.15 Branch, a casualty and a veteran within four weeks in Spain, wrote of such experience from the Military Hospital in Castellan. [39]

Spain was emotive and romantic, a polarising issue around which there were no ambiguities as far as the rank and file union or Party members were concerned. This made the task of collecting funds for Spain not only simple but popular. The total sums collected by NAFTA members is not known but it was substantial and from the surviving records we know that in one Branch (No.15) over £500 was subscribed in a period of two years despite average branch unemployment of 17 per cent.

Ambivalence of thought over Spain was confined to the leadership of the Labour Party and the TUC. Their position was strongly attacked by Alex Gossip. 'We have written to Mr Walter Citrine (note - not Sir Walter Citrine) asking that Ernest Bevin's speech at the International Conference on Spain be published, owing to the conflicting statements which have appeared in the Press. Mr Bevin is alleged to have said he was voicing the opinion of British organised Labour and we naturally desire to know the attitude which 'we' have taken up on this vital question'. [40]

Citrine replied that the Conference was private and the speech could not therefore be published. 'From what has already come out of this', declared Gossip, 'Mr Bevin's comments were a direct betrayal of our Spanish comrades and most certainly did not represent the true feelings of the British worker'.

Bevin had spoken against intervention at the 1936 Edinburgh Labour Party Conference in line with the policy of other British labour leaders, who as G.D.H. Cole reported 'held off support (for Spain) because they could not assure the French of gaining British government support, and were indeed hesitant about invoking this war danger, which stronger pressure, if it had been successful, would have involved'. Alex Gossip was outraged. Spain was a watershed, a recognition that the pacifism of left wing idealism was no longer viable in the face of international Fascism. 'The pacifists from the English universities are said to be most excellent machine gunners', wrote the *Manchester Guardian* correspondent from Spain. [41]

Ideas were changing, so were the personalities, not least those in the old guard of NAFTA. Sir James O'Grady died in January, 1935. 'We regret to announce the passing away of our one time organiser, the late Sir James O'Grady who as plain 'Jim' at one time did splendid work for the Association'. The General Secretary, Assistant General Secretary and members of the EC represented the Association at the funeral. [42]

The parting of the ways from Jim O'Grady had occurred as long ago as 1921 and the ties that had bound him to the Association were those of a different age. He, with Alex Gossip, Fred Bramley, Alf Purcell and Charlie Hawkins, had laid the foundations upon which the Association had stood resolutely throughout the stormy years of the twenties and thirties. 'In his earlier days', Alex Gossip commented at the time of the funeral, 'he was one to be reckoned with in the movement. His latter years were spent in the service of the Imperial Government, a sad epitaph for a former 'genial colleague', formerly up and doing in the cause of the oppressed class to which he belongs'. [43]

Alf Purcell died on Christmas Eve 1935 at the age of 63. Starting life as a polisher he had become the General Secretary of the Amalgamated Society of French Polishers. When that society joined NAFTA he became a District Organiser, Parliamentary Secretary and MP for Coventry and later for the Forest of Dean. He had latterly been the Secretary of the Manchester and Salford Trades Council, 'carrying on that work with the energy and ability which he displayed in our own Association'. Alf Purcell's widow was left in 'rather poor circumstances' and 'in delicate health'. The Association raised over £200 for her support in addition to the monies raised by the Manchester Trades Council. [44]

The Association's Parliamentary Secretary J.P. Gardner died in August 1937, at the age of 54. A sculptor and stone carver born in Belfast he had joined NAFTA when the London Stone Carvers Society amalgamated with the Association in 1912. He was elected as MP for North Hammersmith in 1923 and held the seat until the election of 1931. In 1929 he succeeded Alf Purcell as Parliamentary Secretary and at the time of his death was the candidate for North Salford.

August 1937 also saw the resignation of H.A. Urie from the post of Assistant General Secretary because of failing health. He had joined the Alliance Union in 1884 as a member of No.6 Branch - South London Carvers - and was Secretary of that Branch from 1889 to 1893 when he was elected to the EC and served on the Executive until elected as Assistant General Secretary in 1907. In a long, loyal and hardworking career he was challenged only twice in elections for this post at the tri-annual elections, a measure of the respect and confidence that he won from the membership despite all those long years in the shadow of the General Secretary Alex Gossip.

A happier event of the year was Alex Gossip's 75th birthday in September 1937. To celebrate the event his own Branch No.2 (London West End) held a presentation and public meeting on the 17th September and No.15 Branch (East End United) Held, on behalf of the Association, a Mass Dinner and Ball. Later in the month Alex and his wife travelled to Dublin where a dinner and presentation was given on behalf of the Irish members. This was an international celebration of this great leader's birthday. Messages of congratulation came not only from within the British trade union movement but also from as far afield as Australia, America, Russia, India and Africa.

One of the honours which Alex Gossip cherished most had come in 1934 when he was made a Freeman of the Borough of Fulham, his home for so many years. In his speech on receiving this honour he noted with characteristic candour; 'I have been in the habit of receiving more kicks than anything in my years of militancy. I appreciate the honour you have unanimously conferred upon me. There is an old saying that a prophet is without honour in his own country. This is not true, otherwise I should not be receiving this honour'. [45]

The election for the vacant post of Assistant General Secretary was won by Alf Tomkins, Organiser District No.1 (London ) and the runners-up in the final ballot became Organiser No.1 District (Bernard Rockman) and of the London District Management Committee, (Bill Zak). The vacant Parliamentary Secretary post was filled by F.E. Sweetman who later became the Labour candidate for Chatham.

The political fund which supported both national and local labour candidates was by this time at a very low ebb. Had all the members contracted in in 1937 £2,000 would have been available. In fact only £164 was contributed in that year.

Table

Contributions to Political Fund: 1919 - 1939

| Year | £ | Year | £ | Year | £ |
|---|---|---|---|---|---|
| 1919 | 320 | 1926 | 803 | 1933 | 202 |
| 1920 | 592 | 1927 | 744 | 1934 | 192 |
| 1921 | 676 | 1928 | 605 | 1935 | 180 |
| 1922 | 711 | 1929 | 578 | 1936 | 185 |
| 1923 | 849 | 1930 | 500 | 1937 | 164 |
| 1924 | 950 | 1931 | 340 | 1938 | 166 |
| 1925 | 977 | 1932 | 225 | 1939 | 157 |

As the nineteen thirties drew to a close two problems remained as the main concerns of the union - its apparent inability to organise the unorganised in the industry and the growing spectre of war.

The furniture industry in the thirties had seen the growth of large factories in the northern and eastern areas of London, in Tottenham, Edmonton and Walthamstow. These had proved difficult if not impossible to organise in the early part of the decade. By late 1936, however, a joint campaign was mounted by NAFTA and the AUU to remedy this situation. The old problem of the past, that of acceptance of PBR, was quietly set to one side by the joint statement; 'Some Upholsterers' members favour piece work but it is not AUU policy to enforce this; the NAFTA rules provide for the organising of piece workers with an object in view of getting day work rates whenever this is possible. NAFTA agrees to allow AUU full rein to organise the London Upholsterers and the AUU has agreed to the same conditions for NAFTA where it is already in control'.

The campaign was only marginally successful. Though it aroused enthusiasm among the workers, unemployment was again increasing. There had been a number of recruiting campaigns during the period in Scotland, the North East and in particular at High Wycombe where Ted Rolfe had been brought in as an additional organiser for the period of the campaign.

The industry by the late thirties had developed a three tier structure. The highest pay packets were at the PBR firms; day rates at an acceptabale level were paid by the high quality makers and the economic conditions of the twenties and thirties had created a substantial group at which conditions and rates of pay could fairly be described as 'sweated'.

When trade in the furniture industry was good, the effect upon the market of this third group could be disregarded, but in any downturn in the economy the undercutting effect of the low wages in this sector threatened the very existence of the other 'fair' firms in a price conscious market place. The unions looked for change to rescue the exploited workers, and the employers sought change to protect their businesses, yet neither, whether by recruitment or through Federations and Trade Groups, was able to effect the substantial changes necessary to secure improvement.

The only answer lay in some form of governmental involvement in the form of a Trade Board and this solution was proposed by the 'fair' employers in 1938. The initial reaction of NAFTA was scepticism, tinged with suspicion. Its earlier experiences with a Joint Industrial Council after the 1914-18 war had failed to improve the wages paid or the conditions in the cheap end of the trade; more important was the recognition that its stance on piece work would undoubedly have to be abandoned.

The EC wrote to the membership. 'Regarding the setting up of a Trade Board. The employers are particularly keen to establish same because of the excessively bad conditions in the uncontrolled factories. Your EC is quite ambivalent about the idea, seeing much virtue in the idea, but also the problem that it means an automatic recognition of piece work. The EC is concerned that there seems to be no provision for the control of the number of learner improvers and apprentices in the industry under a Trade Board'. [46]

The response was not a rejection and the mild reference to payment by results was no more than a token gesture to past resistance to this method of payment since, as already shown, it was in practice tolerated where no alternative was practical. In all subsequent negotiations on the Trade Board the question of PBR was quietly ignored.

The next meeting on the subject was held in August when NAFTA, AUU and the Wood Machinists met the Employers' Federation on a formal basis. The joint union proposal was that they were in favour of some form of Trade Board but a self-organised and controlled body without government intervention. Their proposals were, as they must have known, flawed. A voluntary body jointly with the 'fair' employers would have achieved little since it would have lacked the legislative force of a Trade Board to deal with the 'sweaters'. There was a deep concern, however, that a Trade Board under legislation would require a number of government 'appointed members' to the Board and that these members would, almost by definition, be anti-union. The unions feared that they would find themselves in a legislative straightjacket over terms and conditions of employment with which they did not agree. They did not trust a Tory government to be fair to a working class organisation.

However, though they raised objections and produced counter

proposals, the unions were prepared to go on talking. The attitude of the Ministry of Labour was friendly, calm and judicious. All discussions set up to look at the problem were conducted by joint committees of equal numbers of employers and union officers chaired by officials of the Ministry. NAFTA and the other unions became less apprehensive and a very high level of involvement and cooperation developed between the two sides of the industry.

At the meeting on December 14th 1939 the employers and the unions unanimously accepted the introduction of a Trade Board to operate from March 1st 1940. The Agreement fixed the minimum wage to be paid to furniture workers in the United Kingdom as:- Operative males 1/7d. per hour; Labouring males 1/3d. per hour; Female operatives 11d. per hour; Female labourers 9d. per hour. All workers over the age of 17 years were to be entitled to piece work rates on the scales with a minimum of 15 per cent bonus. 47 hours was to be the standard week with all time beyond this paid at overtime rates.

The impact of the Agreement may not be fully appreciated if viewed against the conditions operating in the 'fair firms' of 1/10d. per hour for male operatives, overtime payments and a 47 hour week. Its true value appears when seen against the background of the sweat shops which it set out to eliminate. In these Alf Tomkins reported 'the hours were from 70 TO 80 per week when trade was busy with wages of 1/- or 1/1d. per hour without any overtime payment'. [47] The Trade Board Agreement was, in a very real sense, a watershed for the furniture unions. Prior to the agreement they were essentially in the embattled situation that they had occupied since their foundation. With this Agreement, however, the employers and employees in the industry enjoyed a period of industrial peace and cooperation unbroken to the present day.

The spectre of war which hung over the final negotiations hastened the conclusion of the Agreement. The war itself also presented NAFTA with a moral dilemma. As a union it had been outstanding in its opposition to Fascism at home and abroad; yet it had also an honoured and justified reputation for pacificism both from moral and political conviction.

A.J.P.Taylor has suggested that; 'Until 22nd August 1939 the Labour movement from right to left retained its old principles, or if you prefer, its old illusions. It still held the outlook of Keir Hardie, E.D. Morel, J. Brailsford and J.A. Hobson. Two simple sentences expressed it all. Imperialistic capitalism was the cause of war. Socialists should oopose both war and capitalism'. [48]

Alex Gossip precisely reflected these ideas. He wrote at the time of Munich; 'We protest against the action of the British Cabinet and Prime Minister in betraying Czechoslovakia to the German Nazis, and thereby discrediting and dishonouring our country, and not even consulting Parliament, which is kept in the dark as much as the people generally'. [49]

'A strengthened Italy and Germany will make war almost inevitable in a few years at most, and the British Government will be largely responsible'.

Alex Gossip wrote to the membership of the dilemma which faced all peace loving men at this time. 'Whenever Fascism rears up its ugly head, all sense of decency and respect for human life goes by the board, and unfortunates suffer. And yet what can one do. If no resistance is made, the suffering is no less, and life without liberty is worth nothing'. [50]

He was, however, like all left wing socialists, devasted by the announcement of the German-Soviet pact of 23rd August 1939; 'There may be some things which one may have some difficulty in understanding, as it is a bit difficult to get full details, but which we feel sure will come out right in the end'. [51] Nevertheless, he was able to assure the membership of the justice of the war which had been declared, and he did so with his characteristic perception and incisiveness; 'A mad dog has run amok with a Swastika on his arm, and full of evil desire to dominate the people of Europe and to make it wholly Fascist, and much as we detest war and opposed both the South African war and the war of 1914-18 as both were purely capitalistic and Imperialistic conflicts, there would appear to be no other course left in the present case than to use force to stop the wild career of one to whom ordinary reason does not appeal. We must be very careful and watchfull, however, against any attempt of our own rulers to use the present position to further the interests of the owning and the exploiting class, and to use our hatred of Fascism and Nazism to embroil us in an Imperialistic conquest'. [52] The pity of it all, is that Spain, Austria, Czechoslovakia, etc. were sold and betrayed by the French and British Governments and that of Germany made tremendously stronger than it was before'.

This was the last political message from Alex Gossip to the membership. Now 77 and in failing health he was able to continue in office only for a few more months to see the implementation of the Trade Board before he retired. A great leader, a great Socialist, for 34 years he had led his members through triumph and vicissitude. For Alex Gossip there is no finer memorial than the union itself. In the beginning Alex Gossip was the union and the union was Alex Gossip.

# CHAPTER IX

# *1939 – 1947 : From NAFTA to NUFTO*

The war years opened a new era for NAFTA. The contrast between the attitudes of the Association to the second world war and those which it harboured from 1914 to 1918 was very marked. The first world war was opposed by the union's leadership with substantial support from the membership. Every opportunity was taken both inside and outside the union to publicise its anti-war stance and to demonstrate its opposition. The second world war, on the other hand, it supported wholeheartedly. With one notable exception very little comment is therefore made in its journals upon the progress of the war. In the period 1939-1945 the major preoccupation of the executive committee was with the opportunity to build and consolidate a national union with national negotiation machinery - an enormous task but one which was tackled with imagination and efficiency and enjoyed deserved success.

In 1939 the union had a membership of some 20,000 and its greatest strength lay within the more craft based factories and workshops. By 1947 it had become a highly organised and centralised industrial union with 61,000 members spread across all aspects of the industry from the most modern factory to the smallest craft workshops in the land.

The implementation of a Trade Board agreement for the Furniture Industry had barely begun when the war situation decreed that the production of furniture for the civilian market should be concentrated into 150 production units only compared with the 1,500 furniture factories employing ten or more employees which had previously existed. The consequent reduction in levels of production, coupled with a shortage of furniture due to bombing, led to 'utility' furniture and rationing. 'Priority classes', that is newly marrieds, people setting up house because they were about to have children and victims of the bombing, were issued with 'dockets' which were, in effect, permits to buy furniture up to the value of a certain number of 'units', each utility unit being sold at a given price. Twenty-two articles of furniture only were produced in the utility scheme. Each of these articles had a carefully prescribed timber content, was manufactured in two qualities and usually in three designs. These designs included beds, sideboards, chairs, tables, kitchen cabinets and an armchair, but not three piece upholstered suites 'since these would have used a considerable quantity of scarce materials in their manufacture'. [1]

A Board of Trade enquiry showed that 65 per cent of housewives questioned liked utility furniture and only 20 per cent positively disliked it. Nearly all, it appeared, would have bought the utility kitchen cabinet of choice - though from 1943 there was no choice, since only 'utility' was available. The design panel which was responsible claimed with some justice 'that it is pleasant to look at and easy to keep in condition'. The materials were not, however, always of first quality since manufacturers were constrained to use whatever was available. [2] 'One purchaser of a utility sideboard claimed that when the sun shone on the back under the thin oak veneer he could distinctly see the lettering 'Apples''. [3]

'The chief complaint', notes the author of *People's War,* 'was that there was not enough to go round'. There was no fixed ration for the furniture and only enough units were issued to give the applicants the barest minimum to set up house. The maximum was, at first, sixty units for a couple, plus another fifteen for each child or expected child. In July 1944 this allowance was cut to thirty units, too little even to furnish a single room. Spending the units was an exercise in organisation. For a newly married couple in 1944, a table was six units, four chairs one unit each, a sideboard was eight units and a wardrobe twelve units which used up the whole allowance with no units left for a bed - five units for a double and six for two singles!

An unmerited degree of prejudice has grown up against the utility designs. They were developed under the guidance of a panel of eminent industrial designers and as Angus Calder states, 'were simple and serviceable, and though hardboard was used instead of plywood, and a matt finish instead of the usual high polishes, the utility pieces at their best made an aesthetic virtue out of austerity'. Indeed, it was not only on the grounds of aesthetics that the utility furniture scored. It was substantially better made than a great deal of pre-war production. Alf Tomkins commented on the introduction of the scheme that 'a useful feature of the new furniture is the fixation of constructional details, and it is generally agreed that the standard set by the return of the mortice and tenon and the dovetail instead of the crude forms of jointing which have become the rule in machine production jobs, is a feature which should be retained by Government control after the conclusion of hostilities. [4], [5]

For those factories which were designated furniture production units, a concurrent feature was the operation of the closed shop. There was in reality no compulsion in this matter but as Jock Shanley, then General

Secretary of the AUU relates, 'As soon as we knew the name of a factory which was to produce furniture under the utility scheme we sent an official down to meet the management, and told them, 'We have come to sign up all your work people as you are going on to the utility scheme. The suggestion was that it was a condition of the contract that all workers should be in the union. No one ever questioned it and we established our influence over the whole of the utility making factories very quickly'. [6]

Those factories which were not on the list of 150 units were not, however, without work. The Mosquito, a wooden aeroplane, was produced by more than 400 firms ranging from furniture makers and church pew carvers to pianoforte manufacturers. The gliders used in the invasion of Europe were among the more obvious items to be produced by the furniture industry. So great was the impact of this new production upon the furniture industry that even today parts of the G Plan factory in High Wycombe are known as the 'Glider Shop' and the 'Wing Shop'.

Other manufacturers dealt with the more mundane aspects of war production such as munitions boxes and portable buildings but the most astonishing feature of those years was the levels of output achieved and the size of contracts placed. This is most clearly exemplified by the war production of Ercol furniture which included thirty-six million tent pegs as well as other items.

The impact upon the furniture industry of the time of these new requirements can hardly be underestimated. The most important was the introduction into the industry of specialist technical advisors from agencies such as the Ministry of Aircraft Production, the advent of dispersed sub-contracting with its requirements for absolute adherance to tolerance levels in wooden components to a level never before imagained, and above all the influence upon production of the new urea ormaldehyde based glues and their accelerated curing under heat to produce a moisture resistant joint of greater strength than the wood itself. All were fundamental in establishing the technological base for the furniture trade of the post-war years, as well as the management/control function of an industry which was now based on technology rather than craft.

The one dissenting voice heard in NAFTA during the war was that of Bill Zak, Secretary of the London District Management Committee. He and Alf Tompkins were the union's delegates to the 1940 Trades Union Congress in Southport. His report of the Congress, sharply critical of the role of the General Council, was in its turn roundly criticised by Alf Tomkins. Zak was scathing in his comments on the management of Congress - 'monopolised by the platform', resulting in questions which 'did not receive consideration or proper attention'. His report ended; 'our task is still to guard against the unscrupulous employer and the encroachment of capital'. [7] Alf Tomkins took the unprecedented step of issuing a separate report. 'It would be difficult to find one delegate who attended....with the intention of representing the Trade Unionists who appointed him who would not give full praise to the General Council of the TUC for the service given to the movement. The TUC, like all other responsible administrative bodies, gives judgement on fact and consequently does not need the facility to turn a complete volte-face because of 'advice' or instructions received from outside the Trade Union Movement.'. It was well understood by those in-the-know that this latter reference was to Bill Zak's support for the anti-war People's Convention and his subsequent election as one of the 26 Members of the National Committee of that Convention at its meeting of 12th Janury, 1941. [8] There is no further reference to this incident in any subsequent union documents but it must be assumed that within the furniture union at least the People's Convention had neither impact nor lasting effect.

When the war broke out the furniture industry, though covered by a national Trade Board and Joint Industrial Council, was still essentially regulated at local level. On the employers' side there was a series of locally based societies loosely knit into a number of national, regional and trade federations. On the union side the workers were represented by the three main unions, NAFTA, AUU and the Woodmachinists, though small societies still existed as diverse as the venerable Edinburgh Society of Upholsterers and the specialist Association of Cricket Bat Makers. Agreements with the employers were still on a local basis and there were some 30 different local agreements which notionally covered the whole country but which in reality left considerable areas without any form of agreement at all. These had grown up for historical reasons which one example will suffice to illustrate. The London Agreement covered all factories within the London postal area, and the High Wycombe Agreement an area within a ten mile radius of the Guildhall in High Wycombe. In effect, an employer operating in the Uxbridge-Ruislip area was not party to any working agreement and could, in theory at least, apply any terms and conditions of employment he wished.

In reality the conditions of war emergency production applied and sets of working rules did pertain; however, it was a less than satisfactory arrangement and Alf Tomkins with his Regional Organisers and with the blessing and assistance of the other unions began the task of covering the country with labour agreements. The first step was to agree those working arrangements which operated outside the normal local areas and a series of so-called 'no-man's land agreements' were signed during 1941 and 1942.

By 1943 the employers had reorganised themselves into the British Furniture Trade Employers Confederation. The union side matched this in August of the same year by setting up the National Federation of Furniture Trades Unions with Jock Shanley (General Secretary AUU) as Chairman and Alf Tomkins (General Secretary NAFTA) as Secretary. Neither side operated on the model of the 'battle federation' of the 1930's and earlier. The war years were the start of an almost unbroken era of industrial peace in the furniture industry. Whereas the immediate pre 1914-18 years record expenditure dispute pay of 8/- and 9/- per member per year and similar sums the war; the second world war was marked by the payment of minimal average sums such as three-fifths of a penny or one-eighth of a penny, and even when disruption and strikes were at their highest in the rest of industry in 1944 the union paid out only one-sixteenth of a penny in strike support per member for the year.

It cannot be claimed that the furniture workers were particularly conscious of the part they had to play in the war effort; nor that they had any sense of being cowed into submission by the effect of Order 1305 in the summer of 1940 making strikes illegal; nor is there, despite the traditionally strong left wing bias of the union, any evidence of the Shop Stewards National Council having any effective voice either at local or national level. The inevitable conclusion is that the reason for industrial peace in this formerly turbulent industry was primarily full employment, guaranteed wages and the bonus levels obtained. This, coupled with a most effective local machinery for dispute settlement and the establishment of Joint Production Committees in most furniture factories, proved effective in resolving difficulties at a local and factory level before they were allowed to escalate. The Joint Production Committees though, set up by the Ministry of Supply to discuss at a factory level 'matters relating to production and increased efficiency' were also used throughout the furniture sector to discuss such matters as piece rates, bonuses and working conditions. While it may be mistaken to suggest that all factories were dispute free or that all JPC's were effective, there is no doubt that the situation provided an unparalleled continuity of employment for furniture workers. After the trauma of the thirties when unemployment rarely fell below 20 per cent of union membership and was often as high as 33 per cent with equal numbers on short time working, the war years represented work and a decent wage. In the absence of the militancy of 1914 among national officials, the grass roots level showed no desire to show its teeth, either to employers or to the government.

A factor in stabilising the industry was undoubtedly the adoption of a cost of living related sliding scale for wages in 1940. Coupled with bonus earnings on the continuous flow of war production the labour force saw little reason for militancy. Non-militancy in NAFTA may also have been associated with wartime dilution. This dwarfed the dilution in the first world war. By 1944 there were 9,286 women members in the union out of a total strength of 36,707. There is verbal evidence that women carried out all the tasks which had previously been the preserve of men, with the exception of the saw milling. Equal work did not mean equal pay, a situation which was taken for granted as much in the furniture factory as it was in Parliament where as late as 1944 a move for equal pay for women teachers was denounced by Churchill as 'impertinence' and abandoned as a part of Butler's new Education Bill. In furniture factories women's wages were fixed at two-thirds of the man's rate appropriate to the task. [9] There is no record of any dissent from this position which, indeed, remained normal practice until the equal pay movements of the 1970's.

By 1944 the first moves were taking place to consolidate the relationships which had developed under the umbrella of the National Federation of Furniture Trades Unions into a national union. The only dissenting voice was that of the Wood Machinists who maintained that in 1944 only 1,000 of their 20,000 members worked in the furniture industry, the remainder being in the joinery and carpentry trades. Indeed, many furniture wood machinists had never been members of the Woodcutting Machinists union, seeing NAFTA as the more logical organisation for their membership since they were furniture workers first and foremost and machinists only incidentally.

Progress towards amalgamation was, however, slow, since it was blocked during the war years by a powerful lobby which argued that with so many members in the Armed Forces and with women who could subsequently leave the trade forming such a high proportion of the current membership the decision on amalgamation should be postponed until peacetime conditions prevailed.

The Executive of the union used the wartime period to consolidate local agreements and 'no-man's land agreements' into eight regional agreements. Once again there is no record of dissent from such a move which was accepted as logical and sensible by the membership but which effectively removed a very large measure of local control over negotiation on wages and conditions. Typically, the Regional agreement for the North East Counties, covered Yorkshire, Northumberland and Durham and in one document replaced six existing local agrements.

As the war drew to a close the number of factories engaged on war production was reduced and these were added to those engaged on the manufacture of utility furniture. As in the case of the first 150 utility factories, the union grasped the opportunity to apply for and achieve 100 per cent membership wherever possible.

Concurrent with this change in the pattern of the industry there was also pressure for national agreements to cover the trade. The unions for their part had no wish to return to the catch-as-catch-can wage rates of the pre-war period. The difficulties that such a situation created not only for their members, but also for the retention of membership itself were too dreadful to contemplate, while on the employers' side there was a strong feeling that a common national base for labour rates was a most desirable position for the renaissance of the industry.

In 1945 a series of national agreements were signed for groups within the industry ranging from the National Agreement for the Blind Making Trade, to the National Agreement for the Pianoforte Trade, to the National Agreement for the Cane Willow and Woven Fibre Industry. This succession of agreements culminated in the ceremony in the Connaught Rooms, London on 31st January 1946 at which the employers, represented by the British Furniture Trade Confederation, and the unions associated in the National Federation of Furniture Trade Unions, signed the first National Labour Agreement for the Furniture Manufacturing Industry.

The Agreement, a model of clarity and even brevity, stands to this day as the reference from which all national and local negotiations in the furniture industry begin. The document is a testimonial to the perception of the main architects of the agreement. It has remained largely unchanged to the present time, well able to accommodate the varying directions in which the furniture trade has moved in the post-war years.

The agreement fixed a working week of 44 hours with appropriate overtime rates. These were minimum working rates of two shillings and twopency halfpenny per hour in London and two shillings and a halfpenny in the rest of the country, women workers being paid two thirds of the appropriate rate. In this it was no different from many other trades but clauses providing for homeworkers or outworkers to be paid the union minimum plus fifteen per cent were particularly perceptive. And the statement that 'the provisions of this agreement are minimum and do not prevent the operation by individual employers of wages and conditions more favourable to individual workers', allowed a degree of local autonomy from national control which was most effective in providing the furniture worker with the possibility of a good standard of living while full employment lasted. [10]

With regard to payment by results the provision of a clause requiring that 'evaluation of the task shall be by reference to time and not by price' enabled bonus rates effectively to keep pace with changing wage rates while the provision of a mutual agreement clause for the fixing of times effectively kept the rate fixer out of the furniture factory while allowing time study to become a normal management tool. Furthermore, when time study and payment by results were used in a factory the bonus base had to be fixed such that 'the average productive worker could by appropriate effort earn at least twenty five per cent more than the minimum time rate'.

Holidays with Pay were established and paid day release for all apprentices and learners, but it was in its provision for conciliation machinery that the agreement was most forward looking. Effectively a *status quo* provision was applied in the event of disagreement between employer and employee. Failing this a provisional agreement might be made pending negotiations, subsequently adjustable in any further settlement. Provision was made for factory level negotiations followed by district level discussions and in the event of a failure the referral of the dispute to the National Joint Industrial Council. In all the years of the operation of the agreement there have been few occasions when disputes have gone further than district level, a tribute to the effectiveness of the agreement and the dislike of both union and management to 'wash their dirty linen in public' as one district officer has noted. [11]

After 1939 NAFTA was no longer the active political and compaigning organisation of earlier years. Contributions to the political fund remained low and even when the 'contracting out' procedure for contribution to the political fund was adopted by the new Labour government in 1946, only one-in-six paid their contributions compared to one-in-ten for the wartime period.

The unions sponsored two parliamentary candidates, F.I. Sweetman and Bernard Rockman, but neither was adopted by a constituency for the 1945 election. Two members of NAFTA were, however, returned to Parliament at this election, William Leonard who became Parliamentary Secretary at the Ministry of Supply, and A. Bechervaise. Neither was able to take the role of Parliamentary Secretary because of other commitments. If this is to suggest that NAFTA/NUFTO had become non-political, nothing could be further from the truth. It was ratther that the union's political philosophy and that of the 1945 Labour Party and TUC were closer, and that goals more agreed than had ever previously been the case.

Amalgamation was now an obvious desire on the part of the unions concerned in the industry and was seen as a logical step by the membership. The Edinburgh Upholsteres had joined NAFTA in 1945 with 200 members and £265 in funds. The Association of Cricket Bat Makers joined the union early in 1947 with 55 members and £148 in funds. But the major amalgamation was that which would bring the bedding and upholstery workers together with NAFTA. The benefits of the two unions were uniform; common interest had been established between them. Personalities and positions with the merged union presented some problems, a difficulty which was resolved by the adoption of a Regional and a Group system.

The country was divided up into six regions, each with a national organiser and a number of district organisers as determined by membership numbers. There also was established a Bedding and Spring Mattress Group and an Upholstery and Soft Furnishing Group, each with a group secretary and organisers. In this way the officers of NAFTA, the upholsterers and the bedding workers were absorbed into the new and larger union without offence and without redundancy.

The formal amalgamation to form NUFTO, The National Union of

Furniture Trades Operatives, took place on May 1st, 1947 and brought 46,522 members of NAFTA together with 10,608 members of the AUU. In terms of funds NAFTA was worth £152,000 or £3.20 per member and the AUU about £61,000 or £6.10 per member.

Alf Tomkins OBE, who had been appointed in 1946, became General Secretary of the new union and Jock Shanley, former General Secretary AUU became Assistant General Secretary (Organisation) while Alf Bickness remained as the second Assistant General Secretary with responsibility for Finance and Administration. The AUU organisers moved across to the newly formed specialist soft furnishing group with Reg Carter, the husband of Lilly Carter, the organiser of the 1930 women upholsterers' strike, becoming London District organiser for the group, and J.J. Johnson, the national organiser.

NUFTO ws born, the national union which had been the dream of Alex Gossip and his comrades throughout the early years of the century; a large union, well endowed with funds, highly organised with a corps of experienced and dedicated district officers. This was the union which had been the vision of the pioneers of the early days, the culmination of the years of strife, sacrifice and leadership.

CHAPTER X

# NUFTO to FTAT : 1948 – 1972

Between 1948 and 1972, the final stage of the dream of the early pioneers of furniture trade unionism was realised — the attainment of a single union for the industry. In a series of amalgamations all of the smaller trade societies were gathered into the fold of NUFTO and by the end of the period the Amalgamated Society of Wood Cutting Machinists joined with them to form the Furniture Timber and Allied Trades Union with over 89,000 members, more than £2 million in funds and organising over 95 per cent of all workers in the trade.

In industrial relations terms this was a period of relative peace and cooperation. Such disputes as there were were settled amicably and the vehement denuniciations of an earlier era were reserved for internal disputes and government policies as these were judged adversely to affect the union and its membership. Even these disputes or disagreements were of little real or lasting consequence and in the post-war period the main thrust of union activity was that of improving wages and organisation and of recruitment of membership against a background of immense initial demand for the industry's traditional production, followed by substantial and far reaching changes in the technology and output of the industry.

That a dramatic change in the industry was taking place is made clear by the following statistics. Taking 1946 production levels as an index figure of 100, the output of the industry rose to 199 by 1952. Well aware of this rise in production, the furniture workers felt they were entitled to a share of this prosperity. Not only was production doubled during the period; the increase was achieved with only a 10 per cent increase in manpower. Such an improvement in productivity could be explained away as post-war recovery. Indeed, the industry was by 1946 re-established on a basis of full peacetime production. This could only be explained in relation to changes in the industry itself. Effectively it was well on the way to becoming a 'hand assisted machine production industry' and the trends which were apparent in this period were to accelerate and intensify over the years which followed. [1] [2]

Technical change had its most marked effect upon the number of firms engaged in the trade and over the years 1950 – 1957 the number of companies producing furniture dropped from 3,148 to 1,987. This decline, though sudden and acute, did not affect employment or output and since the industry subsequently stabilised at this number of companies, can be seen as a weeding out of those who could not or would not modernise. Post 1953, the substantial increase in the output of the industry levelled off and though the value of furniture produced in 1962 was £2 millions higher than ten years earlier, volume was unchanged. This was a time of consolidation and reorganisation with a smaller industry absorbing the changes of the machine production era. [3]

The main problems facing the industry throughout the fifties and sixties arose from a change in the purchasing habits of the furniture buying public. Prior to the second world war there was some purchasing of furniture by means of hire purchase agreements. After the war this method became normal, as with most other consumer durables. The consequence of this change came when successive governments in the post-war period used changes in the availability of hire purchase or the levels of deposits associated with such agreements as economic regulators. The sensitivity of furniture production to variations in credit restrictions became an important and destabilising feature of the situation, especially in the 1950s.

From 1960 onwards there was a progressive growth within the industry which, whilst still effected by government policy, was now more firmly established by advertising and promotion of branded trade names as a major recipient of consumer durable spending. By the late sixties the industry was reaping the full benefit of this change and output by value in 1970 was double that of 1950 and had trebled by 1972, as can be seen from the following table:—

Turnover and Employment in the United Kingdom Furniture Industry 1954–1971

| Year | £ Million Turnover | Total | Employment Males | '000's Females | Unemployed |
|------|------|------|------|------|------|
| 1954 | 110 | 135.7 | 100.4 | 35.3 | 2.5 |
| 1955 | 105.6 | 136.7 | 100.6 | 36.1 | 3.4 |
| 1956 | 102 | 129.2 | 94.8 | 34.8 | 3.3 |
| 1957 | 108.1 | 130.8 | 95.2 | 35.6 | 3.7 |
| 1958 | 110.5 | 130.9 | 95.5 | 35.4 | 3.7 |
| 1959 | 122.6 | 137.4 | 100.2 | 37.2 | 2.8 |
| 1960 | 121.7 | 101.8 | 80.7 | 23.2 | 5.4 |
| 1961 | 125.9 | 101.8 | 81.2 | 22.7 | 3.3 |
| 1962 | 126.3 | 99.9 | 79.4 | 21.1 | 6.2 |
| 1963 | 125.3 | 99.3 | 78.5 | 20.5 | 2.0 |
| 1964 | 144.2 | 102.7 | 81.1 | 20.8 | 1.3 |
| 1965 | 156.8 | 102.5 | 80.9 | 21.6 | 1.5 |
| 1966 | 157.3 | 95.7 | 75.5 | 21.6 | 6.1 |
| 1967 | 152.4 | 98.1 | 77.1 | 20.2 | 2.5 |
| 1968 | 181.4 | 97.6 | 76.4 | 21.0 | 2.4 |
| 1969 | 177.9 | 92.7 | 73.6 | 21.2 | 2.24 |
| 1970 | 204.6 | 89.9 | 71.3 | 19.1 | 2.5 |
| 1971 | 253.6 | 93.6 | 74.4 | 18.6 | 3.36 |
| 1972 | 311.7 | 88.0 | 71.3 | 16.7 | 2.70 |

Source:
Department of Trade and Industry, *Economic Review for the Furniture Industry*, 1973, p.6
N.B. The method of accounting for numbers employed etc., in furniture industry was changed by the government in 1960 particularly affecting those peripheral to the upholstery and soft furnishing sectors.

The boom of 1968 saw volume up by 11 per cent and value up by 12.5 per cent on the previous year. By this time a specific concentration within the industry was occurring. Some 3.8 per cent of the firms in the industry were now responsible for more than 50 per cent of the output. The numbers employed in the industry had fallen and continued to fall. The industry could be truly said to have entered an era of machine related high productivity.

The technological change which dominated the new era was above all the development and use of chipboard. This is a man-made product in which soft wood chips are bonded together with urea formaldehyde resin to produce a stable, dimensionally accurate board which can in its turn be covered in wood or paper veneers or melamine foil. This board transformed the industry.

Gone were the designs of an earlier era with their curved surfaces and intricate patterns. In their place the industry produced the flat panelled square edge products so familiar to today's furniture buyer. Given a stable non-variable base material, high speed cutting machines designed automatically to replicate the joints produced over production runs of thousands of parts could now be installed in the modern factory. Linking the machinery together was the next obvious step and when these developments were added to automatic machine sanding lines and to linked finishing and drying equipment, it can be seen that a highly capitalised, high volume, output could be achieved. A small number of highly efficient companies with a limited range of products, whose trade names are household words now dominated the mass market for furniture.

The transformation of production which these changes represented were, of necessity, accompanied by a transformation of skills at a managerial and, more obviously, at a workshop level. The industry of furniture making had always been regarded as based upon separate but inter-related crafts with relatively rigid lines of demarcation between trades. This new spirit of cooperation between employer and employee which characterised the post-war period, coupled with the changing and more intensive nature of the industry, required a re-thinking of attitudes on the matter and progress towards inter-changeability of labour.

Steps in the process of change began with apprentice training. From the late 1920's the certification of apprenticeship had been by way of an examination structure administered by the City and Guilds of London Institute. These courses, known as C & G 103, were both practical and written tests and were trade specific, i.e. for cabinetmakers or chairmakers or upholsterers etc. By the 1960's it became apparent to educationalists, unions and employers that these rigid compartmentalised skills were becoming anachronistic in relation to the changing nature of the industry. As a result of tripartite talks the old C & G 103 series of qualifications were superseded in 1968-69 by the C & G 425 courses (later re-numbered as C & G 555 in 1975-76).

In essence, 425 (or 555) required that apprentices should undertake a first year of study as an introduction to all the craft skills of the industry and only in the second and third years of training concentrate their learning on one specific skill. The only craft exempt from this generalist approach is that of wood machinists. It is an acknowledgement of the now central role of the machine within the furniture industry and of its increasing complexity, that the wood machinist apprentice spends the whole of his three years of training on this one subject.

This change of learning pattern was accompanied by new instructions to the union membership in 1969. NUFTO adopted a policy of acceptance of inter-changeability of skills within any firm such that if a short term shortage of, say, cabinetmakers, occurred then any member of the workforce, no matter what his trade, could be called upon to perform that task. Effectively this was no more than a recognition of a situation which already pertained in those firms which had the very best industrial relations, but it should not, for the bulk of the industry, be seen as simply bowing to a *fait accompli*. Rather it was a particularly far-sighted and progressive move in an industry imbued with a very real sense of mutuality.

In the post-war years NUFTO became in many respects a model union. The relationships with the employers at a national and local level recognised an inter-dependence which strove for a mutually satisfactory settlement to any question. The new attitude is typified in the contrast between Charlie Hawkins' struggles with the firm of Meredew in the twenties and thirties and the cooperation accorded to Charlie Ward, the District Organiser, in the post-war period. Ward noted in his *Monthly Report* 'The management sent all unorganised workers in groups to the canteen, with full pay, to be addressed by me, and we now have a fully 100 per cent organised factory'. [4]

The only disagreement of any consequence was in 1952 when the employers called for a wage freeze and an end to the cost of living sliding scale. This disagreement was resolved at a meeting at the Ministry of Labour under the Chairmanship of Sir Robert Gould, the Chief Conciliation Officer of the Ministry. There was never any further need to use this conciliation machinery for the furniture industry. The 42 hour week was gained in 1960 and this did require a five day ban on overtime working and restriction of payment by results earnings but the 40 hour week gained in 1965 was achieved without need to revert to any industrial action. [5] [6]

Though the battles of former years with employers were now a thing of the past, there appeared within NUFTO a new phenomenon of internal conflict centred round the supposed activities of the Furniture Trade Advisory Committee of the Communist Party within the union.

Alf Tomkins, the General Secretary, had been a member of the Communist Party in the twenties and thirties but had resigned in 1940 and moved politically away from the left wing of the Labour movement. His subsequent struggles with the left began in 1948/9 when a series of small but potentially damaging unofficial strikes broke out in the industry. Alf Tompkins recognised such disputes as a potential threat to the National Labour Agreement and the national negotiating machinery and so in a special message to the membership he wrote; 'Are unofficial disputes necessary? Your union says — emphatically no. We must emphasise that each member of the union is committed to observe the requirements of the conciliation machinery which has been devised to make unofficial stoppages absolutely unnecessary. It is important to note that in nearly every case where a difference has been dealt with by the conciliation machinery, the union submission has been upheld by the Tribunals appointed to adjudicate on the matter. What additional proof is required to establish that time and wages lost as a result of unofficial stoppages is time and wages unnecessarily lost. It is a well worn plea that unofficial action is a demonstration of militancy. If we seriously believe this to be the case, then we should not pledge ourselves through a national agreement to act as a disciplined, an organised body of people. Undisciplined activity is nearer related to anarchy. Militant trade unionism can only be effectively expressed by the membership, moving *en masse* to enforce, when necessry, undetrakings given, or when a challenge is thrown down to agreements made'

Recognising that the General Officials could find themselves out-manoeuvred by a small, militant and highly organised group within the union during elections, a system of individual postal voting for all elections within the union was instituted from July of 1949. The registers of paid-up members were kept as duplicates by the union accountants who then checked the voting papers against their registers and declared the results.

The postal ballot decision, though costly and time consuming, was welcomed and endorsed by the membership as a whole. It had been challenged on a number of occasions at Biennial Conference on the basis of the expense incurred but in each case reaffirmed by the vast majority of members. Postal voting did not reduce the number of members of the Communist Party within the Executive or appointed as General Officials. It has, however, ensured that those members best fitted for union office have been elected on a much broader mandate than would have been achieved at sparsely attended branch meetings.

The most vociferous dispute between Alf Tomkins, CBE, who was appointed in 1951, and his left wing colleagues occurred after the 1953 Biennial Conference. A motion from the right wing proposing to ban members of the Communist party from holding office within the union, was withdrawn on Alf Tomkins' personal plea. In his justification of this action the Genberal Secretary antagonised the party members by claiming that such a vote would 'result in a series of Martyrs' who 'when their task of arousing sympathy was accomplished would be replaced by 'reliable fellow travellers".[7]

This action and the conference report that followed it aroused a hornet's nest of letters from the right and left wings of the union 'strongly deprecating this action', 'insulting', 'distorting the facts' and even; 'What a pity the communists never learned to play cricket!'.[8] Alf Tomkins delayed his reply to this controversy until November when much of the heat had been removed from the issue and whilst claiming communist infiltration within the union, was careful not to re-start the arguments adopting the theme that 'the price of freedom is eternal vigilance'.

Such tetchiness in left-right relations within the union was characteristic of the times and perhaps reflected credit upon no-one, including the General Secretary himself. The affair in no way reduced the number of communist party members who were and are active officers of the union, men who are without exception highly effective, dedicated workers for the benefit of their fellow members, and who, being recognised as such, have been elected and re-elected, often unopposed, or with huge majorities.

The last episode of this skirmish occurred in 1955 when an unofficial strike involving 24 NUFTO members broke out. Alf Tomkins saw this as a communist conspiracy; 'If a tiny minority cannot bear the thought of being bound together in an organisation which is devoted to the task of achieving the greatest good for the greatest number, they should cease to retain their link with their colleagues. The duration of this unofficial strike provides the certainty that financial support is being provided' and is 'a calculated step to weaken the union'.

The General Secretary seems to have over-reacted. The dispute was in an upholstery factory and the very officials who were trying to resolve the dispute through the normal union channels were themselves CP members. In the event the matter was soon resolved and with the Soviet intervention in Hungary in 1956 a period of disenchantment with anything pertaining to Eastern Bloc countries followed. The formerly close links between the union and furniture workers in Eastern Europe were reduced and not resumed until the 1970's.

Despite these problems, Alf Tomkins held his membership together in the post war period with little or no opposition to his middle of the road stance. One of the fundamental factors was the position of the furniture workers in the national wage league table. Before 1939 the industry had been relatively poorly paid. In the post-war era wages for the industry rapidly moved forward to make it one of the better paid industrial occupations as the following table illustrates:—

172    THE FURNITURE MAKERS

Table

Indices of Basic Weekly Wage Rates 1959 – 1968
January 1956 = 100

| Year | All Manual Workers Wage Range | Furniture Workers |
|---|---|---|
| 1959 | 111 – 119 | 117 |
| 1960 | 112 – 122 | 119 |
| 1961 | 118 – 125 | 124 |
| 1962 | 119 – 133 | 133 |
| 1963 | 127 – 138 | 136 |
| 1964 | 130 – 145 | 141 |
| 1965 | 138 – 152 | 146 |
| 1966 | 143 – 161 | 153 |
| 1967 | 146 – 162 | 158 |
| 1968 | 150 – 177 | 170 |

The furniture workers remained near the top of the wages league for 1959-1968 even allowing for the distortion introduced into the table by the inclusion of the category of professional and scientific services, public administration and defence.

Lack of dissent within the union allowed the officers to concentrate upon their organisational role. Despite the business organisation image which such attention produced, the union was not without a political voice. Its disagreements with government policy were at two levels. It objected, in concert with the employers, to the use of the industry as a pawn in the game of economic regulation; as a national union it also made its voice heard both through the TUC and independently on a number of other issues.

Furniture unions have always supported the right of free collective bargaining. This policy was reiterated early in the post-war period. The wage restraint policy of the first Labour Government was not one with which NUFTO agreed and though government policy was supported by TUC the furniture workers produced a dissenting voice. The story began in 1948. The TUC General Council was in favour of a wage freeze in the Autumn of 1949 but at the special conference of Trades Union Executives in January 1950, it could only muster a majority of 650,000 votes. NUFTO was amongst those unions, including the Miners, the AEU and the NUR, who cast 3,600,000 votes against such a policy.

Indeed wage rises at a national level and cost of living sliding scale increases for the furniture workers continued unabated through this period.

On Suez the union was energetic in its protests to the Government. It refused to accept the pay pause of 1962; with great reluctance accepted the wages and prices freeze of the 1966 Labour administration with its attendant 'early warning system' and was strongly against the report of the Donovan Commission. *In Place of Strife,* the Wilson/Castle proposals for industrial relations reform, was in its turn rejected by the union as was the Tory Industrial Relations Act of 1971. In common with the majority of trade unions the Furniture Workers declined to register under that Act.

The trend towards concentration of production within a smaller number of companies increased the need for centralisation and unification of the trade unions involved in the industry. In 1954 the National Union of Carpet, Linoleum and Rubber Planners and Fitters joined NUFTO by transfer of engagements. This arrangement was also used in 1969 when the Midland Glass Bevellers and Kindred Societies and the United French Polishers Society joined NUFTO.

The major amalgamation of the period was, however, with the Amalgamated Society of Wood Cutting Machinists (ASWCM). Over the years there had been many discussions with this society both on its own and on a tripartite basis with the Amalgamated Society of Woodworkers. The first of these meetings was held in 1963 arising out of the 1962 Trade Union Congress recommendations on amalgamation, but after an initial discussion between General Secretaries, the contact was broken. However, in 1965 Charlie Stewart, General Secretary of the ASWCM was invited to the NUFTO Biennial Conference and, in his address to the meeting, spoke particularly on the need for closer ties between the two societies.[8]

The wood machinists were in something of a dilemma about amalgamation. The subject was discussed at their 1963 conference and it appeared that a number of unions were interested in merging or amalgamating. The Building Trade Operatives, the Woodworkers, the Furniture Workers, the General and Municipal Workers and the Transport Workers all had members who were wood machinists and saw some logic in a more substantial link up. Though the discussions that followed were about the nature of the union with which to discuss amalgamation, the real problem for the wood machinists lay in the diversity of industries of which they formed a part. The union had members working in railway workshops, automobile factories and local dockyards though the two largest groups were employed within the building trade and the furniture industry.

The delegates were split in their views as to whether a craft society or a general union was the more favourable group with which to amalgamate. The issue was not put to the vote but referred back to the Executive to 'continue our exploratory talk and possibly by next year some positive proposals will be submitted before conference either for or against change'. [9] At the conference there were many speeches against industrial unionisation. 'We have been fighting bosses for years — we don't want labour bosses', and talk of trade societies as 'a bulwark against the encroachment these days of the great labouring unions'. [10]

The General Secretary, Charlie Stewart, did not at this point make his own feelings known, but after the NUFTO Conference of 1965 the ASWCM set up a sub-committee to meet NUFTO to discuss amalgamation under the chairmanship of the General Secretary. [11] The ASW also called for talks on amalgamation, and these were arranged during the year. This tripartite approach and the playing off of one union against the other continued for a number of years even though all the apparent conditions for amalgamation were being met by both unions.

Many constructions can be put upon the delaying tactics which continued through the 1960's with ASW and NUFTO the ardent suitors and ASWCM the reluctant bride. In essence there was a groundswell of opinion within the unions that some form of amalgamation was essential and that either a joint or tripartite arrangement could and should be arrived at. The latter was explored at a meeting of the General Secretaries of the three unions in May 1969, but this made no more substantial progress than any earlier discusssion. [12]

At the Wood Machinists' conference in 1970 Jim Kooyman, District Organiser, was the main spokesman for amalgamtion with NUFTO. The General Secretary reported that a common rule book had been drawn up with NUFTO but as it contained a clause which allowed for the leader of the Wood Machinists to live in either Edinburgh or Manchester (the existing headquarters of the Wood Machinists) it had been rejected by the Executive Committee on the General Secretary's recommendation. As far as the ASW was concerned the matter of concern was that the Wood Machinists had an asset value of £27 per member and the Executive was very concerned about handing over such accumulated wealth to the ASW which had an asset value of only £6 per member. [13]

Charlie Stewart encouraged the membership to inaction by reminding them that 'when you elected your EC, you placed your trust in the EC to look after your affairs', and the matter of amalgamation was again remitted to the EC for consideration. This delaying tactic of 1970 proved, however, to be the final act of the long drawn out amalgamation drama for it had become patently obvious to the membership of the ASWCM that the existing system of separate unions with separate headquarters and separate district officers was both economically and administratively inefficient. Meanwhile, the balance of opinion with the

Wood Machinists Society had moved to a preference to join the smaller but well organised NUFTO rather one of the larger generalist unions.

In the New Year of 1971 the two unions moved quickly towards amalgamation. In March 1971 a joint executive committee approved the common rule book and as the benefits paid by both unions were comparable, the merger was agreed. In 1964 the Trade Unions (Amalgamations) Act had provided a simplified form of an amalgamation procedure first introduced in 1940. This simply required that the Wood Machinist membership should vote by a simple majority to 'transfer its engagements' to NUFTO, in this instance under the changed title Furniture, Timber and Allied Trade Union. This it did by 5,432 votes to 1,728, and on September 14th 1971 the merger came into being with 84,000 members and £2 million in assets. NUFTO brought 61,788 members and £1,408,464 in assets to the new union; ASWCM 22,106 members and £650,627 in assets.

The father figure of the furniture unions, Alex Gossip had not lived to see his dream fulfilled; he had died on 14th May 1952, aged 89, after a long illness. The union journal quoted from a poem by Joseph Burgess, as a fitting tribute to the man who above all made FTAT possible:—

> They trimmed their lamps all through the murky night
> Guiding their fellow creatures to the light
> Then gratefully their fellows lit the flames
> Which glory shed upon their honoured names.

# Appendix

## Women Workers in the Furniture Trade

There is a myth that furniture making is an exclusively male preserve. In fact women workers have represented a significant proportion of the work force at various times throughout the past century. Actual numbers have varied as a result of external factors such as war and economic recession, but these have always been significant, especially in the upholstery, polishing and soft furnishing branches of the trade.

Numbers are one thing, activity and militancy are another. Despite long term pressures in the industry, women seem not to have played a significant executive role in the various unions in the industry and to have come comparatively late to the politicization process associated with trades union membership.

The earliest record of organised women workers in the industry is that of the Edinburgh Upholsteresses whose rules date from 1871. This is reputed to be the oldest women's trade society in the UK. The Edinburgh Society and the older Edinburgh Upholsterers' Union (founded in 1842) merged in 1891 to form the Amalgamated Union of Upholsterers. At the first delegate meeting of the AUU only two representatives of the Edinburgh Society were present.

Women were a minority group; they were in most instances outworkers in such occupations as caning, rushing, sewing etc. and as such were the first to be affected by any downturn in demand or change in fashion. Even when they were employed in factory situations they were dominated by men. Enquiries among older workers in the trade have established that even where female chargehands were employed they were under the overall control of male foremen and supervisors. Furthermore, women workers in the furniture industry were mercilessly exploited. The rates for High Wycombe in the lock-out of 1913/14 are a graphic example, and when women were brought into the factories during the 1914-1918 war to carry out work which had been traditionally male preserves, such as chairmaking and wood machining, this practice was continued. The men who had done the work had received eightpence halfpenny or so per hour. The Belgian refugees (male) were paid sixpence an hour and the women twopence farthing per hour for the same work.

Eventually, the situation became so embarrassing to the trade that the unions and employers came together in 1916 to sign a national agreement regarding women's wages. It fixed the women's rate at two-thirds of the men's rate for comparable work, and required that all women working in a furniture factory must be members of the appropriate trade union. This latter clause placed women's membership of the unions on on a more official basis and their numbers were recorded in all subsequent statistics of membership. This new found membership, voice and numerical strength (during wartime periods) did not bring with it any protest or declaration of resentment at their subservient position in the trade. The Manchester Agreement of 1918 made the point succinctly. Women polishers and upholsterers were paid, under the new agreement, tenpence per hour, comparable male workers one and twopence per hour and unskilled labourers tenpence per hour. Such a denial of equality was surely a reflection of society's overview of the place of women in trade and industry rather than a specific attitude of furniture makers and workers to female staff. Moreover, the closest scrutiny of the union records and trade press of the period has not brought to light the slightest evidence of dissent from this position from women in the trade.

Having been brought into membership and became part of the official statistics of NAFTA in 1916, numbers of women in the trade increased dramatically in the later years of the war. There was a desire on the part of employers in the trade to retain this new (cheap and docile?) workforce. 'For a long time women and girls have been brought into the cabinet making industry and it is largely due to the quickness with which they have been able to pick up the craft that this industry has been able to carry on so well. In the wood working industry, women and girls are now employed to an extent that would not have been thought possible before the war. Brought in at an early stage as merely emergency workers, they have adapted themselves with wonderful facility to the new duties and the new conditions of factory life, and, except for the unusually heavy work, practically every workshop process known to the trade is now being undertaken efficiently by women workers'.

'Their success in this respect will raise one very important problem after the war. It has been understood from the extent that the trade unions rules and regulations suspended for the time being will have to be re-imposed as soon as possible after peace is declared. This will raise the serious question as to what is to become of the trained and organised body of women workers who have been brought into the service of the nation. It is admitted that we will need a vastly increased output to maintain our financial and commercial stability and it is therefore almost unthinkable that this skilled army should suddenly be disbanded' - 'They have, in short, come into our industrial life to stay'. ('A Trade Review 1917': *Cabinetmaker and Complete House Furnisher,* , December 29th 1917, p.223).

Despite their numerical strength and the wishes of the trade to retain them, women workers left or were removed from the industry as male workers returned from the armed forces and peacetime production was resumed. Two reasons can be suggested for this change. The first was the undoubted pressure exerted at a shop floor level for the return of 'men's work' to men. The second, which was coincident with this view, was that of the manufacturers themselves. Despite the predictions of the trade press, employers perceived the work of the industry as being suitable for men and inappropriate to women. If women were to be employed, they were to be placed in their traditional roles of sewing, upholstery (light work), sandpapering, staining and outwork (caning, rushing etc.). The state of the technology of the industry of this period also had a part to play. There was a rapid introduction of independently, electrically driven machines in place of the lay shaft and belt driven plant of former years. Nevertheless furniture making was still a machine-assisted hand-production industry and physically demanding. Physical strength though not as paramount as in heavy engineering, for example, was nevertheless important. Rightly or wrongly, women were not seen as possessing the necesssary strength or stamina for a long working day spent in timber components through the production process, despite the evidence of the war years.

By 1924 the percentage of women employed in the industry and having membership of the union had fallen to 4 per cent and this figure, with minor variations, remained constant until the beginning of the second world war despite endemic unemployment and short time working. Furthermore there is no record at local or national level of any pressure from the male membership for the displacement of the women from their now well established place in the working of a furniture factory.

The outbreak of total war in 1939 saw a population at war, mobilised and directed, which brought women workers back into the furniture factories in large numbers. By 1944 one-in-four of the workers employed in the industry was female. This influx necessitated a change in the way in which work in the furniture factory was viewed. The physical constraints attendant upon using women workers remained. Machinery was now powered by independent electrical motors, but the furniture factory was still a physically demanding workplace by virtue of the size and weight of the materials handled. A reconsideration, and in many instances, a first time consideration, of materials and handling was undertaken. The mixed labour force necessitated a more reasoned, less physical approach. The universal introduction in the furniture factory of mechanically assisted materials handling dates from this period.

It must not be assumed that all factories prior to the war period were operating a materials handling philosophy of 'sweat and muscle'. Oral evidence attributes a high degree of sophistication in this area by firms such as Harris Lebus and E. Gomme Ltd. These businesses were, however, the leaders of the industry and their internal organisation and process controls were the exception rather than the rule. For most businesses in 1939 the method of moving more materials in the factory was to 'get a bigger wheelbarrow' (George Venables, retired polisher, oral evidence 1981).

Statistics for the end of the war in 1945 show a similar and immediate pattern of reduction of women workers to that which occurred in 1919. Compared with the 5 per cent of women in the union membership before the war, the proportion had settled down in the nineteen fifties and sixties at about 15 per cent. Perhaps the 1946 fall was the result of a clerical error. Since the primary statistical documents for these years have long since been destroyed, there is no way in which such a contention can be verified.

The pattern and type of employment of women in the industry remained constant until the end of the period under consideration. Women were not involved and are still not involved in machining and assembly areas. In general they have tended to remain in upholstery-related occupations. Nevertheless there has been some incursion into the areas of veneering where womens' skills in jointing, matching and cutting light materials can be utilised and when their lower rates of pay provide a cost benefit to the employers. In the polishing and fitting shops they were able, after the war, to retain their hold on the lighter tasks of sanding and fitting out furniture. And so the conservative view of the women's place in the factory has been perpetuated in the post 1945 period, as it was between the wars, and this despite the specific evidence of the effectiveness of women workers in all roles in the wartime factory, and the substantially less physically demanding nature of post-war manufacture.

Since the advent of FTAT the percentage of women workers within the total labour force of the industry has fallen. In what (in 1983) is now a declining employment industry, it is difficult to see any change in this pattern. Given the application of equal pay and the inherent conservation of both management and male workers with regard to women workers, it seems inevitable that the woman in a furniture factory will continue to fulfil her traditional role in the upholstery shop but will find few opportunities of joining her male counterparts in the rest of the factory.

In political terms the women of the furniture unions, have had little impact at a national level. There have been no full-time women officials.

However, at the grass roots level this picture is reversed. Women officials at a branch and district level have been numerous. Executive members of the union accept that they have fulfilled their task with a dedication and tenacity equal to, and in most cases greater than, those shown by their men. Why then have they not found at least some representation amongst the full-time officials? It can only be assumed that the traditions of the industry have perceived furniture making as a man's world and that, in negotiations with the employers (seen by the majority of the union membership as the main function of the district official) it has been felt that this role is still best fulfilled by men.

Women Workers in the Furniture Trades Unions

| Year | Membership | Male | Female | Women's % of Total |
|------|-----------|------|--------|--------------------|
| 1916 | 12,534 | 12,375 | 159 | 1.3 |
| 1917 | 16,123 | 14,820 | 1,303 | 8.1 |
| 1918 | 22,442 | 19,442 | 3,000 | 13.3 |
| 1919 | 30,901 | 28,162 | 2,739 | 8.9 |
| 1920 | 32,987 | 30,607 | 2,382 | 7.2 |
| 1921 | 25,263 | 23,830 | 1,433 | 5.6 |
| 1922 | 22,449 | 21,114 | 1,335 | 5.9 |
| 1923 | 21,819 | 20,536 | 1,283 | 5.8 |
| 1924 | 22,820 | 21,370 | 1,432 | 6.2 |
| 1925 | 23,705 | 22,740 | 965 | 4.0 |
| 1926 | 19,760 | 18,464 | 1,296 | 6.5 |
| 1927 | 19,485 | 18,671 | 814 | 4.1 |
| 1928 | 19,989 | 19,113 | 876 | 4.3 |
| 1929 | 21,071 | 20,023 | 1,048 | 4.9 |
| 1930 | 20,243 | 19,344 | 899 | 4.4 |
| 1931 | 17,874 | 17,067 | 827 | 4.6 |
| 1932 | 15,829 | 15,102 | 727 | 4.5 |
| 1933 | 15,036 | 14,300 | 736 | 4.8 |
| 1934 | 14,902 | 14,197 | 705 | 5.0 |
| 1935 | 16,280 | 15,469 | 811 | 3.7 |
| 1936 | 17,830 | 16,967 | 864 | 4.8 |
| 1937 | 20,391 | 19,424 | 967 | 4.9 |
| 1938 | 21,251 | 20,346 | 903 | 4.4 |
| 1939 | 20,631 | 19,560 | 1,071 | 5.1 |
| 1940 | 23,389 | 22,077 | 1,312 | 5.6 |
| 1941 | 26,834 | 24,517 | 2,317 | 8.6 |
| 1942 | 31,674 | N.a | N.a. | N.a. |
| 1943 | 36,211 | 30,711 | 5,500 | 15.1 |
| 1944 | 36,707 | 27,421 | 9,286 | 25.2 |

Women Workers in the Furniture Trades Unions

| Year | Membership | Male | Female | Women's % of Total |
|------|-----------|--------|--------|--------------------|
| 1945 | 34,642 | 29,177 | 5,465 | 15.1 |
| 1946 | 44,927 | 39,827 | 5,100 | 11.3 |
| 1947 | 61,169 | 51,587 | 9,582 | 15.6 |
| 1948 | 66,376 | 56,277 | 10,099 | 15.2 |
| 1949 | 59,054 | 49,285 | 9,769 | 16.5 |
| 1950 | 74,063 | 62,586 | 11,477 | 15.4 |
| 1951 | 74,746 | 62,329 | 12,417 | 16.6 |
| 1952 | 73,351 | 61,813 | 11,538 | 15.7 |
| 1953 | 72,438 | 61,825 | 10,613 | 14.6 |
| 1954 | 74,815 | 64,645 | 10,170 | 13.5 |
| 1955 | 73,622 | 62,445 | 11,177 | 15.1 |
| 1956 | 70,688 | 60,033 | 10,655 | 15.0 |
| 1957 | 70,356 | 59,319 | 11,037 | 15.6 |
| 1958 | 68,933 | 58,528 | 10,405 | 15.1 |
| 1959 | 69,033 | 58,564 | 10,469 | 15.1 |
| 1960 | 69,733 | 59,124 | 10,609 | 15.2 |
| 1961 | 67,424 | 57,054 | 10,370 | 15.3 |
| 1962 | 64,688 | 54,793 | 9,895 | 15.2 |
| 1963 | 63,488 | 53,882 | 9,606 | 15.1 |
| 1964 | 64,597 | 54,918 | 9,679 | 14.9 |
| 1965 | 63,607 | 54,075 | 8,532 | 14.9 |
| 1966 | 61,517 | 52,178 | 9,339 | 15.1 |
| 1967 | 60,142 | 51,004 | 9,138 | 15.1 |
| 1968 | 59,723 | 51,062 | 8,661 | 14.5 |
| 1969 | 58,759 | 50,160 | 8,599 | 14.6 |
| 1970 | 60,754 | 51,687 | 9,067 | 14.9 |
| 1971 | 83,894 | 75,279 | 8,615 | 10.2 |
| 1972 | 85,377 | 75,458 | 9,919 | 11.6 |

# Footnotes and References

Chapter I

1  S. Lilley, *Men Machines and History*, 1910, p.17
2  W.L. Goodman,*The History of Woodworking Tools* , 1912, p.76
3  Lilley, *op.cit.* p.22
4  Lilley, *op.cit.* p.28
5  Goodman, *op.cit.* p.92
6  Norwich Public Library, *Norwich Index of Freemen* 7  Bristol Archives Office
8  Penelope Eames, *Medieval Furniture,* London, 1977, p.37
9  P.S. Allen, *Selection from Erasmus,* Oxford, 2nd.ed. 1918, p.51
10  William Harrison, *Description of England* (1577), p.60
11  LeRoy Ladurie, *Montaillou,* 1978
12  Warner, *The Patient Countess* (1587), p.17
13  Ambrose Heal, *The London Furniture Makers,* 1953
14  E. Pinto, *Small Woodware Thro' the Ages,* Batsford, London, 1949
15 John Evelyn, *An Account of Architects and Architecture,* 1723, p.76
16  J.L. Oliver, *The Development & Structure of the Furniture Industry,* Pergamon Press, 1966, p.5
17 E.T. Jay, *Some Aspects of the London Furniture Industry in the 18th. Century,* MA Thesis, London University, 1962
18  Anon, *A General Description of all Trades,* 1747
19  R. Campbell, *The London Tradesman 1747,* Augustus M. Kelley, N.Y. 1969, p.171, 172
20  R. Campbell, *op.cit.,*p.171
21  H. Angelo *Reminisences* , Vol.I, 1828, p. 367
22  R. Campbell, *op.cit.,* 1747, p.171
23  R. Campbell, *op.cit.,* p.70 and J. Collyer, *London Trades,* 1749, pp.86-87
24  *London Chronicle* , December 12th 1761, p.6

25 Arthur Marsh and Victoria Ryan, *Historical Directory of Trade Unions*, Gower, 1986

26   A. Heal, *Country Life*, January 23rd 1942 (letter)

27   *Daily Advertiser*, October 10th 1786, p.2

28   L.J. Mayes, *The History of Chairmaking in High Wycombe*, Routledge & Kegan Paul, 1960, pp.2-3

29   E.P. Thompson & Eileen Yeo, *The Unknown Mayhew; Selections from the Morning Chronicle 1840-50*, Merlin, 1971, p.321

30   *op.cit.supra*, p.323

31   *op.cit.supra*, pp.328-329

32   *Furniture Working Party Report*, HMSO, 1946, p.53

33   *Timber its Development & Distribution, An Historical Survey*, 1957, p.53

34   Thompson & Yeo, *op.cit.* pp.334-335

35   C. Bale, *Woodworking Machinery, Its Rise, Progress & Construction*, Lockwood, 1914, *passim*

36   *Cabinetmaker*, June 1908

37   *Ibid*. January 11th and 18th 1908

38   Mayes, *op.cit.*, p.121

39   *Cabinetmaker*, 1892

40   *Ibid*, 1908

41   Records of the Borough of High Wycombe

42   *Bailey's British Directory*, 1784

43   *Kelly's Directory for the Town of High Wycombe*, 1875

44   Mayes, *op.cit.*, p.30

45   H. Pour, *London Labour*, , 1891

46 E.P. Thompson, *The Making of the English Working Class*, Penguin, 1981, p.277 *et seq.* and William Lovett, *Life and Struggles in Pursuit of Bread, Knowledge and Freedom*, 1920 ed., pp.31,32

47   E.P. Thompson, *op.cit.*, pp.278, 279

48   E.P. Thompson & Eileen Yeo, *op.cit.*, pp.367, 368

49   Evidence to the Select Committee of the House of Lords on the Sweating System, Vol.17, 1890, pp.279-281

50   Mayhew, *London Labour & the London Poor*, 1861, p.392

51   *Post Office London Directory* 1881

52   J.J. Sheaham, *The History & Topography of Buckinghamshire*, 1862, p.920

53   R.H. Coe, *The Story of High Wycombe Furniture*, 1951

54   *Chair & Cabinetmaking Book of Prices*, London, 1811, p.2

55   *Bucks Free Press*, February 1854

56   Mayes, *op.cit.*, p.50

57 Truck was made illegal in 1831 but appears not to have disappeared from High Wycombe until 1887.

Chapter II

1  H.A. Clegg, Alan Fox & A.F. Thompson, *A History of British Trade Unions since 1860, Vol.I,* Clarendon Press, 1964, pp.2-3

2  *Alliance Cabinetmakers Records, 1865-1875,* and Lewis Leckie, *Memoir of Lewis Leckie,* Amalgamated Union of Upholsterers 1924

3  *Beehive,* July 14th 1865

4  *Cabinetmaker & Art Furnisher,* November 1st 1881

5  'A Chat about Trade Societies', *Cabinetmaker & Art Furnisher,* May 1st 1890

6  *Beehive,* October 28th 1865

7  *Ibid.* November 25th 1865

8  *Ibid.*

9  *Cabinetmaker & Art Furnisher,* November 1st, 1881

10  Alliance Cabinet Makers Association, *Report* , July 1st 1872

11  *Beehive,* July 20th 1872

12  *Ibid.* July 27th and August 3rd 1872

13  *Ibid.* September 7th 1872

14  'The Cabinetmakers' Wage Movement', *Furniture Gazette,* November 2nd 1872

15  Alliance Cabinet Makers Association, *Minute Book* , May 11th 1872

16  *Furniture Gazette,* November 23rd 1872

17  *Beehive,* October 26th and November 22nd 1872

18  Alliance Cabinet Makers Association, *Report* , January 6th 1873

19  *Ibid. Annual Reports,* 1873, 1874 & 1875

20  *Beehive,* September 14th 1867

21  Alliance Cabinet Makers Association, *Annual Report 1873*

22  Robert Taylor, *The Fifth Estate,* Routledge, 1978, p.189-190

23  ACMA *Report,* July 6th, 1874

24  ACMA *Report* January 4th 1875

25  A letter from Jackson & Graham to the Alliance Cabinet Makers Association, February 10th 1875

26  *Times,* May 6th 1875, p.11

27  *Ibid.* May 7th 1875, p.12

28  Beehive, June 5th 1875

29  ACMA, *Annual Report,* December 31st 1875

30  *Ibid. Report,* July 6th 1874

31  *Ibid. EC Report,* December 31st 1877

32  *Ibid.*

33  Estimates of numbers employed in furniture making for this period are uncertain since they are included with statistics for carpenters and joiners. It can be assumed that some 110,000 males and females were employed in the furniture trades out of the total of 230,000 given in *British Labour Statistics 1841-1921*

34  ACMA *Annual Report* 1888

35  *Ibid. Annual Report* 1896
36  *Ibid. Annual Report* 1897
37  Trades Union Congress, *Annual Report* 1898
38  Colonel Dyer, Letter to *The Times*, September 5th 1879
39  ACMA *Annual Report* 1879
40  *Ibid.*
41  *Ibid.* 1898
42  Alex Gossip, *History of NAFTA,* 1930
43  Gossip, *op.cit.*
44  Gossip, *op.cit.,* p.4
45  Clegg, Fox & Thompson, *op.cit.,* p.160; N. Robertson, *A Study of the Development of Labour Relations in the British Furniture Trade,* University of Oxford, B.Litt Thesis, 1955
46  Shop limits; a traditional practice in furniture factories limiting the output of the workforce by means of an agreement between all craftsmen to put a ceiling on output or earnings in order to spread the work available over the lean periods of the year and to insure continuity of employment.
47  Gossip *op.cit.,* p.5
48  ACMA *Annual Report* 1898
49  *Ibid.* 1899
50  *Ibid.* 1901


Chapter III

 1  NAFTA *Annual Report* 1902
 2  W. Parnell, No.2 Branch London West End
 3  E. O'Hara, Secretary, Manchester No.4 Branch
 4  Thomas Gordon, Manchester No.2 Branch
 5  F. Cooper, Birmingham No.19 Branch
 6  John Watston, No.37 Branch
 7  Letter from J.R. May 1904
 8  This was a very topical issue which attracted a protest rally in Hyde Park on March 26th 1904 with an estimated attendance of between 150,000 and 200,000. Among the speakers were Alex Gossip and Jim O'Grady
 9  *Yorkshire Post,* January 13th 1906
10  *Leeds and Yorkshire Mercury,* January 12th and 15th 1906
11  *Yorkshire Evening Post,* January 9th 1906
12  *Ibid.* January 15th 1906
13  J. O'Grady, NAFTA *Monthly Report,* February 1906
14  NAFTA *Monthly Report* 1906
15  In 1911 Parliament took a decision to pay MPs a salary of £400 per annum. This allowed Jim O'Grady to relinquish his role as Trade Organiser for NAFTA and to retain his links with the union as

Parliamentary Secretary. O'Grady had held the post of Trade Organiser since 1899 and in the words of Alex Gossip 'was a force to be reckoned with'. His successor in the post was Fred Bramley, a cabinetmaker from No.2 West End Branch, the future General Secretary of the TUC. [16] see Duncan Blythell, *The Sweated Trades*, Batsford, 1979

17   John Lovell & B.C. Roberts, *A Short History of the TUC*, 1968 p.42
18   NAFTA, *Monthly Report*, February 1908
19   *Saturday Review*, March 1908
20   *Daily News*, November 20th 1908
21   *Ibid.*
22   NAFTA, *Monthly Report*, May 1909
23   NAFTA, *Monthly Report*, December 1910

Chapter IV

1   NAFTA estimate, 1913
2   NAFTA *Monthly Report*, February 1913
3   *South Bucks Free Press*, January 1913
4   Fred Bramley, *Monthly Report*, June 1913
5   EC *Minutes*, January/February 1913
6   Fred Bramley, *Monthly Report*, March 1913
7   *Birmingham Furnishing Employers Journal*, November 1913
8   *South Bucks Herald*, November 16th 1913 and *NAFTA Journal*, November 1913
9   EC *Minutes*, March 1913
10   Ted Rolfe, *40 Years After, Recollections*, 1913-14
11   Borough of Chepping Wycombe Watch Committee, *Minute Book*, December 1st 1913
12   *South Bucks Herald*, December 20th 1913
13   *Times*, December 18th 1913, p.5
14   *Daily Herald*, December 17th 1913
15   Lord Askwith, *Industrial Problems and Disputes*, Harvester Press, 1974
16   *Times*, February 6th 1914, p.8
17   *Times*, February 7th 1914, p.5
18   *Daily Herald*, February 12th, 1914
19   *Monthly Report*, March 1914
20   *South Bucks Free Press*, December 16th 1913
21   Ted Rolfe, *op.cit.* 22   Watch Committee *Minutes*, December 23rd 1913, January 14th 1914 and February 16th 1914

Chapter V

1   H. Pelling, *Modern Britain*, 1968, p.80
2   *General Annual Reports on the Army*, HMSO, 1921 C ind 1193 p.9; see also Earl of Derby, *Report on Recruiting*, HMSO, Cd. 18149 1916

3  NAFTA *Monthly Report*, November 1914

4  NAFTA *Monthly Reports*, February, March & April 1915

5  *Daily Telegraph*, January 4th 1916

6  NAFTA *Monthly Report*, February 1916

7  NAFTA *Monthly Report*, February 1916

8  NAFTA *Monthly Report*, April 1916

9  NAFTA *Monthly Reports*, March and April 1916

10  NAFTA EC *Minutes*, May 29th 1913

11  NAFTA EC *Minutes*, May 29th 1913

12  NAFTA EC *Monthly Report*, May 29th 1916

13  NAFTA *Monthly Report*, July 1916 14  NAFTA *Monthly Report*, May 1917

15  NAFTA *Monthly Report*, May 1917

16  See also A. Marwick,*Clifford Allen*, 1979,p.28; *Hansard* January 26th 1916 and D. Boulton, *Objection Over-ruled*, MacGibbon & Kee, 1967

17  This Council for Civil Liberties was active during the First World War after which it ceased to operate. The present National Council for Civil Liberties was founded in 1934. The papers of the earlier Council are held in the International Institute of Social History, Amsterdam.

18  National Council for Civil Liberties, *Minutes*, May 18th 1918

19  NAFTA *Monthly Report*, November 1915

20  NAFTA *Monthly Report*, May 1917

21  NAFTA *Monthly Report*, May 1917

22  NAFTA *Monthly Report*, August 1918

23  *Manchester Guardian*, December 31st 1914

24  NAFTA, Executive Council *Minutes*, October, November and December 1915 and January, February, March, April and May 1916

25  NAFTA *Monthly Reports*, December 1915 and January 1916

26  NAFTA *Monthly Report*, February 1916

27  *Engineer*, December 1915; NAFTA *Monthly Report*, May 1916

28  NAFTA EC *Minutes*, May 1916; *Monthly Report*, June and July 1916

29  NAFTA *Monthly Report*, October 1916

30  NAFTA *Monthly Report*, October 1916

31  NAFTA *Annual Report*, 1916

32  ----

33  NAFTA *Monthly Report*, January 1918; see also James Hinton, *The First Shop Stewards Movement*, 1973

34  NAFTA *Monthly Report*, March 1918

35  NAFTA *Monthly Report*, December 1918

36  NAFTA *Monthly Report*, March 1918

37  Document submitted to EC by Ministry of Labour, February 1918

38  Roberts, *op.cit. supra*, p.61; see also P. Johnson *Homes Fit for Heroes*, 1977

39  NAFTA *Monthly Report*, March 1918
40  NAFTA *Monthly Report*, December 1918
41  NAFTA *Monthly Report*, April 1917
42  NAFTA *Monthly Report*, May 1917
43  *Cabinet Papers* 23/1 no.104(5) March 26th 1917; *Cabinet Papers* 23/2 no.107(9) March 28th 1917
44  see also J.M. Winter, 'Arthur Henderson, the Russian Revolution and the Reconstruction of the Labour Party', *Historical Journal*, Vol.XV, No.4, 1972, pp.753-773
45  J. Toland, *No Man's Land*, 1980
46  NAFTA *Monthly Report*, July 1917
47  NAFTA *Monthly Report, July 1917*
48*Times,* July 30th 1917, p.3; see also David Englander and James Osborne, 'Jack, Tommy and Henry Dabb, the Armed Forces and the Working Class', *Historical Journal*, Vol.XXI, No.3, 1978, pp.593-621; also Walter Kendall, *The Revolutionary Movement in Britain 1900-1921*, 1969
49  NAFTA *Monthly Report*, August 1917
50  NAFTA *Monthly Report*, February 1918
51  NAFTA *Monthly Report*, January 1917
52  NAFTA *Monthly Report*, 1917
53  NAFTA *Monthly Report*, February 1919
54  NAFTA *Monthly Report*, April 1917
55  NAFTA *Monthly Report*, August 1918
56  Alex Gossip, *Monthly Report*, November 1917
57  *Evidence Presented to the Board of Trade Enquiry into the Training and Employment of Disabled Servicemen*, 1917
58  NAFTA *Monthly Report*, February 1917
59  NAFTA *Monthly Report*, January 1918
60  NAFTA *Annual Report*, 1918 and NAFTA *Monthly Report*, December 1918

Chapter VI

1  NAFTA *Monthly Report*, February, March, July and September 1919
2  NAFTA *Monthly Report*, July 1919
3  NAFTA *Monthly Report*, August 1919
4  NAFTA *Monthly Report*, January 1920
5  NAFTA *Monthly Report*, March, April and May 1919
6  *Harrods Furniture Catalogues*, May 1920, May 1921
7NAFTA *Monthly Report*, May 1920
8  There were unskilled members especially during the war years but as a floating workforce the unskilled rarely sustained their contributions and were lapsed for non-payment.

9  NAFTA *Monthly Report*, April 1920
10  NAFTA *Monthly Report*, September 1919
11 NAFTA *Monthly Report*, January, February, and March 1919
12  NAFTA *Monthly Report*, July 1919
13  N. Robertson, *op.cit.supra*
14  NAFTA *Monthly Report*, June 1920
15  *New Age*, 1912, various issues
16  MacFarlane, *The British Communist Party*, 1966, p.33
17  MacFarlane, *op.cit.*, p.36
18  See Frank Matthews 'Building Guilds' in Briggs & Saville, *Essays in Labour History, Vol.2*, 1978
19  *Guildsman* and *Guild Socialist*, February 1920; March, April, December 1922; February, March 1923
20  NAFTA *Monthly Report*, June 1925
21  NAFTA *Monthly Report*, July 1925
22  NAFTA *Monthly Report*, January and fFBRYUARY 1923
23  *Tottenham & Edmonton Weekly Herald*, January 12th 1923
24  *Tottenham & Edmonton Weekly Herald*, January 19th 1923; January 26th 1923; March 23rd 1923
25  NAFTA *Monthly Report*, November 1921
26  NAFTA *Monthly Report*, December 1923 and January 1924
27  R.W. Lyman, *The First Labour Government*, 1957
28  *English Review*, January 1924, pp.3-4
29  NAFTA *Monthly Report*, Janujary and February 1924
30  NAFTA *Monthly Report*, June 1924
31  NAFTA *Annual Report*, 1917
32  MacFarlane, *op.cit*, p.117 and p.153
33  *Sunday Worker*, August 16th 1925 and Roderick Martin *Communism and the British Trade Unions*, Clarendon Press, Oxford, 1969, p.53
34  MacFarlane, *op.cit.*, p.149
35  MacFarlane, *op.cit.*, pp.143-148
36  *Sunday Worker*, March 15th 1925; May 17th 1925
37  R. Postgate, 'Lansbury', *Labour Weekly*, October 17th 1925
38  G.D.H. Cole, *History of the Labour Party from 1915*, 1948, p.182
39  NAFTA *Monthly Report*, July 1925
40  NAFTA *Annual Report*, 1919
41  NAFTA *Monthly Report*, November 1925
42  NAFTA *Monthly Report*, July 1925
43  J. Symons, *The General Strike*, 1957, p.41
44  Symons, *op.cit.*, p.52 45  G.A. Phillips, *The General Strike*, 1979, pp.138-139
46 NAFTA *Monthly Report*, August 1926
47  NAFTA *Monthly Report*, September 1926
48  *Sunday Worker*, May 23rd 1926
49  *Sunday Worker*, June 13th 1926

50  *Sunday Worker,* June 20th and October 1st 1926
51  NAFTA *Monthly Report,* December 1926

Chapter VII

 1  NAFTA *Monthly Report,* May, June and September 1927
 2  NAFTA *Monthly Report,* May 1927
 3  NAFTA *Annual Report,* 1927
 4  *Sunday Worker,* January 21st, July 12th, July 19th, August 8th, September 20th, October 4th, November 8th 1925
 5  NAFTA *Monthly Report,* October 1927
 6  Documents of TUC Library
 7  NAFTA *Monthly Report,* January 1928
 8  NAFTA *Monthly Report,* March 1928
 9  NAFTA *Monthly Report,* March 1928
10  NAFTA *Monthly Report,* April 1928
11  G.D.H. Cole, *History of the Labour Party,* pp.203-204, *op.cit.*
12  *Morning Post,* September 28th 1928
13  NAFTA *Monthly Report,* 1930
14  NAFTA *Monthly Report,* April 1928
15  NAFTA *Monthly Report,* March 1929
16  *Gloucestershire Echo,* February 25th 1929
17  NAFTA *Monthly Report,* September 1929
18  Verbal evidence
19  NAFTA *Monthly Report,* July and August 1931
20  NAFTA *Monthly Report,* August 1931
21  G.D.H. Cole, *History of Labour Party,* p.254, *op.cit.*
22  G.D.H. Cole, *History of Labour Party,* p.258 *op.cit.*
23  NAFTA EC *Minutes,* September 1931

Chapter VIII

 1  George Venables, verbal evidence
 2  Jock Shanley, verbal evidence, April 1981
 3  B.R. Mitchell & Phyllis Deane, *Abstract of British Historical Statistics,* CUP, 1962, p.67
 4  See table
 5  NAFTA *Monthly Report,* August and October 1932
 6  NAFTA *Monthly Report,* October 1932
 7  NAFTA *Monthly Report,* February and March 1933
 8  NAFTA *Monthly Report,* May 1933
 9  NAFTA *Monthly Report,* June 1934
10  NAFTA *Monthly Report,* October 1934
11  NAFTA *Monthly Report,* November 1934
12  *Furniture Record,* June 18th 1937

13  NAFTA *Monthly Report,* July 1935
14  NAFTA EC *Minutes,* September 1935
15  NAFTA *Monthly Report,* September 1935
16  John Middleton Murry *The Necissity of Communism,* Cape, London, 1932
17  *Labour Party Conference Report,* 1933
18  NAFTA *Monthly Report,* June 1934
19  Lily Carter, verbal evidence, February 18th 1981
20  C.R. Hawkins, *Monthly Report,* February 1933
21  Lily Carter, Shop Steward, Maples, verbal evidence, February 18th 1981
22  NAFTA *Monthly Report,* July 1934
23  George Venables, Polisher, High Wycombe, verbal evidence
24  Gossip, August 1934
25  NAFTA *Monthly Report,* September 1924; Pamphlet of the General Council of Labour Defence, July/August 1924
26  Douglas Hyde, *I Believed,* Heinemann, London 1951, p.79
27  John Strachey *Theory & Practice of Socialism,* Secker & Warburg, 1936, p.53
28  NAFTA *Monthly Report,* April 1933
29  NAFTA *Monthly Report,* May 1933
30  NAFTA *Monthly Report,* July 1933
31  NAFTA *Monthly Report,* July 1934
32  NAFTA *Monthly Report,* August 1934
33  NAFTA EC *Minutes,* March 1936
34  NAFTA *Monthly Report,* August, September and October 1936
35  *East London Pioneer,* December 6th 1936
36  NAFTA *Monthly Report,* February 1937
37  Neil Wood, *Communism and the British Intellectual,* 1939, p.46
38  Louis MacNiece, *Collected Poems,* Faber & Faber, 1949
39  see also George Orwell, *Homage to Catalonia,* 1939
40  NAFTA *Monthly Report,* 1937
41  Quoted by Cicely Hamilton, *Modern England,* 1938
42  NAFTA EC *Minutes,* January 1935
43  NAFTA *Monthly Report,* July 1914
44  NAFTA EC *Minutes,* January, February and March 1936
45  S. Harrison, *Alex Gossip,* Lawrence & Wishart, London 1962, pp.62-63
46  NAFTA *Monthly Report,* May 1938
47  *Annual Report,* 1941
48  A.J.P. Taylor, *The Troublemakers,* Panther, London, 1969, p.180
49  NAFTA *Monthly Report,* October 1938
50  NAFTA *Monthly Report,* July 1939
51  NAFTA *Monthly Report,* September 1939
52  NAFTA *Monthly Report,* October 1939

Chapter IX

1 *Furniture: An Enquiry made for the Board of Trade*, 1945
2 Board of Trade, *Utility Furniture*, 1945
3 Norman Longmate, *How We Lived Then*, Hutchinson, London, 1971, p.261-262
4 A. Caulder, *Peoples War*, 5   NAFTA *Annual Report*, 1942
6 Jock Shanley, verbal evidence
7 NAFTA EC *Bulletin*, January 1941
8 Nita Bowes, unpublished MA Thesis, Warwick, 1976
9 Caulder, *Peoples War*, p.466 *op.cit.*
10 National Labour Agreement for the Furniture Industry, 1946
11 Verbal evidence from un-named District Officer

Chapter X

1 Board of Trade Index Figures 1952
2 Organiser's Reports, *NAFTA Journal*, 1946
3 FIRA *Statistical Survey Furniture Industry*, 1958
4 NUFTO *Record*, May 1949
5 NUFTO *Annual Report*, 1960
6 NUFTO *Annual Report*, 1965
7 *Biennial Conference Report*, July 1953
8 NUFTO *Record*, July, August, September and October 1953
9 NUFTO *Annual Report*, 1963
10 ASWCM *Conference Minutes*, 1963
11 ASWCM *Conference Minutes*, 1964
12 ASWCM EC *Minutes*, January 29th 1966
13 ASWCM EC *Minutes*, May and June 1969

# Index

# C

Cabinet & Chairmakers, Manchester & District United Society of   30
Cabinet & Chairmakers Society, Nottingham Local   30
Cabinet and Chairmakers of Scotland, United Operative Society of Scotland   39
Cabinetmakers, Amalgamated Union of   81
Cabinetmakers, Continental Society of   30
Cabinetmakers, East London Society of   25, 27
Cabinetmakers, Friendly Society of   25, 27, 30
Cabinetmakers, Hebrew   36
Cabinetmakers, London Federation of   36, 118, 126
Cabinetmakers, London Society of   9
Cabinetmakers, Photographic   36
Cabinetmakers, Society of Cutlery, Sheffield   30
Cabinetmakers, Society of Fancy   30
Cabinetmakers, United Society of   9, 15
Cabinetmakers, West End Society of   24, 25, 27
Campbell, R.   7, 8
Campbell, Stephen I., MP, 114
Cantley, Henry Struther,   47
Carlyle, Thomas   45
Carpenters and Joiners, Amalgamated Society of   24, 35, 102
Carter, Lilly   164
Carter, Reg   164
Cartwright   12

Carver   7
Chairmakers & Carvers, East London Society of   30
Chairmakers Protection Society   21
Chamberlain, J.   33
Charles II, King   4, 5
Chaucer, Geoffrey   3
Chippendale, Thomas   5
Churchill, Winston   114
Citrine, Walter   123, 142, 149
City and Guilds of London Institute   168
Civil Liberties, National Council for   76, 77
Clarke, A.J.   61
Cleasby, Baron   32
Cohen, B. & Sons   20
Cohen, Jack   83, 93
Cole, G.D.H.   105, 131
Collins, Jack   103
Collyer   8
Communist International   112
Communist Party   105, 106, 111, 112, 113, 114, 128, 143, 146, 169, 170, 171
Conciliation Board, National   97, 101
Conscientious objectors   76
Conscription   70, 73
Cook, Arthur   113, 114, 125
Cook-Maxton Response   122, 125
Coronation   143
Coronation chair   2
Cotton Spinners, Amalgamated Association of Operative   35
Couley, A.   123
Cox   12
Cox, James & Son   63
Crawford, Helen   114
Criminal Law Amendment Act   31

# L

# M

# N